WARWICK STUDIES IN
LITERAT

General editor: Da

In both philosophical and literary studies much of the best original work today explores both the tensions and the intricate connections between what have often been treated as separate fields. In philosophy there is a widespread conviction that the notion of an unmediated search for truth represents an over-simplification of the philosopher's task, and that the language of philosophical argument requires its own interpretation. Even in the most rigorous instances of the analytic tradition, a tradition inspired by the possibilities of formalization and by the success of the natural sciences, we find demands for 'clarity', for 'tight' argument, and distinctions between 'strong' and 'weak' proofs which call out for a rhetorical reading – even for an aesthetic of argument. In literature many of the categories presupposed by traditions which give priority to 'enactment' over 'description' and oppose 'theory' in the name of 'lived experience' are themselves under challenge as requiring theoretical analysis, while it is becoming increasingly clear that to exclude literary works from philosophical probing is to trivialize many of them. Further, modern literary theory necessarily looks to philosophy to articulate its deepest problems and the effects of this are transmitted in turn to critical reading, as the widespread influence of deconstruction and of a more reflective hermeneutics has begun to show. When one recalls that Plato, who wished to keep philosophy and poetry apart, actually unified the two in his own writing, it is clear that the current upsurge of interest in this field is only re-engaging with the questions alive in the broader tradition.

The University of Warwick pioneered the graduate study of the intertwinings of philosophy and literature, and its recently established Centre for Research in Philosophy and Literature has won wide respect. This new Series brings the work of the Centre to a larger public in volumes which combine a sense of new direction with traditional standards of intellectual rigour. The Series will be further developed by the inclusion of monographs by distinguished academics.

WARWICK STUDIES
IN PHILOSOPHY AND LITERATURE

Edited by Andrew Benjamin

Books in the series include:

EXCEEDINGLY NIETZSCHE
Edited by David Farrell Krell and David Wood

POST-STRUCTURALIST CLASSICS
Edited by Andrew Benjamin

THE PROVOCATION OF LEVINAS
Edited by Robert Bernasconi and David Wood

THE PROBLEMS OF MODERNITY: Adorno and Benjamin
Edited by Andrew Benjamin

ABJECTION, MELANCHOLIA, AND LOVE: The work of
Julia Kristeva
Edited by John Fletcher and Andrew Benjamin

THE BIBLE AS RHETORIC
Edited by Martin Warner

WRITING THE FUTURE
Edited by David Wood

PHILOSOPHERS' POETS
Edited by David Wood

JUDGING LYOTARD
Edited by Andrew Benjamin

ON PAUL RICOEUR: Narrative and interpretation
Edited by David Wood

NARRATIVE IN CULTURE

*The Uses of Storytelling in the Sciences,
Philosophy, and Literature*

Edited by

CRISTOPHER NASH

London and New York

First published 1990
by Routledge
11 New Fetter Lane, London EC4P 4EE
29 West 35th Street, New York, NY 10001

Reprinted 1991, 1993
Paperback edition 1994

© *1990 University of Warwick Centre for Research in Philosophy*
and Literature

Typeset in Plantin by
Mayhew Typesetting, Bristol, England

Printed and bound in Great Britain by
T. J. Press (Padstow) Ltd, Padstow, Cornwall

British Library Cataloguing in Publication Data
A catalogue record for this book is available from the British Library.

Library of Congress Cataloging in Publication Data
A catalogue record for this book has been requested.

ISBN 0–415–04156–2 (hbk)
ISBN 0–415–10344–4 (pbk)

Contents

List of Contributors   vii
Foreword   xi
Acknowledgements   xv

NARRATIVE AND 'FACT'

Social Science
1 Storytelling in Economics   5
   Donald N. McCloskey
2 Narrative Theories and Legal Discourse   23
   Bernard S. Jackson
3 Self-knowledge as Praxis: Narrative and Narration in   51
   Psychoanalysis
   J.M. Bernstein

Physical Science
4 Some Narrative Conventions of Scientific Discourse   81
   Rom Harré
5 Making a Discovery: Narratives of Split Genes   102
   Greg Myers

NARRATIVE AND 'FICTION'

Philosophy and Literature
6 Narrative and Invention: The Limits of Fictionality   131
   Peter Lamarque
7 Ill Locutions   154
   Christine Brooke-Rose

Contents

8 How Primordial is Narrative? 172
  Michael Bell
9 Slaughtering the Subject: Literature's Assault on 199
  Narrative
  Cristopher Nash

Index 219

List of Contributors

DONALD N. McCLOSKEY, Professor of Economics and of History at the University of Iowa and Director of the Project on Rhetoric of Inquiry, has been a fellow of the Guggenheim Foundation, the Institute for Advanced Study (Princeton), Honorary Research Fellow of Birkbeck College (London), and the recipient of numerous grants from major research bodies around the world including the National Science Foundation and the National Endowment for the Humanities. Among his books are *Economic Maturity and Entrepreneurial Decline*; *Enterprise and Trade in Victorian Britain*; *The Applied Theory of Price*; *The Rhetoric of Economics*; *The Writing of Economics*; and *Econometric History*. He is working on *Risky Ground: The Open Fields of England* and *The Storied Character of Economics*.

BERNARD S. JACKSON, until recently Professor of Law at the University of Kent at Canterbury, is now Queen Victoria Professor of Law in the University of Liverpool. Having first specialized in ancient law (*Theft in Early Jewish Law* and *Essays in Jewish and Comparative Legal History*), he has more recently become interested in the development of a semiotic theory of law (*Semiotics and Legal Theory*; *Law, Fact and Narrative Coherence*). He is Secretary-General and Treasurer of the International Association for the Semiotics of Law/Association Internationale de Sémiotique Juridique and a member of the editorial board of the *International Journal for the Semiotics of Law/Revue Internationale de Sémiotique Juridique*. In preparation is his book *Wisdom-Laws*, based on his Speaker's Lectures in Biblical Studies delivered in the University of Oxford.

J.M. BERNSTEIN is Senior Lecturer and Chairman of the Department of Philosophy at the University of Essex. His PhD work at the University of Edinburgh was on Kant's philosophy of science. An increasingly vital figure in contemporary debate focusing on that crucial area where political theory comes to interrogate afresh traditional philosophical and psychological modes of thought affecting, for example, aesthetics and metaphysics, he is the author of *The Philosophy of the Novel: Lukács, Marxism and the Dialectics of Form* and *Art, Metaphysics and Modernity: The Fate of Aesthetics from Kant to Derrida*, forthcoming. He is the editor of the *Bulletin* of the Hegel Society of Great Britain, and is presently at work on a study provisionally entitled *Political Love and Tragic Culture*.

ROM HARRÉ obtained a BSc in Engineering and Mathematics and an MA in Philosophy and Anthropology at the University of Auckland. A seminal scholar in the modern analysis of the rhetoric of science, he began as a physics and mathematics teacher at Kings College, Auckland, was Lecturer in Applied Mathematics at the University of the Punjab, Research Fellow at the University of Birmingham, Lecturer in Philosophy of Science at the University of Leicester, and has been University Lecturer in Philosophy of Science, Oxford, since 1960, and a Fellow of Linacre College, Oxford, since 1963. Among his books are *An Introduction to the Logic of the Sciences*; *Matter and Method*; *The Anticipation of Nature*; *The Principles of Scientific Thinking*; *The Philosophies of Science*; and *Great Experiments*.

GREG MYERS, Lecturer in Modern Languages at the University of Bradford where he teaches linguistics and translation, has taught rhetoric at the University of Texas and literature at the University of Lancaster. His book, *Writing Biology: The Social Construction of Scientific Texts*, is soon to be published, and other recent publications include 'The pragmatics of politeness in scientific articles' (*Applied Linguistics*) and 'Every picture tells a story: illustrations in E.O. Wilson's *Sociobiology*' (*Human Studies*). One of the most forcefully acute in the new generation of analysts of the strategies of professional and public discourse, he is currently working on a sociological study of the relations between linguistics and artificial intelligence research in Britain.

PETER LAMARQUE, Lecturer in Philosophy at the University of Stirling, has written on metaphor and extensively on fiction in, for example, his 'Truth and art in Iris Murdoch's *The Black Prince*' (*Philosophy and Literature*); 'How can we fear and pity fictions?'; 'Bits and pieces of fiction' (*British Journal of Aesthetics*); and 'Fiction and reality' (in a volume edited by him, *Philosophy and Fiction: Essays in Literary Aesthetics*), while in *Mind, Psychoanalysis and Science* he has published 'On the irrelevance of psychoanalysis to literary criticism'. He is currently at work with Stein Haugom Olsen on a book on 'Literature, fiction and truth', and among his considerations of Noh theatre an essay entitled 'Expression and the mask: the dissolution of personality in Noh' is soon to appear.

CHRISTINE BROOKE-ROSE, a distinguished novelist and critic, was, until her recent retirement, Professor of American Literature at the University of Paris VIII, where she had taught since 1969. Among the honours conferred upon her have been the Travelling Prize of the Society of Authors, the James Tait Black Memorial Prize, the Arts Council Translation Prize and, in 1988, the degree of Hon. LittD from the University of East Anglia. Among her publications are the novels *The Languages of Love*; *The Sycamore Tree*; *The Dear Deceit*; *The Middlemen*; *Out*; *Such*; *Between*; *Thru*; *Amalgamemnon*; and *Xorandor*; and books of criticism, *A Grammar of Metaphor*; *A ZBC of Ezra Pound*; and *A Rhetoric of the Unreal*. Her new novel, *Verbivore*, is to appear in 1990.

MICHAEL BELL, Senior Lecturer and until recently Chairman of the Department of English and Comparative Literary Studies at the University of Warwick, has taught in France, Germany, Canada, and the United States. Principally interested in the novel with an emphasis on philosophical, interdisciplinary, and comparative issues, he has edited the collection of essays *Context of English Literature: 1900–1930*, and published books on *Primitivism*; *The Sentiment of Reality: Truth of Feeling in the European Novel*; and *F.R. Leavis*. He is currently writing books on language, being, and representation in D.H. Lawrence and on narrative treatments of the theme of authority and education.

CRISTOPHER NASH graduated *summa cum laude* in English from the University of California at Los Angeles where he had been elected to Phi Beta Kappa 'and other honorary academic societies', received an MA in Romance Languages and Literatures and a PhD with Double Distinction in Comparative Literature from New York University. After two years' Fulbright Fellowships to France he was lecturer in the City University of New York before settling in English at the University of Warwick where he helped found the Graduate School of Comparative Literature. His most recent work includes *World-Games: The Tradition of Anti-Realist Revolt*; and its sequel, *Deadlocks: The Limits of Anti-Realist Revolt*, and a novel are to come in 1990.

Foreword

What has made it possible to conceive of a book like this one is that the preoccupation with discourse – the forms of our utterances and their functions and effects – is no longer the private province of specialists in literature and language (as if it ever should have been). The matter has itself become one of the prepossessions, if not an obsession, of our era; that our sensations and understandings are inextricable from the systems of signs through which we articulate them to ourselves. The culture begins to speak to itself about the nature and import of its own speech. That alone raises a lot of questions that need answering. In the meantime, whole movements have sprung up (within ethno-methodology, psycholinguistics, social constructionism, critical legal studies), groups in the physical sciences, the social sciences, the professions, seeking to apply techniques first largely evolved in literary and linguistic studies to the scrutiny of their own patterns of communication, conception and perception.

We no longer need, then – if we ever did – to be told that the narrative mode of discourse is omnipresent in human affairs. We're obliged to consider the ungainly fact that in our culture, where we least expect it and even most vociferously disclaim it, there may actually be storytelling going on, and that the implications may indeed be 'considerable'. Narrative, we've heard, is central to our essential cognitive activities (Ricoeur), to historical thinking (White), to psychological analysis and practice (Lacan), to political critique and praxis (Lyotard); the 'movement of language and writing across time' is 'essentially narrative', Fredric Jameson has declared in sympathy with this synthetic vision; 'the all-informing process of *narrative*' is 'the central function or *instance* of the human mind'.[1]

My aim in this book of vastly diverse 'voices' is to provide contemporary readers with a glimpse both of the proliferation of arenas in which the often unexpectedly aggressive if subtle action of narrative is now proclaimed to be found at work, on the one hand, and on the other hand, of the more precise and *immediate substantive* experience of those delving 'at the coal face' in some of those fields as they encounter and grapple with the phenomenon, in their own divergent terms.

Thus in the following pages an international economist, Donald McCloskey, argues that economics is a form of 'poetry' and specifically of storytelling, whose analysis as such makes possible the apprehension – and the partial resolution – of deep disagreements between economists themselves, and between economists and commercial/community interests, which can never otherwise be bridged. A professor of law, Bernard Jackson, offers a model of legal processes which, through its emphasis upon the narrative construction of legal discourse, offers parallel accounts of the construction and justification of facts and the law itself. A doyen of the modern philosophy of science, Rom Harré, proposes that the authority of apparently neutral scientific evidence and argument is greatly dependent on narratives of heroism and virtue covertly propounded by scientists themselves as members of an elite 'moral community'; and in a magisterial piece of archival analysis Greg Myers shows that texts in the natural sciences may reveal, at each stage in the dissemination throughout the community's consciousness of a new 'discovery', a new potentially fictitious story generated to assist in its successful propagation.

Meanwhile, in psychological (in tandem with political–historical) theory, via a rereading of Habermas on Freud, Jay Bernstein argues that disturbances of identity are always disturbances of the temporal ordering of existence that can only be made intelligible through a process of (re-)narration, a narration of a kind that would be inherently self-reflective; and, reappraising a perennial issue in his own professional discipline, philosopher Peter Lamarque indicates that postmodern efforts in narrative to problematize distinctions between 'truth' and 'fiction' are nevertheless subject

1 Fredric Jameson (1981) *The Political Unconscious*, Ithaca, NY: Cornell University Press, 13.

to logical exigencies requiring that such distinctions continue to be made. At the same time, Christine Brooke-Rose, as a professor of literature and as a novelist producing the most radical experiments in British fictional narrative of the last two decades, makes out the case that contrary to traditional views of the operation of language (as described for example in conventional realist readings of the novel), there are – notably in free indirect 'speech' – modes of narration that are, in human social terms of communication, 'unspeakable' and that exist literally only in literature. And finally, while my own sketch suggests that recent literary theory and practice, directed by philosophical indeterminism, seek to overturn foundational conceptions of narrative and aim to substitute an ideal 'pure narration' that would essentially make writing socially unaccountable, Michael Bell asks whether there is a manner of speaking of 'narrative' that does not actually place it in a category that empties it of its current popularly assumed significance, and illustrates a way that must be of a relative kind, situated dialectically in the multiplex tension between its world and the world of the reader.

The collection, then, expresses what might be called a second, perhaps more pragmatic 'wave' (following the first flush of sometimes ethereal if not ecstatic general theorizing) in the history of the comparative study of narrative discourse at work in contemporary culture. It is still only a beginning. Casebooks to come could easily include representative studies from religion, cybernetics and information science, education, medicine, the arts, journalism and the advertising media, commerce and industry, and from government and the military establishments (where, lest for a moment this seem improbable, the uses of the scenario, for example, are now avowedly fundamental to decision-making processes affecting our daily lives).

The implications of such investigations' results, too, can do with further exploration. The authors speaking here describe narrative by-and-large as a technique for getting coherence. (I use this rough predicate – 'getting' – to leave open, as I think they are disposed to do, the issue as to whether the process alluded to is the discovery or the production of coherence.) What theory, what premises lie behind this 'getting', and how convincing are they? Are narratives occasion-specific (more suitable to certain conditions and motives than others)? Can we reform our narratives, our narrative models? By what criteria would we proceed? Can we determine precisely the relative effects of 'factual' and 'fictional' narrative? Can we discard narratives? Narrating itself? What would be the shape and texture of (for example, mental) 'events' at those points where it had disappeared? Along the way in this book, answers *are* offered; it's hoped that, for the benefit of a culture in the making, it may have flushed into the open even better questions.

Cristopher Nash

Acknowledgements

The impetus for this volume arose from a forum on Narrative in Culture (a series of lecture-seminars on Narrative as an Instrument of Culture and a conference on Narrative as Mode of Cognition and Legitimation) held in the spring of 1987 under the auspices of the Centre for Research in Philosophy and Literature in the University of Warwick. The editors wish to point out and acknowledge with thanks where appropriate the appearance of related material in other publications, viz.: a revised French version of C. Brooke-Rose's essay appears as 'La Controverse sur le discours indirect libre: Ann Banfield vs. les littéraires' in *Théorie, littérature, enseignement*, Presses Universitaires de Vincennes, no. 6 (1988), 77–89; a summary of G. Myers' essay appears in *Three Papers on the Popularisation of Science*, Centre for Science Studies and Science Policy, University of Lancaster (1987), 39–42; an early version of passages in R. Harré's essay appears in his *Varieties of Realism*, Oxford: Blackwell (1986); an abbreviated version of C. Nash's essay appears as 'Playing Havoc' in *PN Review*, vol. 15, no. 4 (1989), 21–4.

NARRATIVE
AND 'FACT'

SOCIAL SCIENCE

· 1 ·

Storytelling in Economics

DONALD N. McCLOSKEY

It is good to tell the story of science and art, economics and the nineteenth-century novel, the marginal productivity theory of distribution and the tradition of the Horatian ode as similarly as possible. I intend to do so. Economists are tellers of stories and makers of poems, and from recognizing this we can know better what economists do.

There seem to be two ways of understanding things; either by way of a metaphor or by way of a story, through something like a poem or through something like a novel. When a biologist is asked to explain why the moulting glands of a crab are located just as they are he has two possibilities. Either he can call on a model – a metaphor – of rationality inside the crab, explaining that locating them just *there* will maximize the efficiency of the glands in operation; or he can tell a story, of how crabs with badly located glands will fail to survive. If he is lucky with the modelling he will discover some soluble differential equations. If he is lucky with the storytelling he will discover a true history of some maladapted variety of crabs, showing it dying out. Metaphors and stories, models and histories, are the two ways of answering 'why'.

It has probably been noticed before that the metaphorical and the narrative explanations answer to each other. Suppose the biologist happens first to offer his metaphor, his hypothetical individual crab moving bits of its body from here to there in search of the optimal location for moulting glands. The listener asks, 'But why?' The biologist will answer with a story: he says, 'The reason why the glands must be located optimally is that if

5

crabs did a poor job of locating their glands they would die off as time passed.' A story answers a model.

But likewise a model answers a story. If the biologist gives the evolutionary story first, and the listener then asks, 'But why?', the biologist will answer with a metaphor: 'The reason why the crabs will die off is that poorly located glands would serve poorly in the emergencies of crabby life . . . .' The glands would not be located according to the metaphor of maximizing: that's why.

Among what speakers of English call the sciences, metaphors dominate physics and stories dominate biology. Of course, the modes can mix. That we humans regard metaphors and stories as antiphonal guarantees they will. Mendel's thinking about genetics is a rare case in biology of pure modelling, answered after a long while by the more usual storytelling. In 1902 W.S. Sutton observed homologous pairs of grasshopper chromosomes. He answered the question put to a metaphor – '*Why* does the Mendelian model of genes work?' – with a story: 'Because, to begin with, the genes are arranged along pairs of chromosomes, which I have seen, one half from each parent.'

The modes of explanation are more closely balanced in economics. An economist explains the success of cotton farming in the antebellum American South indifferently with static, modelling arguments (the South in 1860 had a comparative advantage in cotton) or with dynamic, storytelling arguments (the situation in 1860 was an evolution from earlier successes). The best economics, indeed, combines the two. Ludwig von Mises' famous paper of 1920 on the impossibility of economic calculation under socialism was both a story of the failures of central planning during the recently concluded war and a model of why any replacement for the market would fail (Lavoie 1985: 49).

The metaphors are best adapted to making predictions of tides in the sea or of shortages in markets, simulating out into a counterfactual world. (One could use here either an evolutionary story from the history of science or a maximizing model from the sociology or philosophy of science.) Seventeenth-century physics abandoned stories in favour of models, giving up the claim to tell in a narrative sense how gravity reached up and pulled things down; it just did, according to such-and-such an equation – let me show you the model. Similarly a price control on apartments will yield shortages; don't ask how it will in sequence; it just will, according to such-and-such an equation – let me show you the model.

On the other hand the storytelling is best adapted to explaining something that has already happened, like the evolution of crabs or the development of the modern corporation. The Darwinian story was notably lacking in models, and in predictions. Mendel's model, which offered to explain the descent of man by a metaphor rather than by a story, was neglected for thirty-four years, all the while that evolutionary stories were being told.

The contrast carries over to the failures of the two modes. When a metaphor is used too boldly in narrating a history it becomes ensnared in logical contradictions, such as those surrounding counterfactuals (McCloskey 1987). If a model of an economy is to be used to imagine what would have happened to Britain in the absence of the industrial revolution then the contradiction is that an economy of the British sort did in fact experience an industrial revolution. A world in which the Britain of 1780 did not yield up an industrial revolution would have been a very different one, before and after 1780. The model wants to eat the cake and have all the ingredients, too. It contradicts the story. Likewise, when a story attempts to predict something, by extrapolating the story into the future, it contradicts some persuasive model. The story of business cycles can organize the past, showing capitalist economies bobbing up and down. But it contradicts itself when it is offered as a prediction of the future. If the models of business cycles could predict the future there would be no surprises, and consequently no business cycles.

The point is that economists are like other human beings in that they both use metaphors and tell stories. They are concerned both to explain and to understand, *erklären* and *verstehen*. I am going to concentrate here on storytelling, having written elsewhere about the metaphorical side of the tale (McCloskey 1985). What might be called the poetics or stylistics of economics is worth talking about. But here the subject is the rhetoric of fiction in economics.

I propose to take seriously an assertion by Peter Brooks, in his *Reading for the Plot*: 'Our lives are ceaselessly intertwined with narrative, with the stories that we tell, all of which are reworked in that story of our own lives that we narrate to ourselves . . . . We are immersed in narrative' (Brooks 1985: 3). As the historian J.H. Hexter put it, storytelling is 'a sort of knowledge we cannot live without' (Hexter 1986: 8). Economists have not lived without it, not ever. It is no accident that the novel and economic science were born at the same time. We live in an age insatiate of plot.

Tell me a story, Dr Smith. Why, of course:

A pension scheme is proposed for the nation, in which 'the employer will pay half'. It will say in the law and on the worker's salary cheque that the worker contributes 5% of his wages to the pension fund but that the employer contributes the other 5%. The example is a leading case in the old quarrel between lawyers and economists. A law is passed 'designed' (as they say) to have such-and-such an effect. The lawyerly mind goes this far, urging us therefore to limit the hours of women workers or to subsidize shipping. The women, he thinks, will be made better off; as will the ships. According to the lawyer, the workers under the pension scheme will be on balance 5% better off, getting half of their pension free from the employer.

An economist, however, will not want to leave the story of the pension plan in the first act, the lawyer's and legislator's act of laws 'designed' to split the costs. She will want to go further in the drama. She will say: 'At the higher cost of labour the employers will hire fewer workers. In the second act the situation created by the law will begin to dissolve. At the old terms more workers will want to work than the employer wishes to hire. Jostling queues will form outside the factory gates. The competition of the workers will drive down wages. By the third and final act a part of the "employer's" share – maybe even all of it – will sit on the workers themselves, in the form of lower wages. The intent of the law', the economist concludes, 'will have been frustrated.'

Thus in Chicago when a tax on employment was proposed the reporters asked who would pay the tax. Alderman Thomas Keane (who as it happens ended in jail, though not for misappropriation of economics) declared that the City had been careful to draft the law so that only the employers paid it. 'The City of Chicago', said Keane, 'will never tax the working man.'

Thus in 1987, when Senator Kennedy proposed a plan for American workers and employers to share the cost of health insurance, newspapers reported Kennedy as estimating 'the overall cost at $25 billion – $20 billion paid by employers and $5 billion by workers'. Senator Kennedy will never tax the working man. The manager of employee relations at the US Chamber of Commerce

(who apparently agreed with Senator Kennedy's economic analysis
of where the tax would fall) said, 'It is ridiculous to believe that
every company . . . can afford to provide such a generous array of
health care benefits.' The US Chamber of Commerce will never tax
the company.

The case illustrates a number of points about economic stories.
It illustrates the delight that economists take in unforeseen consequences, a delight shared with other social scientists. It illustrates
the selection of certain consequences for special attention: an
accountant or political scientist would want to hear how the
pension was funded, because it would affect business or politics in
the future; economists usually set such consequences to the side.
It illustrates also the way economists draw on typical scenes – the
queues in front of the factory – and typical metaphors – workers
as commodities to be bought and sold. Especially it illustrates the
way stories support economic argument. Since Adam Smith and
David Ricardo, economists have been addicted to little analytic
stories, the Ricardian vice. The economist says, 'Yes, I see how the
story starts; but I see dramatic possibilities here; I see how events
will develop from the situation given in the first act.'

It is not controversial that an economist is a storyteller when telling the story of the Federal Reserve Board or of the industrial
revolution. Plainly and routinely, ninety per cent of what
economists do is such storytelling. Yet even in the other ten per
cent, in the part more obviously dominated by models and
metaphors, the economist tells stories. The applied economist can
be viewed as a realistic novelist or a realistic playwright, a Thomas
Hardy or a George Bernard Shaw. The theorist, too, may be
viewed as a teller of stories, though a non-realist, whose plots and
characters have the same relation to truth as those in *Gulliver's
Travels* or *A Midsummer Night's Dream*. Economics is saturated
with narration.

The analogy on its face seems apt. Economics is a sort of social
history. For all their brave talk about being the physicists of the
social sciences, economists do their best work when looking
backwards, the way a biologist or geologist or historian does. Journalists and politicians demand that economists prophesy, forecasting the social weather. Sometimes, unhappily, the economists will
take money for trying. But it is not their chief skill, any more than
earthquake forecasting is the chief skill of seismologists, or election

forecasting the chief skill of political historians. Economists cannot predict much, and certainly cannot predict profitably. If they were so smart they would be rich (McCloskey 1988). Mainly economists are tellers of stories.

Well, so what? What is to be gained by thinking this way about economics? One answer can be given at once, and illustrates the uses of the literary analogy, namely: storytelling makes it clearer why economists disagree.

Disagreement among scientists is suggestive for the rhetoric of science in the same way that simultaneous discovery is suggestive for its sociology. The lay person does not appreciate how much economists agree, but he is not entirely wrong in thinking that they also disagree a lot. Economists have long-lasting and long-disagreeing schools, more typical of the humanities than of the sciences. Why then do they disagree?

When economists themselves try to answer they become sociological or philosophical, though in ways that a sociologist or philosopher would find uncongenial. When in a sociological mood they will smile knowingly and explain that what drives monetarists or Keynesians to 'differentiate their product', as they delight in putting it, is self-interest. Economists are nature's Marxists, and enjoy uncovering and then sniggering at self-interest. When they are in a more elevated and philosophic mood they will speak sagely of 'successive approximations' or 'treating a theory merely *as if* it were true'. Some have read a bit of Popper or Kuhn, and reckon they know a thing or two about the Methodology of Science. The stories that result from these ventures into ersatz sociology and sophomore philosophy are unconvincing. To tell the truth, the economists do not know why they disagree.

Storytelling offers a richer model of how economists talk and a more plausible story of their disagreements. The disagreement can be understood from a literary perspective in more helpful ways than saying that one economist has divergent material interest from another, or a different 'crucial experiment', or another 'paradigm'.

It is first of all the theory of reading held by scientists that permits them to disagree, and with such ill temper. The over-simple theory of reading adopted officially by economists and other scientists is that scientific texts are transparent, a matter of 'mere communication', 'just style', simply 'writing up' the 'theoretical results' and 'empirical findings'. If reading is so free from difficulties, then naturally the only way our readers can fail to agree with us is through their ill will or their dimness. (Leave aside the unlikely chance that it is we who are dim.) It's right there in black and white. Don't be a dunce.

A better theory of reading, one that admitted that scientific prose like literary prose is complicated and allusive, drawing on a richer rhetoric than mere demonstration, might soothe this ill temper. The better theory, after all, is the one a good teacher uses with students. She knows well enough that the text is not transparent to the students, and she does not get angry when they misunderstand. God likewise does not get angry when His students misunderstand His text. In fact, like scientists and scholars, God writes obscurely in order to snare us. As Gerald Bruns has noted, St Augustine viewed the obscurity of the Bible as having 'a pragmatic function in the art of winning over an alienated and even contemptuous audience' (Bruns 1984: 157). He quotes a remark of Augustine about the difficulty of the Bible that might as well be about the latest proof in mathematical economics: 'I do not doubt that this situation was provided by God to conquer pride by work and to combat disdain in our minds, by which those things which are easily discovered seem frequently to be worthless.'

One source of disagreement, then, is a naïve theory of reading, the theory that would ask naïvely for the 'message' in a poem, as though poems were riddles in rhyme. Another source of disagreement is likewise a source of disagreement about literature: compression, a lack of explicitness. Partly this is economic. Had she but world enough and time the writer could make everything explicit. In a world of scarcity, however, she cannot. Yet explicitness is no guarantee of agreement, because if the writer has all the time in the world the reader does not. I cannot listen long enough to understand some of my Marxist friends (though I ask them to keep trying). Similarly, the mathematician in economics has an expository style based on explicitness and a zero value of time. Everything will be clear, he promises earnestly, if the readers will but listen carefully to the axioms. The readers grow weary. They cannot remember all the axioms and anyway cannot see why one would wish to doubt them. They do not have the toleration for such speech that the mathematician has.

The point involves more than the economic scarcity of journal space and of the leisure time to read. It involves the anthropology of science, the customs of its inhabitants and their ability to read a language. A scientist convinced of what she writes will come from a certain background, supplied with a language. Unless her reader knows roughly the same language – that is, unless he has been raised in approximately the same conversation – he will misunderstand and will be unpersuaded. This is an unforgivable failure only if it is an unforgivable failure to be, say, non-Javanese or non-French. The reader comes from another culture, with a different tongue. The training in reading English that a D.Phil. in English provides or the training in reading economics that a Ph.D. in economics provides are trainings in rapid reading, filling in the blanks.

A third and final source of disagreement in literature and in economics, beyond the naïve theory of reading and the limits on understanding foreign speech, is an inability of the reader to assume the point of view demanded by the author. A foolishly sentimental poem has the same irritating effect on a reader as does a foolishly libertarian piece of economics. The reader refuses to enter the author's imaginative world, or is unable to. A literary critic said, 'A bad book, then, is a book in whose mock reader we discover a person we refuse to become, a mask we refuse to put on, a role we will not play' (Gibson 1950: 5). The reader therefore will of course misread the text, at least in the sense of violating the author's intentions. We do not submit to the authorial intentions of a badly done greeting card. In a well-done novel or a well-done scientific paper we agree to submit to the authorial intentions, so far as we can make them out. The entire game in a science such as biology or chemistry or economics is to evoke this submission to authorial intentions. Linus Pauling commands attention, and his readers submit to his intentions, at least outside of vitamin C; Paul Samuelson likewise, at least outside of monetary policy.

The argument can be pushed further. An economist expounding a result creates both an 'authorial audience' (an imagined group of readers who know that this is fiction) and a 'narrative audience' (an imagined group who do not). As Peter Rabinowitz explains (Rabinowitz 1980: 245) 'the narrative audience of "Goldilocks" believes in talking bears'; the authorial audience knows it is fiction. The split between the two audiences created by the author seems weaker in economic science than in explicit fiction, probably because we all know that bears do not talk but we do not all know that marginal productivity is a metaphor. In science the 'narrative audience' is fooled, as in 'Goldilocks'. But the authorial audience is fooled, too (and commonly so also is the literal audience, the actual readers as against the ideal readers the author wishes into existence). Michael Mulkay (1985) has shown how important is the choice of authorial audience in the scholarly correspondence of biochemists. The biochemists, like other scientists and scholars, are largely unaware of their literary devices, and become puzzled and angry when their audience refuses to believe in talking bears. Small wonder that scientists and scholars disagree, even when their rhetoric of 'What the facts say' would appear to make disagreement impossible.

Taking economics as a kind of writing, then, explains some of the disagreements of economists. Economists go on disagreeing after the 'theoretical results and empirical findings', as they put it, have been laid out for inspection not merely because they are differentiating their product or suffering from inflammation of the paradigm but because they read a story or a scientific paper written in an unfamiliar language inexpertly, yet do not realize it. They are like the British tourist in Florence who believes firmly that Italians really do understand English, and can be made to admit it if one speaks very slowly and very loudly: 'WHERE . . . IS . . . YOUR . . . STORY??!'

Telling the stories in economics as matters of beginnings, middles, and ends has many attractions. One can start with pure plot, breaking 100 economic stories down into their components as Vladimir Propp did in 1928 for 100 Russian folk tales (Propp 1968: 19–24): the capitalization of Iowa corn prices tale, the exit from and entry to computer selling in the 1980s tale, the correct incidence of the Kennedy health insurance tale, and so forth. The tales can then be analysed into 'functions' (Propp's word for actions). And, to Proppize it entirely, one can ask whether the sequences of functions prove to be constant, as they are in Russia.

The task sounds bizarre. But in a way economics is too easy a case. Economics is already structural, as Ferdinand de Saussure suggested long ago (Saussure 1916: 79, 113). The actions of an economistic folklore are few: entry, exit, price setting, orders within a firm, purchase, sale, valuation, and a few more. It is indeed this self-consciously structural element that makes economics so irritating to outsiders. Economists say over and over again: 'action X is *just like* action Y' – labour is just like a commodity, slavery is just like capitalization, children are just like refrigerators, and so forth. The economist's favourite phrase would please Claude Lévi-Strauss: 'Underneath it all.' Underneath it all, international trade among nations is trade among individuals, and can be modelled in the same way. Underneath it all, an inflated price is earned by someone as an inflation wage, leaving average welfare unchanged. Underneath it all, we owe the national debt to ourselves, though the people who pay the taxes might wonder about this. In such a highly structured field, whose principles of storytelling are so well known by the main storytellers, it would be surprising to find as many as thirty-one distinct actions, as Propp found in his 100 Russian folk tales (Propp 1968: 64). He found seven characters (ibid: 80). That seems more likely: David Ricardo in his economic tales got along with three.

Tale-telling in economics follows the looser constraints of fiction, too. The most important is the sense of an ending, as in the story of the pension scheme. Go all the way to the third act. The 5% pension gained by the workers is 'not an equilibrium', as economists say when they do not like the ending proposed by some unsophisticated person. Any descendant of Adam Smith, whether by way of Marx or Marshall or Menger, will be happy to tell you the rest of the story.

Many of the disagreements inside economics turn on this sense of an ending. To an eclectic Keynesian the story idea 'Oil prices went up, which caused inflation' is full of meaning, having the merits that stories are supposed to have. But to a monetarist it seems incomplete, no story at all, a flop. As A.C. Harberger says, it doesn't make the economics 'sing'. It ends too soon, half-way through the second act: a rise in oil prices without some corresponding fall elsewhere is 'not an equilibrium'. From the other side, the criticism of monetarism by Keynesians is likewise a criticism of the plot line, complaining of an ill-motivated beginning rather than a premature ending: where on earth does the money *come* from, and why?

There is more than prettiness in such matters of plot. There is moral weight. The historian Hayden White has written that 'The demand for closure in the historical story is a demand . . . for moral reasoning' (White 1981: 20). A monetarist is not morally satisfied until she has pinned the blame on the Bank of England. The economist's ending to the pension story says, 'Look: you're getting fooled by the politicians and lawyers if you think that specifying the 50–50 share in the law will get the workers a 50% cheaper pension. Wake up; act your age; look beneath the surface; recognize the dismal ironies of life.' Stories impart meaning, which is to say worth. A *New Yorker* cartoon shows a woman looking up anxiously from the telly, asking her husband, 'Henry, is there a moral to *our* story?'

The sense of adequacy in storytelling works in the most abstract theory, too. In seminars on mathematical economics a question nearly as common as 'Haven't you left off the second subscript?' is 'What's your story?' The story of the pension scheme can be put entirely mathematically and metaphorically, as an assertion about the incidence of a tax on a system of supply-and-demand curves in equilibrium:

$$w^\star = - [E_d/ (E_d + E_s)]\ T^\star$$

The mathematics here is so familiar to an economist that he will not require explanation beyond the metaphor. But in less familiar cases he will. Like the audience for the biologist explaining moulting glands in crabs, at the end of all the modelling he will ask insistently *why*; 'What's your story?' His question is an appeal for a lower level of abstraction, closer to the episodes of human life. It asks for more realism, in a fictional sense, more illusion of direct experience. It asks to step closer to the nineteenth-century short story, with its powerful and unironic sense of *being there*.

And of course even the most static and abstract argument in economics, refusing to become storylike and insisting on remaining poetic and metaphorical, is part of 'that story of our own lives which we narrate to ourselves'. A scholar has a story in which the work in question is an episode: this is why seminars so often begin with 'how I came to this subject', because such a fragment of autobiography gives meaning to it all. You will hear mathematicians complain if a seminar has not been 'motivated'. The motivation is a story, frequently a mythic history about this part of mathematics or about this speaker. The audience wishes to know why the argument might matter to the speaker, or to the audience itself. The story will then have a moral, as all good stories do.

Economics-as-story provides some places from which to see the plot of economics. To repeat, the author is either a narrator or a poet, a user of either a story or a metaphor. But the reader, too, figures in economic thought. A distinction has been drawn by Louise Rosenblatt between *aesthetic* and *efferent* reading. In efferent reading (*effero*, carry off) the reader focuses on what she will carry off from the reading. Efferent reading is supposed to characterize model-building and science. In aesthetic reading the reader focuses on her experience at the time of the reading, which is supposed to characterize storytelling and art. Yet an aesthetic reading of a scientific text commonly carries the argument. The feeling 'Yes: this is right' in the last stanza of 'Among school children' resembles the feeling that comes upon one when concluding the ancient proof that the square root of 2 cannot be expressed as the ratio of two whole numbers. Rosenblatt supposes that 'To adopt an aesthetic stance . . . toward the directions for constructing a radio is possible, but would usually be very unrewarding' (Rosenblatt 1978: 34). Well, yes, usually. Yet the computer repairman takes an aesthetic attitude toward the schematics for a Murrow computer: 'A nice little machine', he says, and smiles, and is brought to this or that solution. The physicist Steven Weinberg argues that aesthetic readings govern the spending of millions of dollars in research money (Weinberg 1983). The pleasure of the text is sometimes its meaning, even in science.

Rosenblatt anticipates such an argument, noting that theories of literature that do not stress the reader's role are left puzzled by pleasurable nonfiction, such as *The Decline and Fall of the Roman Empire* or, one might add, the best applied economics. The reader's response gives a way of keeping track of the aesthetic readings when they matter. The usual theory of scientific reading claims that they never do.

The telling of artful stories has its customs, and these may be brought to economics, too. Take for instance the bare notion of genre, that is, of types of literary production, with their histories and their interrelations. The scientific report is itself a genre, whose conventions have changed from time to time. Kepler wrote in an autobiographical style, spilling his laboratory notes with all their false trails onto the page; Galileo wrote in urbane little dramas. It was Newton, in some other ways also an unattractive man, who insisted on the cramping literary conventions of the

Scientific Paper (Medawar 1964). An economist should be aware that he adopts more than a 'mere' style when he adopts the conventions.

Pure theory in economics is similar to the literary genre of fantasy. Like fantasy it violates the rules of 'reality' for the convenience of the tale, and amazing results become commonplace in a world of hypothesis. That animals exhibit the foibles of human beings is unsurprising in a world in which animals talk. No blame attaches. The task of pure theory is to make up fantasies that have a point, in the way that *Animal Farm* has a point. Pure theory confronts reality by disputing whether this or that assumption drives the result, and whether the assumption is realistic. The literary analogy, by the way, puts the debate about the realism of economic assumptions into a strange light. Is it the talking animals or the flying carpets, both of which are unrealistic, that makes *The Arabian Nights* on the whole 'unrealistic'? The question is strange to the point of paradox, but economists talk routinely as though they can answer it.

To speak of pure theory as fantasy, I repeat, is not to put it at a low value. *Gulliver's Travels* is fantasy, too, but pointed, instructive, useful fantasy for all that. Theorists usually know what genre they are writing. Their awareness reveals itself in their little jokes, of 'turnpikes' along the way to economic growth and 'islands' of labour in the economy. Yet the Ricardian vice is most characteristic of high theory: the vice of allowing fancy too free a rein. Auden remarks, 'What makes it difficult for a poet not to tell lies is that, in poetry, all facts and all beliefs cease to be true or false and become interesting possibilities' (quoted in Ruthven 1979: 175). The hundredth possible world of international trade gives the impression of a poetry gone to Bedlam. Economists would do well to know what genre they are reading or writing, to avoid misclassifying the fantasy and to assure that they are doing it well.

Good empirical work in economics, on the other hand, is like realistic fiction. Unlike fantasy, it claims to follow all the rules of the world. (Well . . . all the *important* ones.) But of course it too is fictional.

The modernist schoolmasters so long in charge of our intellectual lives would reply crossly that it is my analysis that is the fantasy and the fiction. They will complain that the proper scientist *finds* the story; no fiction about it.

The answer to such an assertion has long been understood. The storyteller cloaks himself in Truth – which is what annoyed Plato about alleged imitations of life in sculpture or poetry. Just 'telling the story as it happened' evades the responsibility to declare a point of view. Realist fiction does this habitually – which shows another use for the literary analogy, to note that realist 'fiction' in science can also evade declaring a point of view. Michael Mulkay notes in the epistolary arguments of biologists a Rule 11: 'Use the personal format of a letter . . . but withdraw from the text yourself as often as possible so that the other party continually finds himself engaged in an unequal dialogue with the experiments, data, observations and facts' (Mulkay 1985). The evasion is similar in history: 'the plot of a historical narrative is always an embarrassment and has to be presented as "found" in the events rather than put there by narrative techniques' (White 1981: 20).

Admitting that the Battle of Waterloo has more promising material than today's breakfast, still it is true that nothing is given to us by the world in story form already. *We* tell the stories. John Keegan has nicely illustrated the point in reference to Waterloo in his book *The Face of Battle* (1977). He speaks of the 'rhetoric of battle history' (ibid: 36) as demanding that one cavalry regiment be portrayed as 'crashing' into another, a case of 'shock' tactics. Yet an observant witness of such an encounter at Waterloo reported that 'we fully expected to have seen a horrid crash – no such thing! Each, as if by mutual consent, opened their files on coming near, and passed rapidly through each other' (ibid: 149). A story is something told to each other by human beings, not something existing ready-told in the very rocks or cavalry regiments or mute facts themselves. Niels Bohr once remarked that physics is not about the world but about what we as human beings can say about the world.

Stories, in other words, are selective. In this they are similar to metaphors and models, which must select, too. We cannot portray anything literally completely, as another Niels Bohr story illustrates. He asked his graduate class to *fully* describe a piece of chalk, to give *every* fact about it. As the students found, the task is impossible unless radically selective. We cannot know about the history of every atom in the chalk, or the location of every atom that bears any relation to the atoms in the chalk, since every atom bears some relation, if only by not being that atom in the chalk.

We decide what matters, for *our* purposes, not for God's or Nature's.

The fictional writer selects like the scientist, and invites the reader to fill in the blanks. Stories or articles can give only a sample of experience, because experience is overwhelmed by irrelevance: taking out the rubbish, bumping the table, scratching the back of one's head, seeing the title of the book one was not looking for. What distinguishes the good storyteller and the good scientific thinker from the bad is a sense of pointedness.

The vaunted parsimony of scientific stories is not the result of some philosophy commending parsimony. It is a result of the way we read science, our ability to fill the blanks, telling stories in our culture. The economist can read the most unreadable and compressed production of his fellows, but only if they participate in the same community of speech. Wholly fictional stories are parsimonious in the same way.

Skilful fiction, whether in the form of *Northanger Abbey* or *The Origin of Species*, 'stimulates us to supply what is not there', as Virginia Woolf remarked of Austen: 'What she offers is, apparently, a trifle, yet is composed of something that expands in the reader's mind and endows with the most enduring form of life scenes which are outwardly trivial' (Woolf 1953: 142). Remarking on Woolf in turn, Wolfgang Iser put it this way:

> What is missing from the apparently trivial scenes, the gaps arising out of the dialogue – this is what stimulates the reader into filling the blanks with projections [the image is of the reader running a motion picture inside his head, which is of course why novels can still compete with television] . . . . The 'enduring form of life' which Virginia Woolf speaks of is not manifested on the printed page; it is a product arising out of the interaction between text and reader.
>
> (Iser 1980: 110–11)

As Arjo Klamer (1987) has shown for the postulate of economic rationality, scientific persuasion, too, is like that. Persuasion of the most rigorous kind has blanks to be filled at every other step, if it is about a difficult murder case, for example, or a difficult mathematical theorem. The same is true of a difficult piece of economic storytelling. What is unsaid – but not unread – is more important to the text as perceived by the reader than what is there on the page. As Klamer puts it (ibid: 175), 'The student of the rhetoric of economics faces the challenge of speaking about the unspoken, filling in the "missing text" in economic discourse.'

The running of different motion pictures in our heads is going to produce different texts as perceived. The story here circles back to disagreement. Tzvetan Todorov makes the point: 'How do we explain this diversity [of literary readings]? By the fact that these accounts describe, not the universe of the book itself, but this universe as it is transformed by the psyche of each individual reader' (Todorov 1980: 72). And elsewhere: 'Only by subjecting the text to a particular type of reading do we construct, from our reading, an imaginary universe. Novels do not imitate reality; they create it' (ibid: 67f.). Economic texts also are made in part by the reader. Obscure texts are often therefore influential. Keynes left many opportunities for readers to run their own internal motion pictures, filling in the blanks.

What, then, is to be done? Should economists go on pretending that scientific texts are transparent and complete in themselves? If economists read texts differently, and know that they do, is economics left in chaos? Will admitting that economics like other sciences depends on storytelling lead to the war of all against all, and low wages?

No. In grim little wars of misreading the chaos already exists. A literary turn might bring a peace of toleration and trade. A community of readers is built the same way a community of listeners to music or a community of businesspeople is built, by making them sophisticated readers and listeners and businesspeople, willing to try other ways of reading or listening or dealing.

Perhaps there is something to treating economics as stories. The advantage would be self-consciousness, though self-consciousness itself is disparaged by certain economists anxious to manipulate the rules of conversation. Economists would do better to know what they are talking about. Looking on economics as poetry or fiction – or for that matter, as history – gives the economist a place to look in from outside. It is a better place than is provided by the usual philosophies of science; it is a great deal better than the homespun sociologies and philosophies that economists commonly use.

There is another advantage, to the larger culture. Economics should come back into the conversation of mankind. It is an extraordinarily clever way of speaking, which can do much good. The way to bring it back is to persuade economists that they are not so very different from poets and novelists. They do not have to abandon their lovely mathematics. For a long time now they have been standing aside, believing they have only the mathematical sciences as models. They practise a physics-worship that misunderstands both physics and themselves. Economists could get their gods from poetry or history or philology and still do much the same job of work, with a better temper and with better results.

Reunifying the conversation of mankind is best accomplished with hard cases. Economics is a hard case, wrapped in its prideful self-image as Science. If even economics can be shown to be fictional and poetical and historical its story will be a better one. Technically speaking it will be a comedy, comprising words of wit, an amused tolerance for human folly, stock characters colliding at last in the third act, and, most characteristic of the genre, a universe in equilibrium and a happy ending.

Bibliography

Brooks, Peter (1985) *Reading for the Plot: Design and Intention in Narrative*, New York: Vintage.

Bruns, Gerald L. (1984) 'The problem of figuration in antiquity', pp. 147–64 in G. Shapiro and A. Sica (eds) *Hermeneutics: Questions and Prospects*, Amherst: University of Massachusetts Press.

Gibson, Walker (1950) 'Authors, speakers and mock readers', *College English* 11 (Feb. 1950), reprinted pp. 100–6 in Jane P. Tompkins (ed.) (1980) *Reader-Response Criticism*, Baltimore: Johns Hopkins University Press.

Hexter, J.H. (1986) 'The problem of historical knowledge', unpublished MS, Washington University, St Louis.

Iser, Wolfgang (1980) 'The interaction between text and reader', pp. 106–19 in Susan R. Suleiman and Inge Crosman (eds) *The Reader in the Text: Essays on Audience and Interpretation*, Princeton: Princeton University Press.

Keegan, John (1977) *The Face of Battle*, New York: Vintage Books.

Klamer, Arjo (1987) 'As if economists and their subjects were rational', pp. 163–83 in John Nelson, Allan Megill, and D.N. McCloskey (eds) *The Rhetoric of the Human Sciences*, Madison: University of Wisconsin Press.

Lavoie, Don (1985) *Rivalry and Central Planning: The Socialist Calculation Debate Reconsidered*, Cambridge: Cambridge University Press.

McCloskey, D.N. (1985) *The Rhetoric of Economics*, Madison: University of Wisconsin Press, in the Series on the Rhetoric of the Human Sciences.

—— (1987) 'Counterfactuals', article in *The New Palgrave: A Dictionary of Economic Theory and Doctrine*, London: Macmillan.

—— (1988) 'The limits of expertise: if you're so smart, why ain't you rich?', *The American Scholar*, spring.

Medawar, Peter (1964) 'Is the scientific paper fraudulent?', *Saturday Review* Aug. 1, pp. 42–3.

Mulkay, Michael (1985) *The Word and the World: Explorations in the Form of Sociological Analysis*, Winchester, Massachusetts: Allen & Unwin.

Propp, V. (1968 (1928)) *Morphology of the Folktale*, 2nd edn. trans. L. Scott and L.A. Wagner, American Folklore Society, Austin: University of Texas Press.

Rabinowitz, Peter J. (1980) ' "What's Hecuba to us?" The audience's experience of literary borrowing', pp. 241–63 in Susan R. Suleiman and Inge Crosman (eds) *The Reader in the Text: Essays on Audience and Interpretation*, Princeton: Princeton University Press.

Rosenblatt, Louise M. (1978) *The Reader, the Text, the Poem: The Transactional Theory of the Literary Work*, Carbondale: Southern Illinois University Press.

Ruthven, K.K. (1979) *Critical Assumptions*, Cambridge: Cambridge University Press.

Saussure, F. de (1916) *Course in General Linguistics*, trans. R. Harris (1983) London: Duckworth.

Todorov, Tzvetan (1980 (1975)) 'Reading as construction', pp. 67–82 in Susan R. Suleiman and Inge Crosman (eds) *The Reader in the Text: Essays on Audience and Interpretation*, Princeton: Princeton University Press.

Weinberg, Steven (1983) 'Beautiful theories', revision of the Second Annual Gordon Mills Lecture, unpublished MS, University of Texas, Austin.

White, Hayden (1981) 'The value of narrativity in the representation of reality', pp. 1–24 in W.J.T. Mitchell (ed.) *On Narrative*, Chicago: University of Chicago Press.

Woolf, Virginia (1953 (1925)) *The Common Reader. First Series*, New York and London: Harcourt Brace Jovanovich.

· 2 ·

Narrative Theories and Legal Discourse

BERNARD S. JACKSON

Introduction

Narrative models of different kinds have been used in and around legal studies for a number of different purposes. Lawyers have used them, for example, to *justify* some of the inferential processes of fact-finding in court, while social scientists have used them in a descriptive account of the processes of construction of truth by the jury. Lawyers have also begun to study the rhetorical implications of the presentation of facts by judges in their published judgments, and have noted particularly the relationship between fact and law which is implicit in that practice. Psychologists have considered the role of narrative in the operation of memory and other psychological processes – an issue clearly important for our assessment of the construction of legal facts. Some semiotic approaches, notably that of Greimas, place considerable importance upon narrative in the deep structure of signification of any form of discourse; this approach, too, has been applied to legal discourse.

In this chapter, I first review these various uses of narrative in the legal context, and then offer my own recipe for their inter-relationship. It is a recipe which adopts semiotics as its overall conceptual structure, and which in so doing endorses a Saussurian-based semiotics. By using this recipe, I seek to achieve an integrated model of legal processes: one which, through its emphasis upon the narrative construction of the pragmatic as well as the semantic dimension of legal discourse, is able to offer parallel accounts of the construction and of the justification of facts, and of the construction and justification of law within (and outside) the processes of the courtroom.[1] While more traditional accounts stress (or presuppose) the difference between 'fact' and 'law', my approach attaches greater importance to the distinction between the often unconscious processes of decision-making on the one hand and the explicit rationality of the justification of decisions on the other[2] – whether those decisions concern fact or law.

Narrative in the Rhetorical Presentation of a Case

Twining, in a recently completed book,[3] considers a view some-times expressed by practising advocates, and endorsed by some American realists, that the statement of facts can often be formu-lated so as to advance a particular legal argument: 'The statement of facts is the heart of the case.' He offers as an example the opening passage of Lord Denning's judgment in the case of *Miller* v. *Jackson*.

In summer time village cricket is the delight of everyone. Nearly every village has its own cricket field where the young men play and the old men watch. In the village of Lintz in County Durham they have their own ground, where they have played for these last 70 years. They tend it well. The wicket area is well rolled and mown. The outfield is kept short. It has a good club-house for the players and seats for the onlookers. The village team play there on Saturdays and Sundays. They belong to a league, competing with the neighbouring villages. On other evenings after work they practise while the light lasts. Yet now after these 70 years a judge of the High Court has ordered that they must not play there any more. He has issued an injunction to stop them. He has done it at the instance of a newcomer who is no lover of cricket. This newcomer has built, or has had built for him, a house on the edge of the cricket ground which four years ago was a field where cattle grazed. The animals did not mind the cricket. But now this adjoining field has been turned into a housing estate. The newcomer has bought one of the houses on the edge of the cricket ground. No doubt the open space was a selling point. Now he complains that, when a batsman hits a six, the ball has been known to land in his garden or on or near his house. His wife has got so upset about it that they always go out at weekends. They do not go into the garden when cricket is being played. They say that this is intolerable. So they asked the judge to stop the cricket being played. And the judge, much against his will, has felt that he must order the cricket to be stopped: with the consequences, I suppose, that the Lintz Cricket Club will disappear. The cricket ground will be turned to some other use. I expect for more houses or a factory. The young men will turn to other things instead of cricket. The whole village will be much the poorer. And all this because of a newcomer who has just bought a house there next to the cricket ground.[4]

Twining notes that this example of the presentation of facts by a judge is sometimes regarded as extreme, or 'in some undefined way unjudge-like'. It seems to be arguing a case, 'in favour of cricket, against the Millers personally, or against property developers, or private property',[5] rather than merely to provide a neutral description.

To my mind, what is interesting is the manner in which the rhetoric is expressed in a narrative form. There is a picture of a community bonded together by this common interest: in summer, they all go and enjoy the cricket. Cricket even unites the young and old (an oppositional pair within which conflict is often expected). In Lintz, the villagers are so wedded to cricket that they have actually purchased their own ground, and have looked after it with love and attention. This is not a bias in favour of 'cricket' in the abstract, but rather in favour of the traditional playing of cricket, with all the associations which its narrativization presents. These value-laden associations are not legally relevant, yet they are inextricable from the narrative understanding of the situation.

This first narrative (of traditional cricket-playing) is then put into a wider narrative framework. The fact that the villagers have always (or at least for seventy years) played cricket on this site implies that they want (and are entitled) to continue to do so.[6] But along comes an opponent, 'a newcomer who is no lover of cricket'. We have immediately the narrative framework of an outsider who comes along and tries to interfere with traditional practices. This comes laden with social disapproval. Not only that. The outsider gets 'a Judge of the High Court' to order them to stop playing. Another 'disapproved' narrative is here introduced: the person in authority who interferes with the traditional pleasures of the people. Moreover, the effect of the judge's order might well prove socially detrimental: Lord Denning conjures up a narrative of young men, deprived of their traditional pursuits, who turn to violence. All this, of course, is 'factual' description. But then, the *coup de grâce*: 'And all this because of a newcomer who has just bought a house there next to the cricket ground.' This refers obliquely (and disapprovingly) to the legal rule that it is no defence that the plaintiff 'came to the nuisance'. Here, the activity existed before the Millers arrived. They had the choice not to buy a property affected in that way. Lord Denning has clothed his opposition to the application of the legal rule in a vivid, narrative presentation of the facts. The effectiveness of that strategy of persuasion is attested by its recurrent use from ancient[7] to modern times.[8]

In discussing this passage I have sought to identify only those underlying narrative frameworks which appear to have affected Lord Denning's decision as to the proper rule to apply. There are many other features of the passage which are worthy of attention (such as the relative lack of interest in the background of the Millers – 'This newcomer has built, or has had built for him' – as compared to that of the cricketers) which contribute, at the rhetorical level, to the justifiability of the conclusion, albeit in non-legal terms. In the event, this persuasion was – at least in terms of the narrative structure here presented – successful: the outcome of the case was that the order of the High Court judge was reversed. The cricket club was allowed to continue – although with a requirement to compensate if the cricket balls caused damage.

The reason why the judgment stands out as unusual, and – to Twining and some of his students – 'deviant', is because Lord Denning appears here to have misjudged, according to the conventions of at least these types of audience, the dividing line between those factors in decision-making which conventionally remain private, and those which may be used publicly in the processes of justification. That dividing line is imposed to a large extent by the content of rules of law: it is the content of the substantive rules which determines 'relevance' ('relevance', of course, as understood for legal purposes). Where the judge does stray, in his presentation of the facts, from those issues which the law regards as relevant, we may reasonably hypothesize that he is giving an account of (some of) those non-legal factors which have actually influenced his decision-making.

This is one part of the answer to an obvious methodological difficulty: if the judgment is a justificatory discourse, how can we use it to provide evidence of the anterior processes of decision-making? Judicial discourse, I suggest, leaves traces of decision-making to the extent that it is 'deviant', and breaches conventions as to what may legitimately be said within justificatory discourse. But this is not our only resource for the detection of decision-making. Even where the facts recounted are limited to those which are 'relevant' in terms of the legal rules,[9] we may still have recourse to the rhetorical construction of the narrative. For though the law may define that which is relevant, it cannot define how the relevant facts, in a particular case, are to be expressed. Nor can the judge's presentation of the facts ever be entirely neutral. It reflects – by its inclusions and exclusions, the emphases of its sentence construction, and the structures of its argumentation – choices which, precisely because they are deployed spontaneously in the act of writing, may well be relevant to the subconscious, decision-making level.

Narrative and the Assessment of Probabilities

Neil MacCormick has offered a conception of 'narrative coherence' as 'a test of truth or probability in questions of fact and evidence upon which direct proof by immediate observation is unavailable'.[10] He compares detective fiction, as exemplified by the Sherlock Holmes stories: the reason something strikes us as plausible in literature, and equally in life, is that 'we treat the natural world as explicable in terms of explanatory principles ("laws") of a causal and probabilistic kind, and the world of human affairs as explicable in terms of explanatory principles of a rational, intentional and motivational as well as a causal and probabilistic kind'. That narrative coherence, for MacCormick, comes into play only in the absence of truth based upon observation (and communicated through referential language) is well illustrated by his account of the difficulty in the notorious Edinburgh murder case of Burke and Hare:

The police witness says he found a human corpse in a box in William Burke's house. The corpse bore marks of bruising. The juror *knows* that was said. If the juror believes that the witness is honest and has a sound memory and is remembering facts he had the opportunity carefully to observe (all of which features of witnesses and their evidence it is the task of the cross-examination by defence counsel to test), then the juror has reason to believe that the testimony is true, or more or less probably true depending on the credibility (that is, the honesty, accuracy and reliability) of the witness.[11]

If coherence comes into play only when direct observation stops, it also falls short, for MacCormick, of providing a sufficient means of assessing possible inferences from the observed facts. What it provides is no more than one or more coherent *theories*. In order to assess the relative weight of such theories, he suggests, we must hand over to the analyst of probabilities.[12] At the end of the day MacCormick is apparently not satisfied by the commonsensical status of narrative coherence; he seeks, at the least, to validate narrative coherence through recourse to a more specific form of justificatory discourse.

Narrative and Plausibility: The Modern Jury Trial

It is a mistake, I would suggest, to limit the role of 'narrative coherence' to the assessment of *inferences from* direct testimony. At least as important is the assessment of the truth-claims of that direct testimony itself. While paying substantial attention to different types of inference, Bennett and Feldman apply narrative models to the assessment both of direct evidence (that which the witness claims personally to have observed) and of inferences which the jury is invited to draw from such direct evidence.[13] Taking their inspiration from frame analysis in sociology, they sought to test a hypothesis derived from their observations of jury trials, combined with discussions with participants, through the use of social-psychological experimentation.

Their hypothesis was that the construction of truth within the courtroom was primarily a matter of the *overall* narrative plausibility of the story told. They argue that it is not the weighing of individual elements of the story, each in terms of the evidence for that element, which renders a case persuasive or not, but rather the plausibility of the story structure taken as a whole. One argument for this lies in the fact that several different witnesses are called to construct a single story. 'In the end,' they argue, 'it is the fit of the symbolised element into the larger structure, and not the pure documentation for the element itself, that dictates final judgment . . . alternative definitions are available for virtually any fact or bit of evidence. Once again, the key issue is how the chosen definition fits within the competing accounts of the incident' (Bennett and Feldman 1981: 113ff.).

In order to test this, they set up an experiment within which two groups of undergraduates told stories to the rest of the class, the one group telling true stories (involving themselves), the other group telling false stories (also involving themselves), and the audience rating the truth of each story. They then determined whether audience judgments varied independently of the truth status of the story, by comparing audience guesses to each story-teller's claim about his or her story. The stories were scored for ambiguities by each author, and 80 per cent agreement on all the various aspects of the coding task was achieved. Their results indicated no statistical association between the actual truth status of stories and their perceived truth status. Moreover, they found that the structure of a story had a considerable impact on its credibility; as structural ambiguities in stories increased, credibility decreased, and vice versa.

Bennett and Feldman claim, in effect, that judgements as to truth are based upon comparison with common-sense knowledge, and that this knowledge is itself constructed as narrative. But we must distinguish (perhaps more clearly than Bennett and Feldman do) between narrative structures on the one hand and substantive narrative typifications of behaviour on the other. Narrative structures are structures of understanding which allow us to recognize discourse presented to us as an intelligible story; it has much in common, in this respect, with 'story grammar' as developed by some social psychologists,[14] and indeed with the syntagmatic level of the 'deep structures of signification' of Greimasian semiotics.[15] Bennett and Feldman present an account of narrative structure in terms of setting, concern, central action, and resolution:

The setting usually includes the time, the place and some of the characters. The concern is an action that, given the setting, creates a climactic (eventful, ironical, suspenseful) situation. For example, if someone is rock-climbing (as was the case in one of our stories) and slips and falls, slipping and falling are the concern. If the story ended at this point, the audience would be left wondering: what happened to the climber? Was he hurt or killed? A complete story will provide an answer to these questions. This stage is the resolution. The central action is the structural element that creates the central question the story must resolve. The resolution normally resolves both the predicament created by the problem and the questions the listeners might have had about the outcome. In the rock-climbing story the resolution consisted of telling the audience that the climber was taken to hospital for treatment. (ibid: 79)

However, plausibility to the jury is not merely a matter of intelligibility of the discourse as a (well-structured) story: it is a matter also of comparison with known substantive narrative typifications of behaviour. Every society (and, we may suggest, particular subgroups within it) has its own stock of substantive narratives, which represent typical human behaviour patterns known and understood within that society or social group. This is the form in which social knowledge is acquired and stored, and which provides the framework for understanding particular stories presented to us in discourse.

That is not to suggest that only such discourse as conforms exactly to one or other typification will be intelligible. Intelligibility, rather, is a question of degree, consisting of the relative similarity of that which is told to a framework of existing social knowledge. Racial stereotypes would form one – extreme – example. Criminal stereotypes are another. The jury in a criminal trial would come equipped, for example, with expectations as to the typical motives of criminals, their typical methods of operation, etc. They would equally come equipped with expectations regarding circumstances which constitute justification or excuse. On all these matters, of course, the law seeks to impose its own definitions. But those definitions, however strongly they are urged by the judge, cannot completely suppress the social knowledge of the jury. For this latter may be taken to operate largely at the subconscious level.

The weak point of Bennett and Feldman's account consists in their treatment of the pragmatic level. Many trial lawyers would argue that plausibility turns not only on the content of that which is told, but also on the manner of telling it. Professional manuals exist to assist the advocate in presenting his or her case – even through the medium of questioning – in the manner which will appear the most convincing. Clearly, rhetorical factors have a role to play in the construction of truth in the courtroom. However, Bennett and Feldman seek to reduce this pragmatic dimension to the semantic level of the content of the stories told in court. Bias, they argue, operates (only) *through* socially-acquired frameworks. Adopting a holistic approach, they claim that 'it makes very little sense to concentrate on the surface properties of the courtroom in isolation from their bearing on the story structure in a case' (ibid: 165). Again, 'various characteristics of case, crime, defendant, law, and lawyer will affect the judgment of a case only when they trigger particular understandings constrained by the strategic stories orchestrated by the lawyers' (ibid: 165). Middle-class witnesses, for example, may prove more effective witnesses than members of sub-cultures because the former provide testimony that can be translated into standard story form intelligible to the average white middle-class juror. A similar argument is adopted with respect to the courtroom rhetoric of the lawyers: 'When surface rhetorical tactics lose touch with the underlying story . . ., they lose their effectiveness' (ibid: 141ff.). Rhetorical moves are not to be regarded as 'self-contained events that can be evaluated in terms of their intrinsic drama, their immediate impact, or their demonstrable success in creating the impression desired by the speaker' (ibid: 143). Yet at the same time, Bennett and Feldman note the importance of the confidence of witnesses as a factor in credibility, and the use of qualifications (e.g. of expert witnesses) in order to validate testimony.

What Bennett and Feldman fail to realize is that the pragmatics of the courtroom are themselves intelligible via narrative frameworks. We have narrative typifications not only of what members of various groups do outside the court, but also of how truthfully they give evidence, how reliable their memory may be, and (in the case of lawyers) what counts as a successful tactic. The courtroom enunciations – of both witnesses and lawyers – are not mediated through the content of the stories being told; they constitute an independent level of narrative discourse – a filter, even, through which the content of the stories told is translated.

The Narrative of Psychological Processes

Bennett and Feldman concern themselves with the narrative structures of the enunciations of witnesses. However, there is another tradition within social psychology which directs our attention to the role of narrative structures in the psychological processes which lead up to, and are prior conditions of, those witness enunciations. I refer to story grammar in psychology, which suggests that there are several comparable narrative stages earlier, in the *witness's* own observation, recall, and testimony. Thus the witness perceives and encodes what the information source transmits to him/her; selectively stores the message in memory; later recalls (retrieves) that message; and finally tells the court what was observed. Only then can the jury process that which is transmitted. In the work of Mandler and Johnson[16] narrative models are seen to influence *memory* – successful recall. Thus narrative forms a link between perception and communication. Elsewhere the psychological literature suggests the importance of narrative models also in the initial processing of information – encoding or perception. But the processes may not be identical at the perceptual, recall and communicational stages. Semiotics, too, would look for separate analyses of these various sense-producing activities, rather than a linear account of information transmission and distortion which thus endorses a traditional correspondence account of the construction of truth, as being in principle attainable even if obstructed by contingent factors in particular cases.

In fact, the work of Mandler and Johnson suggests that the schemata are more important for recall than for initial perception. They stress the difference between encoding and retrieval: more will be encoded than will be recalled; the effect of story schemata will be more apparent during retrieval than during encoding.[17] A story with poor structure, in the sense that nodes are omitted or causal connections are replaced by temporal ones, may be reasonably well comprehended and recalled if tested soon after presentation. A story may also contain departures from the expected order of propositions. If these sequence inversions are clearly marked in the surface structure, the story may be well comprehended and recalled for a time. However, the longer the delay between telling and recall, the more recall will come to approximate to ideal schemata instead of the actual story heard. The importance of such findings for the judicial process are obvious, and lend indirect credibility to the thesis of Bennett and Feldman, since by the time the witness comes to court, s/he must rely substantially upon idealized narrative schemata even for recall – to say nothing about persuasion.

The distinctions between perception, recall, and telling have more than purely conceptual interest. The work of Mandler and Johnson suggests that the schemata used to guide encoding and recall are related but *not* identical. A similar view is taken by de Beaugrande and Miller:

Another factor of story recall has received too little attention: a recall protocol is a story text in its own right. Here, readers are using their stored schemas actively rather than re-actively . . . . If we look only at percent of accurate recall (or even: verbatim recall), we are throwing out a good deal of our best data, and subconsciously subscribing to a one-sided trace-abstraction/trace-retrieval outlook. Surely the changes, omissions, and additions readers make in recalling story texts tell us as much about understanding, storage, and retrieval strategies as do accurate reproductions.[18]

Mandler and Johnson also found a developmental aspect in the deployment of schemata.[19] In their experiment, adults recalled more than fourth-graders, who in turn recalled more than first-graders. In fact, the recall of first-graders formed two clusters: 'settings, beginnings, and outcomes were well recalled, and attempts, endings, and reactions were poorly recalled'.[20] It is noticeable that this account of story grammar focuses upon the level of underlying narrative structure; indeed, the categories it uses – beginnings, outcomes, reactions, etc. – are not dissimilar to those of Greimasian semiotics. Not surprisingly, Mandler and Johnson are amongst the psychological story grammarians who see themselves as working in the tradition of Propp.[21]

Narrative as an Epistemological/Semiotic Conception

Greimasian semiotics provides a possible framework for our perception of the homologous but distinct operation of semantic and pragmatic levels, and of the place of narrative theories of both social and psychological construction of reality, such as those noted in the preceding sections. Within this wider framework, we may observe the multiplicity of levels at which narrative models may contribute to the construction of sense. We may call them, for convenience, the sociolinguistic level (comprising both the form and content of the particular utterance), the thematic level, and the structural level. The sociolinguistic level comprises both the manner of expression of the text – whether oral or written – and the content of the particular discourse, and belongs exclusively to what some semioticians call the 'surface' (v. 'deep') level of the text, or the 'level of manifestation'. The thematic level is the stock of social knowledge organized in narrative terms, irrespective of the particular manner of its expression on a particular occasion. By definition, this level of narrative content must be socially and culturally contingent. However, a claim can be made – and is made in some semiotic theories – that the intelligibility of such discourse depends upon (though is not sufficiently accounted for by) a universal level of signification, which is the underlying structure of discourse – here termed the structural level. The movement from the thematic to the structural level can be represented as that from Propp to Greimas, the former reducing a large number of folk tales in a particular culture to variations upon a finite number of themes, the latter seeing these themes as themselves manifestations of a more abstract universal structure of signification. Thus, we can distinguish both the form and content of the utterance, the substantive schemata invoked by it, and the underlying structures which render it intelligible. For the structural level, we may have recourse to the 'semio-narrative' theory of A.J. Greimas.

Through a re-analysis of Propp's Russian folk tales, and the thirty-one narrative structures derived by Propp from them, Greimas derived a more abstract, general (and, as he claimed, universal) 'actantial' model, which (in combination with a paradigmatic level, inspired by Saussure and Hjelmslev) he takes as representing the 'deep level' of all discourse. This actantial model consists in a 'narrative syntagm', with three elements: the setting of goals ('contract'), the achievement (or non-achievement) of those goals ('performance'), and the acknowledgement of the performance (or non-performance) of those goals ('recognition'). Involved in this narrative syntagm are a set of *actants*, subject-object, sender-receiver, helper-opponent. A sender invests a receiver as 'subject' of the story, by communicating a goal to him/her. In achieving this goal ('object'), or performing this task, the subject may be assisted by a 'helper', or obstructed by an 'opponent'. At the end of the syntagm there is another communicational element, the sending and receiving of recognition of what has occurred. The *actants* and *fonctions* which make up the semio-narrative level may be expressed at the level of manifest discourse by a variety of *acteurs* (real people in social life; 'characters' in literature), each one of whom may perform different actantial roles at different times. But the fact that we are able to make sense of social action (whether real or literary) at all is due to the fact that these basic structures underlie the discourse. The model is sometimes called 'polemic', because of the presence within it of the 'helper' and 'opponent' – as manifest in Russian folk tales, for example, by the dragon guarding the castle where the princess is imprisoned, and obstructing the subject of the narrative, the hero, from effecting the rescue.

We may compare Greimasian semiotics with psychological story grammars on a number of parameters. As already implied, the semio-narrative level of the deep structure of signification is not concerned directly with the interpretation of the story (whether oral or written) but with what makes the text meaningful at all (*not* what endows it with a particular meaning). This distinction leads to others, of a more operational character. Mandler and Johnson define 'a simple story' by the fact that it has a single protagonist in each episode;[22] their story grammar has difficulty with conversational stories, which have at least two protagonists in any one episode. For this reason their version of story grammar would encounter considerable difficulty in analysing courtroom cross-examination, whereas Greimasian semiotics can account for this quite readily in terms of polemic narrative structures operating within the pragmatics of the courtroom itself.

The Narrativization of Pragmatics in the Common Law Trial

Conventionally, the 'battle' which occurs in the courtroom is assumed to be between the two parties to the litigation: plaintiff and defendant in civil cases, prosecutor and accused in criminal. But it does not take long to observe the fact that the two parties to the dispute very rarely engage in the combat. There will be no occasion in the trial during which the parties confront each other, as speaking subjects. Indeed, it is only in relatively modern times that parties to a dispute have been permitted to give evidence on their own behalf.

Perhaps, then, the combat manifest in the trial (I do not speak, metaphorically, of the underlying conflict of interests) is engaged in by champions, as representatives of the two parties? This is closer to the truth, but still far distant from it. Occasionally, counsel for the two sides clash directly, as where one objects to a particular question put to a witness by the other,[23] or where there is a dispute on a point of law, on which the opposing counsel are invited to make submissions to the court. But most of the time of the lawyers is spent in examining and cross-examining witnesses. And that is where the most perceptible battles take place. Every single witness may be 'cross-examined', a form of hostile questioning designed to plant doubts in the mind of the judge or jury as to the credibility, truthfulness, or accuracy of the witness. In terms of the Greimasian narrative syntagm the witness is a subject for whom a goal has been set, to perform the task of persuading the court of the truth of certain propositions. S/he has a helper and an opponent. The helper is counsel for the party who called the witness, and who commences the examination of the witness in a 'friendly' manner; indeed, s/he is normally not allowed by the court to indulge in 'hostile' examination of his/her own party's witness. The opponent is the counsel for the opposing party, who conducts the 'cross-examination'. The subject of the narrative syntagm thus undergoes a test; later, there is a recognition of it, in the judge's summing up, and ultimately, but less explicitly, in the decision of the court.

It may, however, be argued that while this analysis accounts for a greater part of the observable phenomena of the trial than do alternative formulations of the trial-by-battle theory, it would be artificial to reduce the trial process to just this. To this, there are two answers. First, such a Greimasian analysis is not reductive; it provides an account of necessary elements in the construction of meaning but does not claim to provide a sufficient account of all the semiotic characteristics of the 'level of manifestation'. Second, Greimasian theory insists upon a distinction between *actants* and *acteurs*. For example, the opposing counsel (*acteurs* at the level of manifestation) may play the roles (as *actants*) of helper and opponent in the narrative syntagm just described. Clearly, each one regularly changes from helper to opponent as the witnesses of the other party take the stand. But they may also play other roles at the very same time. And indeed, each also has a personal task to perform – to advance his/her career by impressing the judge. In this context, s/he is a subject. In some trials there may be more than the normal element of professional opposition involved between the rival counsel. And, given this theoretical orientation, we need not exclude from our analysis the battle between the opposing parties. In other words, even at the 'deep' level of the analysis, the trial may be seen as an overlapping series of contests. It is intelligible as such: the jury observes the contest, understands the respective goals of the participants, forms a judgment as to who has 'won', i.e. succeeded in the objective of persuasion, and gives recognition to that fact. It is this story – that of the pragmatics of the trial – which the judge or jury observes;[24] it is only through this process that they have access to the facts whose truth or otherwise is to be established; and the possibility of this latter objective is contingent upon the intelligibility of that through which it is mediated – the pragmatics of the trial.

The above proposal encompasses a vitally important theoretical claim as to the structure of semiotics, quite apart from its potential for providing an explanatory model of judicial discourse. Its theoretical claim is that we cannot separate the semantic and pragmatic dimensions of a text, or (to use different terminology) its semiotic and rhetorical features. The two are inextricably intertwined. Purpose and audience affect discursive structure. To many, this will appear obvious, commonplace and banal. But in current debates regarding legal semiotics, it is a theoretical position not to be taken for granted. For there are many who portray the viewpoint of the Greimasian school as excluding pragmatics from semiotics entirely.

Rhetoric does not here provide a model antithetical to the role of narrative coherence in the construction of truth – as Bennett and Feldman appear to fear. Rhetorical practices simply manifest a second level of narrative, that which I term 'the story of the trial' in contrast to 'the story (told) in the trial'.[25] That 'story of the trial' is as much subject to the constraints of narrative coherence as is 'the story (told) in the trial'. For the 'story of the trial' is at root just another piece of human action, no different in kind from 'the story (told) in the trial'. We have conventional narrative frameworks for the understanding of the former no less than for the latter. We know what it takes – who, how, etc., – to persuade. Any theory of narrative coherence must take due account of the narrativization of pragmatics.

BERNARD S. JACKSON

Law Construction: The Role of Narrative in Judicial Decision-Making

Lawyers conventionally distinguish fundamentally between the processes of fact construction on the one hand and of law determination and application on the other. This sacred distinction even influenced American realism, within which separate schools, or approaches, known as 'rule-scepticism' and 'fact-scepticism' were generated. The separation, of course, is crucial to the image of the lawyer as an expert, a member of an autonomous profession, one separated from society as a whole through its peculiar science. However, adoption of a semio-narrative viewpoint, such as has been sketched in the earlier sections of this article, leads us to reject any fundamental distinction between 'fact' and 'law'. As I argue at some length in *Law, Fact and Narrative Coherence* (Deborah Charles Publications, 1988), the very same semio-narrative concepts are fully applicable to the construction of law and to decision-making by reference to it. This applies even to the processes of conversational interaction in the arguing of points of law. In the context of appeals to the House of Lords, judge – counsel interaction takes centre-stage. Paterson quotes a QC who described the dialogue between Bar and Bench as '. . . like a football game: you only play as well as the opponents let you – and by opponents I mean the tribunal'.[26]

In deciding a case, the judge has two tasks to perform: first, to make a decision regarding the disposal of the case; second, to justify that decision – to a number of audiences, perhaps, but most especially to the audience of the legal profession. I take the view that, even in 'easy' cases, decision-making is not a simple result of (justificatory) legal reasoning: if it were, the principal goal of reform of our legal system would be the substitution of judges by computers. In fact, decision-making necessarily takes account of the subconscious as well as the conscious reasoning of the judge, and this subconscious reasoning is necessarily informed by ordinary social knowledge, constructed and maintained through narrative frameworks.

This is sometimes apparent in areas of doctrinal difficulty: series of cases which are difficult to reconcile in purely doctrinal terms, but where the individual decision in each one is understandable, taking account of narrative structures. An instance of such a set of cases occurs in the English law regarding contracts induced by fraud, where the fraud relates to the identity of one of the contracting parties. Typically, a 'rogue' (as the law constructs him) buys goods misrepresenting his/her identity to be that of some other person whose credit-worthiness is capable of being established. S/he obtains the goods in exchange for a cheque, which turns out to be worthless. S/he then disposes of the goods to an innocent purchaser, and absconds with the proceeds. Can the original owner recover the goods from the innocent purchaser? This depends on whether the mistake in the fraudulent transaction rendered the contract 'void' or merely 'voidable'.

Where the fraudulent transaction was conducted face-to-face, the courts have encountered particular difficulties in determining this question. In *Phillips* v. *Brooks Ltd*,[27] a rogue entered a shop, represented himself to be Sir George Bullough residing at a certain address, and gave a cheque in the name of Bullough in exchange for pearls and a ring. Before accepting the cheque and parting with the goods, the jeweller took the precaution of checking the directory to verify that Bullough (whose name, in fact, was known to him) did reside at that address. By the time the fraud was discovered, the rogue had pledged the ring to an innocent third party, the defendant. When the jeweller sued the latter for recovery of the ring, the court held that the fraudulently-induced mistake did not here render the contract void, since the shopkeeper intended to deal with the person in the shop, provided that he was satisfied as to his credit-worthiness (which he was, on verifying the address given to him). The contract therefore was merely voidable, so that the transaction had remained valid until such time as the seller discovered the mistake and decided to avoid the contract. But by that time, the defendant had already obtained rights in the ring, which the jeweller could not override.

Compare this with the case of *Ingram* v. *Little*.[28] Here, the sellers were defrauded into parting with their car by a rogue who claimed to be P.G.M. Hutchinson of a certain address. The sellers had not heard of P.G.M. Hutchinson, but took the trouble of verifying from the telephone directory that there was a P.G.M. Hutchinson at the address the rogue had given, before accepting the cheque. When the cheque turned out to be worthless, they sought recovery of the car from the innocent third party to whom the rogue had, in the meantime, resold it. Here, the court held that the contract was void, and not merely voidable, so that the sellers were able to recover the car, notwithstanding the fact that the fraud came to light only after the car had been resold to an innocent purchaser.

If we construct the facts in terms only of those categories which the legal rules claim to be relevant, then no reasonable explanation can be given of this case.[29] There are, however, pertinent *narrative* distinctions between this case and *Phillips* v. *Brooks Ltd*, although, in purely legal terms, the two appear indistinguishable. The differences relate to the narrative roles of the participants in the respective stories. In *Phillips* v. *Brooks Ltd*, the seller seeking to recover his goods was a shopkeeper, while in *Ingram* v. *Little* the sellers were private individuals (two sisters) disposing of their second-hand car. The judges have at least two alternative narrative frameworks from which to choose. On the one hand, there is the narrative of the shopkeeper[30] – here, almost by definition, a retailer of fairly valuable commodities (such as the jeweller in *Phillips* v. *Brooks Ltd*), not the corner sweetshop – who, in the course of business, is bound on occasion to part with goods in return for worthless cheques, and on the other hand the story of the 'innocent' (in both senses) private seller, defrauded by an (habitual) rogue.

What influences the choice between these two stock narratives? The comparison is informed not only by neutral perceptions of degree of similarity, but by the force or pertinence (or 'relevance') of those particular narrative traits which distinguish the two schemes. And this relevance is a function of an *evaluation* of the situation. Narratives come laden with tacit social evaluations. In that of the shopkeeper defrauded by a dud cheque, though our sympathies may be with him, we do not sympathize with him as fulfilling the role of an innocent victim in quite the same way that we do when regarding the narrative of the private individual who has been defrauded by the same means. The representation of the plaintiffs as 'two sisters' (implied of the elderly maiden variety) evokes further sympathy, and reinforces our evaluation that they are victims who ought to be assisted (even as against an innocent third-party purchaser).

Of course, one might argue that the law has simply added a further distinction: the consequences of a mistake as to credit-worthiness differ according to whether the mistaken party is a retailer or a private individual. The courts had an opportunity to decide just that, a few years later, in another case involving the private sale of a second-hand motor car. In *Lewis* v. *Averay*,[31] the rogue posed as Richard Greene, a well-known film actor (who played Robin Hood in the television series of that name – information provided by Lord Denning[32]). As proof of identity he produced an admission pass to a leading British film studio, Pinewood, bearing the name 'Richard A. Green', a photograph (of the rogue) and an official stamp. The plaintiff then handed over the car and its log-book in exchange for a (stolen) cheque signed R.A. Green. By the time the fraud came to light, the car had been sold to an innocent purchaser, from whom the plaintiff then sought to recover it. The Court of Appeal could have endorsed a distinction between *Phillips* v. *Brooks Ltd* and *Ingram* v. *Little* along the lines here suggested. It chose rather to follow *Phillips* v. *Brooks Ltd* and disapprove *Ingram* v. *Little*: the contract was merely voidable, had not been avoided in time, and therefore the innocent third-party purchaser was protected against the claims of the original owner.

At the level of legal doctrine, the result is confusing, unless one simply takes a predictive view based upon the weight of authority *after Lewis* v. *Averay*, and concludes that in practice *Ingram* v. *Little* is unlikely to be followed in future cases: doctrinally, it is not distinguishable from the other cases, but must be treated simply as an anomaly. If, however, we look at these cases against typical narratives with their accompanying social evaluations, the results of the decision-making may not appear quite so strange. Even the different results in *Ingram* v. *Little* and *Lewis* v. *Averay* become intelligible. Although in both, the plaintiff was a private individual, not a retailer, in the one case we *sympathize* with the victim of the fraud (the two sisters in *Ingram* v. *Little*) while in the other we are *amused*: the plaintiff here appears more as a stupid dupe than as a victim. How many people would believe a stranger when he turned up out of the blue and told them he was a famous actor? If he was so famous, the plaintiff should not have been fooled; he should not have accepted the evidence of the admission pass; and he should have realized that the name on the cheque presented to him was spelled differently from that of the real Richard Greene.

This is reinforced by Lord Denning's narrative constructions of the parties in this case: the plaintiff was 'a young man who is a postgraduate student of chemistry', while the defendant was also young: 'at the time under 21. He was a music student in London at the Royal College of Music.' In terms, then, of the two 'innocent' parties competing not to carry the loss, there was not much to choose. But added point is given to the underlying pattern by the fact that the duped plaintiff was a person of some intelligence (if it is permissible so to construct postgraduate students of chemistry). Hence, when it comes to comparison of the litigants, the plaintiff's youth is suppressed: 'Now Mr. Lewis, the original owner of the car, sues young Mr. Averay.'

The overall impression given by the narratives in *Ingram* v. *Little* and *Lewis* v. *Averay* is therefore different; the two sisters may have been defrauded, but Lewis was actually *fooled*. That being so, the contest between plaintiff and defendant is no longer one between two equally innocent parties: it is between a fool and an innocent, and the fool is at least partly the victim of his own stupidity. The culpability of the plaintiff here may not amount to that required by the law to deprive him of a remedy: i.e. that the true situation would have been *obvious* to a reasonable person. Nevertheless, decision-making reflects the social evaluation of the case, which is here typified by laughter rather than sympathy.

Narrative in the Justification of Legal Decisions

Both judges and academic writers internalize (some, of course, more successfully than others) narrative rules as to those types of justificatory strategy which are most likely to prove acceptable according to the conventions of the audience concerned. Here, we do indeed move away from the social construction of ordinary, common-sense knowledge, into the sphere of the construction of the knowledge of a particular sub-group. However, the processes are essentially the same, even if the 'semiotic group'[33] and the 'codes' they use are different. Knowledge of rhetorical strategy, of the kinds of arguments which are likely to persuade, and the modes of presenting those arguments, are far from adequately represented in doctrinal textbooks. They depend upon internalization of observed behaviour – in particular, through observation of those forms of behaviour which are 'sanctioned' (recognized) with approval by the sub-group concerned and those which provoke a hostile reaction. In this way, narrative typifications of successful persuasion are built up, generating what Karl Llewellyn termed the 'trained intuition of the lawyer'.

Such rules are internalized not simply as strategies of persuasion, but as truth-creating procedures, so that certain types of argument do genuinely appear to be more persuasive than others. This may well come about by conversion of the practical effect of the argument into a quality of the argument perceived to be inherent in it. But of course, the plausibility of justificatory discourse is not a purely semantic matter. There is no one best answer in terms of the argument (in the abstract) most likely to succeed. For the narrative rules concerned specify typifications not only of arguments but of enunciations of arguments: who proposes the argument (the authority of the enunciator), how it is proposed (the rhetoric of its presentation), when and where it is proposed (the context of the enunciation). Through everyday interaction, and sometimes in highly institutionalized forms (such as dining together at the Inns of Court in England), narrative typifications of the pragmatics of courtroom interaction are built up. These apply to doctrinal justification as much as to courtroom tactics.[34] The point is worth stressing in relation to doctrinal justification, in the light particularly of the 'narrative' theories of Ronald Dworkin.

Dworkin has suggested that the reasoning of judges in 'hard cases' presents significant parallels with the practices of a different group of professional interpreters, the literary critics.[35] Legal argument employs a form of coherence which is not a purely legal construct. Legal reasoning is a 'holistic' form of meaning, which depends upon semiotic processes similar to those found in literature. At the same time, Dworkin does not claim that the semiotic processes are identical in the two forms of discourse: his 'Hercules' is not interchangeable with Northrop Frye, Frank Kermode, or Umberto Eco. Because of the particular democratic values underlying the legal system – the values which Dworkin seeks to affirm and promote through his analysis of legal reasoning – the discretion of the judge is limited in particular ways. There exist, for example, two different types of legal sign, which the judge must distinguish: 'principles' and 'policies'. In my opinion, Dworkin (like Bennett and Feldman) makes a significant contribution to the study of legal signification, by pointing to a level of analysis which may be regarded as between the 'deep level' of Greimasian analysis and the 'surface level' which we find in sociolinguistics. However, he commits an error very comparable to that here attributed to Bennett and Feldman. He reduces to a single semantic level an activity whose pragmatics equally call for narrativization.

At different times, Dworkin has used two different models of literary activity, which he appears to regard as interchangeable, but which are better regarded as distinct. The first is the activity of the literary critic, looking back on a completed text, and asking questions about it. He invites us to imagine, for example, a meeting of literary critics discussing Dickens' novel *David Copperfield*.[36] One asks: did David have a homosexual relationship with Steerforth? There is nothing in the novel which explicitly says that he did, or did not; nor is there anything in the novel (he assumes) from which either a positive or a negative answer to that question can necessarily be inferred. Nevertheless, Dworkin argues, the literary critics could intelligibly debate this question, on the basis of what hypothesis as to the nature of David's relationship with Steerforth best coheres with the facts actually stated in the novel. For this notion, Dworkin proposes the name 'facts of narrative consistency'. The discovery of law in difficult cases is, he claims, like that. The law is to be regarded as a literary whole, but one consisting of norms rather than facts.

Elsewhere, Dworkin uses the model of a 'chain novel'. One author writes the first chapter of a novel, and gives it to a second author, who must write the second chapter. The latter passes the 'story so far' (chapters 1–2) to a third author, and s/he adds the third chapter. The construction of the novel proceeds in this way, until it is completed (whatever that means). At each point of the chain, Dworkin suggests, the freedom of action of the author becomes more limited, as the amount of data with which the new chapter must 'fit' increases. Each successive author is thus progressively more constrained. Increasingly, s/he discovers what is implicit in what goes before, rather than creates something entirely new.

There is, of course, a significant difference between these two models. In the first, the text is completed before the literary critics set to work; in the second, the literati are engaged in the construction of the text. Dworkin might object that each author in the chain novel already has no less finite a text (from which to derive criteria of 'fit') than do the literary critics in surveying *David Copperfield*. Nevertheless, I suggest that Dworkin here reveals what at worst is the ambiguity, and at best the complexity, of the nature of judicial activity itself. The judge *is* at one and the same time both author and critic. At one and the same time the judge is addressing a variety of different audiences. But each of these audiences constitutes a semiotic group with its own narrativized conventions. In rendering judgment on contested legal issues, the judge addresses doctrinal audiences (who will indeed view the decision in terms of its 'fit' with a pre-existing body of doctrine), judicial audiences (fellow-judges, whose criteria of a good decision may be somewhat different), and most particularly the audience of that particular litigation, for whom s/he has to make a specific decision, and to whom the nature of that decision is far more important than the legal grounds on which it is given. There is no doubt, in this latter respect, that the activity of the judge is creative: when the decision is given, an entirely new legal speech-act is performed, which creates a new state of affairs for the parties to the litigation. In short, the judge takes part in several different stories, of fact discovery, of law discovery, and of the (theoretically separable) activity of adjudication, whereby legal rules are 'applied' to facts. In those stories, s/he performs a multitude of different actantial roles. Dworkin's failure to recognize the difference between such stories as discussion amongst critics on the one hand and participation in a chain novel on the other reflects his neglect of the pragmatic level. Criteria of plausible justification are as much a function of success or failure in playing a particular role in the narratives of successful criticism or successful adjudication as of the inherent reasonableness of what is said in the justificatory discourse.

Narrative Competence, Narrative Negotiation and Truth

The claims made in this chapter raise important conceptual issues. Traditionalists may object to the apparent reduction of truth to narrative. Relativists may argue, contrariwise, that narrative frameworks provide too fixed, too rule-bound, a model; in fact, truth is a matter simply of politics and negotiation. In this final section, I approach these questions in semiotic terms, by asking about the nature and status of the multitude of semiotic systems considered in this account of narrative models.

My conception of the relationship of narrative to truth can perhaps be illuminated by consideration of a different semiotic structure, the depiction of reality in painting. Suppose that I walk through a portrait gallery. What I see may provoke judgments of a number of different kinds. Occasionally, I may 'know' (or think I know) the subject of the portrait. I have seen film, for example, of the Queen sufficiently often on television to make me believe that I know what she really looks like, so that I can judge whether a particular portrait is a 'true' likeness. But most of our judgments, in walking through a portrait gallery, are not of this variety. On the one hand, we realize that the artist is trying to tell us something *about* the subject, and not merely 'depict' the subject in some neutral fashion. Here, the description is necessarily tied to a (personal, not social) evaluation of some kind: the subject is kind, haughty, elegant, different, etc. If we have no 'knowledge' of what the subject 'looks like', this latter form of judgment is (almost) the only kind which we can make about the subject (I do not say about the painting). Moreover, our very assumption that this portrait is 'of' (or 'about') a determinate human subject, the one whose name (and sometimes dates) appears below the portrait, is taken very much on trust. The portrait itself does not 'refer' to that real person, the subject. It is only by the separate speech-act of referring, made by naming the subject below the portrait, that this act of identification is effected.[37] Without that, we may note, the portrait could be of any number of human beings whose features happen to resemble those of the portrait. Moreover, and most important, the portrait would still 'make sense' without any such act of reference at all. Indeed, in our walk through the portrait gallery, we may pass paintings labelled 'portrait of an unknown woman' or even portraits without any designation at all. These are still recognizably portraits: they make the same type of sense as those with identifiable referents, even though this particular portrait may have no referent at all.

I have chosen here the portrait gallery for my argument (rather, for example, than the landscape gallery – to which the same analysis could be applied), because it brings into play a theory of Noam Chomsky's, which may be useful to us in the present context. In an essay entitled 'Language and unconscious knowledge',[38]

Chomsky discusses the relationship between language and other semiotic systems. His view is that (contrary to the structuralists) non-linguistic semiotic systems are not necessarily modelled in the same way as language (for example, with the whole range of syntactic, semantic and pragmatic dimensions), but have their independent structures. Nevertheless, such structures – while perhaps simpler than those of language – may also be 'deep' (in a generative sense). Moreover, the same type of 'innateness' hypothesis may be advanced in respect of them, as in respect of language: namely, that without such a hypothesis, it becomes difficult to explain how we can emit and process an infinite variety of signs, on the basis of acquiring (inferring) rules in childhood based upon a much more limited input of signs. One such simpler semiotic system, Chomsky suggests, is that of face recognition.[39] There may well be, argues Chomsky, some innate capacity for face recognition, indeed a 'grammar of face recognition'. This gives us a competence to identify persons whom we meet at various stages of our lives, on the basis of a single past encounter. (It is, of course, arguable that there are good evolutionary reasons for the development of such a human competence.)

This aspect of Chomsky's thought ought, perhaps, to be attached to the Greimasian view of narrative. In particular, it is needed in order to bridge the gap between 'deep structures of signification' on the one hand (which, of themselves, have no 'investment' as particular narratives) and socially-constructed typifications of behaviour, which represent substantive narratives. It is clearly not the case that human behaviour is recognizable only in so far as it conforms exactly to an existing, socially-constructed narrative typification of behaviour. Indeed, the very term 'typification' implies a much looser relationship. Thus it is that in assessing the plausibility of a particular narrative, we make *comparisons* with the typifications which are socially constructed, but within an existing semiotic constraint: the narratives are recognizable as such in so far as they are generated by a single grammar. But once we have the grammar, we can construct an infinite number of new narratives, and can judge their relative similarity to existing typifications. This, I suggest, is precisely what we do when we walk though a portrait gallery, and form judgments not only about the personality of particular portraits, but also whether the portrait 'looks true'. However, these judgments are not made in the abstract, at a purely 'semantic' level. In the art gallery, as much as in the courtroom or in everyday life, the narrativization of semantics is mediated through the narrativization of pragmatics. Much will depend upon how the portrait or landscape is presented within the gallery: in what kind of room, in what kind of position, in what kind of lighting. But even this narrativization of pragmatics – though it may entail a certain 'competence' – is not to be regarded as the mechanical operation of rules. Narratives provide constraints upon – and perhaps even, at the substantive level, presumptions for – the construction of sense, but within these constraints negotiation remains possible.[40] The narratives of pragmatics tell us *how* negotiable, but these narratives too are negotiable.

Narrative frameworks and speech-acts are inextricably intertwined. Narratives can only be understood in the context of their enunciation, but their enunciation can only be perceived through the narrativization of pragmatics. This is not, however, to set up a tension between rules (speech-acts) and metaphors (narratives). For a powerful case has been made that the operation of speech-acts itself involves interpersonal negotiation.[41]

Notes

1　What follows largely summarizes, but also to an extent glosses and criticizes, my *Law, Fact and Narrative Coherence* (Merseyside: Deborah Charles Publications, 1988).

2　See my 'Conscious and unconscious rationality in law and legal theory', in *Reason in Law, Proceedings of the Conference Held in Bologna, 12–15 December 1984*, ed. Carla Faralli and Enrico Pattaro (Milan: Giuffrè, 1988) III 281–99.

3　W.L. Twining, *Rethinking Evidence* (Oxford: Blackwell, 1989) Ch. 7: 'Lawyers' stories'. I am grateful to Professor Twining for making available this chapter in advance of publication.

4　[1977] 3 All ER 338, 340–1.

5　Twining's account here is based upon his observation of student reactions to the passage.

6　'Contract', in the Greimasian sense; see later, 'Narrative as Epistemological/Semiotic Conception'.

7　For the ancient world, see, e.g., the story of the daughters of Zelophehad in the Bible (Numbers 27); the tale of Susanna in the Old Testament Apocrypha (for a discussion of which see my 'Susanna and the singular history of singular witnesses', *Acta Juridica* (1977) 37–54);

and the story recounted by Aulus Gellius, and attributed to Labeo, about one Lucius Veratius who amused himself by taking advantage of the effects of inflation on the fixed fine in the Twelve Tables penalties for assault, by striking free men in the face, and having his slave immediately tender the appropriate payment – this in order to explain the departure from the Twelve Tables penalties which had occurred (*Noctes Atticae*, 20.1.13).

8   E.g. the argument of Ed Meese against the accused's right of silence, 'Promoting truth in the courtroom', *Vanderbilt Law Review* 40/2 (1987) 278.

9   Strictly, such a limitation can never be complete in practice, since general rules are by definition indeterminate as to person, time, place, etc.

10 'Coherence in legal justification', in *Theorie der Normen, Festgabe für Ota Weinberger zum 65 Geburtstag*, ed. W. Krawietz *et al.* (Berlin: Duncker & Humblot, 1984) 48. The text as printed has 'unavoidable' rather than 'unavailable': that this is an error is verified by the hand of MacCormick on the offprint in my possession. Cf. MacCormick's formulation in 'The coherence of a case and the reasonableness of doubt', *The Liverpool Law Review* 2 (1980) 46, where he presents coherence 'not as a theory about the meaning of "truth", but as a theory about procedures for proof of all such statements as cannot be directly checked for their present correspondence with present facts'.

11 *The Liverpool Law Review* 2 (1980) 47.

12 Op.cit., 50.

13 W.L. Bennett and M.S. Feldman, *Reconstructing Reality in the Courtroom* (New Brunswick: Rutgers U.P., 1981). Trial lawyers have not infrequently remarked upon the importance of narrative structures in persuading a court (particularly in a jury trial) of the truth of a particular story. See D.A. Binder and P. Bergman, *Fact Investigation* (St Paul, Minn.: West Publishing House, 1984) 45; M. Stone, *Proof of Facts in Criminal Trials* (Edinburgh: W. Green & Sons Ltd, 1984) 269; see further my 'Narrative models in legal proof', *International Journal for the Semiotics of Law/Revue Internationale de Sémiotique Juridique* 1/3 (1988) 228.

14 See next section, 'The Narrative of Psychological Processes'.

15 See later, 'Narrative as an Epistemological/Semiotic Conception'.

16 J. Mandler and N.S. Johnson, 'Remembrance of things parsed: story structure and recall', *Cognitive Psychology* 9 (1977) 111–51.

17 Op.cit., 112, 132.

18 R. de Beaugrande and G.W. Miller, 'Processing models for children's story comprehension', *Poetics* 9 (1980) 181–201.

19 Mandler and Johnson, 1977: 42ff.

20 ibid., 145.

21 ibid., 129 n. 7. Propp is recognized as a precursor by Bennett and Feldman (1981: 189 n. 5), story grammarians, and semioticians alike.

22 Mandler and Johnson, 1977: 114.

23 For a semiotic analysis of this process, see Jackson, 1988: 117–28.

24 In 'Narrative models in legal proof', *International Journal for the Semiotics of Law/Revue Internationale de Sémiotique Juridique* 1/3 (1988) 225-7, I have illustrated this point through the analysis of a courtroom cartoon.

25 Cf. Schum's figure of a play within a play: D.A. Schum, 'Probability and the processes of discovery, proof, and choice', *Boston University Law Review* 66/3-4 (1986) 830, 846.

26 Alan Paterson, *The Law Lords* (London: Macmillan, 1982), 21 and 51.

27 [1949] 2 KB 243.

28 [1961] 1 QB 31.

29 Cf. M.P. Furmston (ed.) *Cheshire, Fifoot and Furmston's Law of Contract*, 11th edn. (London: Butterworths, 1986) 244ff., noting that the fact that the plaintiffs in *Ingram* v. *Little* had not heard of the person whom the rogue represented himself to be in fact made their case weaker than that of the plaintiff in *Phillips* v. *Brooks Ltd*.

30 Cf. Pearce, L.J. in *Ingram* v. *Little*, [1961] 1 QB 31, 57, where he constructs two opposing narratives – of a shopkeeper, and a private individual commissioning a portrait from someone he thinks to be a famous artist. In this case, he argues, 'the facts lie in the debatable area between the two extremes'.

31 [1971] 3 All ER 907.

32 [1971] 3 All ER 908h – who speaks only of the 'series', leaving the television provenance to implication!

33 See further Jackson, 1988: section 5.1.

34 On the narrative frameworks operating in the latter, see Jackson, 1988: section 4.7.

35 For a fuller discussion, see my *Semiotics and Legal Theory* (London: Routledge and Kegan Paul, 1985) ch. 9; Dworkin's most recent major statement is to be found in his *Law's Empire* (London: Fontana, 1986).

36 R. Dworkin, 'No right answer?', in *Law, Morality and Society*, ed. P.M.S. Hacker and J. Raz (Oxford: The Clarendon Press, 1977) 58-84, on which see Jackson, 1985: 203-11.

37 Adopting here a Strawsonian position. For a discussion, in the context of the normative syllogism, see Jackson, 1988: ch. 2.

38 In *Rules and Representations* (Oxford: Blackwell, 1980) ch. 6.

39 Op.cit., at 248f.

40 Consider, in this context, Lord Denning's negotiation of the conventions regarding fact-telling in *Miller* v. *Jackson*, discussed earlier.

41 M. Sbisà and P. Fabbri, 'Models (?) for a pragmatic analysis', working papers and pre-publications, Centro Internazionale di Semiotica e di Linguistica, Università di Urbino, Serie A, 91 (1980); a later version in *Journal of Pragmatics* 4 (1980) 301-19.

· 3 ·

Self-knowledge as Praxis:
Narrative and Narration in
Psychoanalysis

J.M. BERNSTEIN

Habermas's reading of Freud in *Knowledge and Human Interests* has often been criticized both in its role as a plausible model for a critical theory of society and as a reading of Freud.[1] In what follows I want to suggest that Habermas's reading of Freud exceeds the role assigned to it in his argument; and in so doing it provides a more powerful and radical model for critical theory than has been recognized.

Implicitly, and indeed in ways Habermas has tacitly come to recognize in his *rejection* of Freud and turn toward Piaget, Kohlberg, and evolutionary history, reconstructed Freudian theory delineates an emphatic sense of history and historical praxis incompatible with the universalistic and transcendental structures that are generally regarded as the Achilles' heel of the Habermasian programme.[2] To put the same point otherwise: Habermas interprets Freudian metapsychology in terms of a theory of depth hermeneutics; hence critical theory is to become a critical hermeneutics. Habermas believes that the 'critical' element of this project can be sustained only if a universalistic and transcendental moment is presupposed by depth hermeneutical practice. This moment, the moment of the ideal speech situation, is not only not required for a depth hermeneutic modelled on psychoanalytic theory, it is incompatible with it. This incompatibility is a consequence of the central and pivotal role of narrative in Habermas's account. Because of its narrative element depth hermeneutics remains hermeneutics – historical, contextual, productive.

Depth Hermeneutics: Representation or Interpretation?

Habermas challenges the hermeneutical claim to universality, as forwarded by Gadamer (and Winch), on the grounds that its identification of social reality with the shared consciousness of its participants dissolves any critical appearance/reality distinction. Not only do social agents often fail to grasp the interconnection between the various aspects of the meaning complexes they inhabit, that is, fail to recognize the nature of the determinations operating on the different parts of their symbolic totalities (hence failing to see them as totalities), but equally they are made blind by their understanding of given meaning complexes to the non-normative causes and conditions for those very same complexes. When communication between social agents is systematically and causally inhibited, then the going consensus about beliefs and norms must be deceptive or false. The difficulty for hermeneutics with such a case is that the situation is *as if* there were a real consensus about beliefs and a free acknowledgement of norms as just; but a consent cannot be free if it is based on a systematic inhibition of communication. Because hermeneutics regards the given meaning complex as the point of departure and the terminus for social analysis it cannot adequately distinguish between a real and a deceptive consensus, between true communication and pseudo-communication.

What is required for social analysis might be termed a 'depth hermeneutic', that is, a hermeneutic which connects agents' self-interpretations to the 'depth-grammar' of social relations which, operating like a natural force upon them (but behind their back), distorts and mutilates their communicative actions. What such depth-grammars reveal are the moments and causes of systematically distorted communication in the life processes of individuals and societies. By making the causes of distorted communication visible a depth hermeneutic places an individual or a collective in a position to remove the source of the distortion, and thereby to be able to give voice to inhibited meanings. The point of such analyses, then, is to allow for the abolition of the quasi-causal mechanisms they detect, to allow repressed meanings, interests and desires to be formed and communicated. Since such depth hermeneutical theories allow quasi-causal mechanisms to be dissolved by being made visible, and since such theories hence operate in the name of emancipation, Habermas denotes them self-reflective sciences. They combine hermeneutical theory's concern for meaning with objective theory's concern for detecting causal structures.

According to Habermas a depth hermeneutic is always a double hermeneutic: we come to understand the *meaning* of a deformed language game with and through the *explanation* provided of the origin of this deformation. Habermas's model of a depth hermeneutic adds to hermeneutics' interpretive procedure an explanatory dimension. The unique linking of interpretation with explanation in a depth hermeneutic is meant, again, to provide a conceptual schema for a science of self-reflection. In *Knowledge and Human Interests* Habermas offers an account of Freudian theory as an epistemological or methodical model for a science of self-reflection, and hence as a model which accurately delineates the respective contributions which explanation and understanding make to such a science.[3] In what follows I want to consider Habermas's analysis of Freud in precisely this light; that is, what is at issue in this reconstruction of Freud is not the truth or falsity of his theory (or theories) in general, nor will it concern itself with the question of whether there may be other kinds of therapy and other possible sources of mental disorder than those Freud proposes.

According to Habermas, Freud misunderstood his enterprise as forwarding an empirical, causal, theory of the psyche, and consequently he misunderstood analytic practice as an instrumental application of a natural scientific metapsychology. In so doing, Habermas argues, Freud was in danger of sacrificing the very point of the psychoanalytic enterprise: emancipation through self-reflection.

Freud surely surmised that the consistent realization of the program in a 'natural-scientific' or even rigorously behavioristic psychology would have had to sacrifice the *one intention* to which psychoanalysis owes its existence: the intention of enlightenment, according to which ego should develop out of id. But he did not abandon this program, he did not comprehend metapsychology as the only thing it can be in the system of reference of self-reflection: a universal interpretation of self-formative processes.

(Habermas 1972: 254)

All the tensions in Habermas's account derive from the discordances among the three elements following the colon in the final sentence of this passage. What is at issue is an *interpretation*, but unlike interpretations generally, where context-dependence and limitedness are conditions of possibility, this interpretation is to attain to *universality*. Worse still, the interpretation is of self-formative processes, that is, processes of development for beings who possess the capacity for altering their agency through altering their comprehension of themselves.

Not only is Freudian metapsychology about a temporal sequence, and hence narrative in form; but it is derived from and refers back to the analytic situation of dialogue (ibid: 237–45, 252–4), and hence is realized in a praxis of self-narration that is a self-transformation. Habermas acknowledges these aspects of Freudian theory as placing a constraint or restriction on the kinds of corroboration and falsification to which it is subject. These constraints, above all the fact that psychoanalytic inquiry cannot establish a 'methodologically clear separation of the object domain from the level of theoretical statements' (ibid: 262), are what distinguish it from the strict empirical sciences. Nonetheless, Habermas believes that in acknowledging these constraints and restrictions he is explicating the way in which general interpretations can attain to universality despite their specific differences from the strict empirical sciences. This acknowledgement is not sufficient. The gap between narrative form (the general interpretation) and narrative praxis is not the same as the gap between a universal and a particular it covers or can be predicated of; nor is it identical with a type and a token of that type (ibid: 264); nor is the situation here governed by a logic of exemplification. Rather, the realization of the Freudian narrative form in the narrative praxis of an analysand involves the queer idea of the narrative form *becoming true* because of the praxis it enjoins. Narrative praxis, it will be argued, is an excess beyond narrative form in virtue of which the latter gains its cognitive validity; the excess of narrative praxis beyond narrative form hence realizing at the cognitive level the excessive, self-transcending character human existence possesses in virtue of its temporal constitution.

So construed, one might object that narrative excess is nothing but the excess of human freedom itself; and hence that psychoanalytic narration is but another version of triumphal, self-mastering human subjectivity; the idea of becoming true a thinly disguised pragmatism. Such an objection would be true if psychoanalysis were nothing but an emancipatory project, another practice of self-liberation. It is not; according to Habermas, psychoanalytic self-transformations work through the operation of the Hegelian causality of fate. As we shall see this causality involves the acknowledgement (recognition) of an always already presupposed alterity which in its alterity conditions the self-possession of the subject. The narrative form that articulates the movement of the causality is tragedy. Emancipation is only possible as tragedy.

Narrative Reason: Theory and Therapy

One of the ways human beings assess and interpret the events of their life is through the construction of plausible narratives. Narratives represent events not as instances of general laws but rather as elements of a history where a continuing individual or collective subject suffers or brings about dramatic, i.e. meaningful, changes. A change is meaningful in virtue of its relation to past and future events. Eating an apple is a pleasant but not generally meaningful act; Eve's eating of that apple, motivated by curiosity, is in that context an act of disobedience and defiance, which leads to banishment from the Garden, and the unending toil of men. Constructing narratives involves eliciting connections between events by describing them in one way rather than another. Sleeping with your wife is morally and legally acceptable, not to say desirable; but if your wife is your mother, tragedy is afoot. To describe an action correctly, then, means describing it under descriptions relevant to the story being told. Typically, we call the conceptual structure which binds the events of a story together a plot. Plots are not events, but structures of events. The meaningfulness of plot-structures is analogous to the meaning of human action in that they are governed by a teleological or purposive movement: 'A story's conclusion is the pole of attraction of the entire development . . . [A] narrative conclusion can be neither deduced nor predicted (in the logical or scientific sense) . . . rather than being predictable, a conclusion must be acceptable.'[4]

Human self-reflection is dominantly, if not exclusively, either structural or narrative. In structural self-reflection we engage in self-evaluation, measuring character and personality traits against either accepted norms or their suitability for realizing desired ends. In narrative self-reflection we rehearse past events as turning points in a life-history. Only certain construals of past events cohere with present circumstances and self-understanding; but those construals, the descriptions narratively appropriate to them, can, and often do, fail to coincide with our original understanding of what had occurred. The understanding of past events, then, can require the searching out of new descriptions if our inarticulate sense of their meaningfulness is to be preserved. Sometimes this involves employing a language or vocabulary and concepts not available at the time the events in question took place. Psychoanalytic theory is such a language, and our childhood such a past.

The model of the three mental agencies, id, ego, and superego, permits a systematic presentation of the structure of language deformation and behavioural pathology . . . . They elucidate the methodological framework in which empirical substantive interpretations of (a) self-formative process can be developed . . . They are interpretations of early childhood development (the origins of basic motivational patterns and the parallel formation of ego functions) *and serve as narrative forms that must be used in each case as an interpretive scheme for an individual's life history in order to find the original scene of his unmastered conflict.*

(ibid: 258; emphasis mine)

The model of the three mental agencies (derived from the experience of analytic dialogue), together with the roles, persons, and patterns of interaction arising from the structure of the family, and the mechanisms of action and learning (object-choice, identification, internalization, and the like) are the materials which allow sufferers to form the narrative which would make their misery comprehensible in the first instance. Where pointless behaviour was, there narrative shall be. Therapy just is, in part, the constructing of a narrative, the making of a generalized biography into a specific autobiographical tale. The analyst

makes interpretive suggestions for a story the patient cannot tell . . . they can be verified only if the patient adopts them and tells his story with their aid. The interpretation of the case is corroborated only by the successful continuation of an interrupted self-formative process.

(ibid: 260)

Around this feature of the analytic enterprise three essential philosophical problems of psychoanalysis crystallize: the validity of particular psychoanalytic interpretations; the validity of psychoanalytic theory generally; and the effectivity of therapy. Roughly, Habermas believes that the acceptability of particular analytic insights depends upon their acceptability to the analysand; and since analysis is the only place where the general theory meets reality, and the theory is a narrative schema, a generalized biography which becomes an *auto*biography through its acceptance by the analysand, then the empirical accuracy of the theory as a whole 'depends not on controlled observation and subsequent communication among investigators but rather on accomplishment of self-reflection and subsequent communication between the investigator and his "object"' (ibid: 261). Stated in this manner, Habermas appears to be merely specifying the kinds of evidential and corroborative constraints applicable to psychoanalytic theory in virtue of its narrative form and the significant place which an analysand's acceptance of interpretations has in the theory's projection on to the world. He does not appear to be arguing, for example, that psychoanalytic theory should be interpreted instrumentally. Rather, he is pointing toward the way in which the peculiar relation between universal and particular in psychoanalytic theory and practice distorts the standard picture of how theories are tested, corroborated or refuted. For all that, once we take account of these constraints on testing, psychoanalytic theory itself can still be interpreted 'realistically', not of course in accordance with the mechanistic energy-distribution model, but in accordance with the model of intentional structures pathologically deformed by the causality of split-off symbols and repressed motives. Now I want to argue that such an attempt to preserve a realistic core in our reading of psychoanalytic theory radically underestimates the significance of the materials which are used to demonstrate the necessity for there being alterations in our established procedures for theory evaluation.

In order to show what is at issue in this claim, let me instance a passage where Habermas is pressing beyond the bounds of his own interpretation.

The process of inquiry can lead to valid information only via a transformation in the patient's own self-inquiry. *When valid, theories hold for all who can adopt the position of the inquiring subject. When valid*, general interpretations hold for the inquiring subject and all who can adopt its position only to the degree that *those who are made the object of individual interpretations know and recognize themselves in these interpretations*.

(ibid: 261–2; emphasis mine)

As is all too obvious, the two 'when valids' of this paragraph are epistemically idle since they can refer to nothing beyond and nothing stronger than the *consequences* of the acceptance of the general interpretation for the analysand. And the reason for this is not simply that no firm methodological line can be drawn between theoretical statement and object domain, but rather that there is no firm distinction because the *existence* of the object domain is contingent upon the acceptance of the theory. The application of the general interpretation is, as Habermas insists, a translation (ibid: 264); further, 'the conditions of application define a *realization* of the interpretation, which was precluded on the level of general interpretation itself' (ibid: 266). The logic of 'realization' and what is 'precluded' on the level of the general interpretation reveals the non-representational core of the general interpretation. The relation between the patient's ordinary language and the language of the theory hence corresponds most closely to the Gadamerian notion of a fusion of horizons.[5]

Hence, what is properly, if obliquely, being stated by Habermas, despite himself, is that the scheme of psychoanalysis can become true if agents can recognize themselves in it, and through that recognition continue their interrupted self-formative process and thereby gain emancipation. Nor is this claim surprising if human agents are the sorts of being who can modify and alter their agency through altering their conception of themselves.

Nonetheless, the radically historical conception of truth implied by this, the thought that a theory may be neither true nor false in itself but become true through its employment, since it contradicts even our mildest representational (realist and/or naturalist) assumptions, is in need of backing, drawing on familiar materials. What we learn from a consideration of these materials turns out to be something already known to us from the history of narrative.

Emotion, Thought and Therapy

At the centre of Habermas's reconstruction of Freud is the thesis that the talking cure, the reversal of repression carried out through the analytic dialogue, would be incomprehensible unless the object of repression were itself linguistic. So, for example, he contends that instead of thinking of instinctual demands unable to find an acceptable outlet, we should 'conceive of the act of repression as a banishment of need interpretations themselves' (ibid: 241). On Habermas's reading, then, the id represents charged, split-off symbols, symbols charged because they have been split off and semantically privatized. The consequence of privatization, the binding of a symbol to a particular event or cluster of events in a life-history, is the formation of a symptom.

In urging these thoughts Habermas is pointing to the familiar analytic thought that therapy would be impossible unless our emotional life had a large intentional component. Emotions which take objects logically require the having of some types of thoughts, and inversely, certain types of emotion are either appropriate or inappropriate to particular types of thought. To be angry, for example, one must have an object about, by, or at which one is angry; therefore one must have certain true or false beliefs about this object; normally one will have appraised the object in question in unfavourable ways; and the content of those appraisals will be relevant to the justification of one's being angry if this is challenged as being in some manner inappropriate. The immediate object of an emotion must be an intentional object since only under an appropriate description can one have that emotion toward that object. This in itself generates two ways in which an emotion can be inappropriate: first, one's belief may be false ('You see, there is nothing to be afraid of'); or second, the appraisal may be inaccurate ('But the snake is harmless; it has no harmful – fear-provoking – properties'). Finally, objectless emotions are usually deemed to be caused, although we are willing to admit that conjectures, beliefs, doubts and related cognitive states may have a place in their genesis. Which is not to deny that joy, depression, free-floating anxiety, and the like, even if inaugurated by a belief, seem able to persist independently of that or any related belief, and hence without an object.

Even from this it is clear that a change in belief can under appropriate circumstances inaugurate a transformation in our emotional states; and finding the belief at the source of an objectless emotion *may* be the first step in dispelling that state. Now, as a first approximation, one might hazard that apparently pointless actions (or 'neurotic' feelings) are logically akin to objectless emotions, and hence what can yield relief from that latter may equally permit release from the former. Nonetheless, the analogy between neurotic feeling and activity, and objectless emotions is not altogether accurate, for in pathological cases the root cause of the emotional states and actions in question may be temporally quite remote from their occurrence. On further reflection, we shall also have to recognize that what makes neurotic activity or feeling differ from their self-deceptive analogues is that the falsity or inappropriateness of the subject's beliefs about his state's object is often quite evident to him. Phobics and obsessives are often quite aware of the irrationality of their fears or the irrationality of their actions, and the same can often be said for other forms of pathological behaviour. Hence, in order to account for such behaviour we need to dig deeper.

In neurotic emotions, desires and beliefs, the object of the state in question is not its true target. This simple form of displacement is familiar from everyday cases of, for example, venting the anger one feels against one's boss against one's wife. Here it seems right to say that the cause and ultimate target of your anger is what (you believe) your boss did, while your wife is its object. In neurotic cases the causes are remote and the objects often superficially heterogeneous: your anger at your boss is really an anger at all authority figures which is really an anger at your father. When dealing, then, with intractable emotions we, to use Amelie Rorty's lovely formulation, 'look for the intentional component of the significant cause of the dispositional set that forms the intentional component of the emotion'.[6] This procedure offers us a generalized account of the method of 'scenic understanding' which Habermas adopts from the work of Alfred Lorenzer.[7] Scenic understanding seeks to establish equivalences between three locations: the everyday scene, the transference scene, and the original scene. The establishing of these equivalences *is* the finding of the intentional component of the significant cause (the unmastered conflict of the original scene) of the dispositional set that forms the intentional component of the emotion. The construction of the scenes and the locating of equivalences is the means whereby symptoms are translated (or retranslated) into symbols. Despite its reliance on intentional language, there is nothing in this procedure itself, either in Rorty's generalized formula or in the Habermas/Lorenzer account, which prevents us from regarding it as being the case in a naturalistic and objectivist mode; objectively, this is being offered as the correct, naturalistic analysis of intractable and anomalous emotions and forms of behaviour. However, I want to argue, the intentional components of this analysis do not really mesh with any form of naturalism, realism or objectivism.

While there are a number of different aspects of the situation which might be used to support this claim, I want to focus on what may be termed the remoteness problem. Roughly, this refers to the fact that we tend to regard intractable emotions as rooted 'elsewhere' than in a person's present, for if merely present then it is difficult to see how anything other than conflicted desires or beliefs could be at issue; and if this were so then a moral and/or 'existential' case would be the natural solution. And, indeed, this is precisely our attitude to akratics and self-deceivers. But our sense that not all emotional intractability is of this sort leads us to search elsewhere, for a remote cause of the disorder. *Our* conception of childhood as formative for the 'character' of our adult mental life licenses and is congruent with the idea that present intractability represents a disturbed self-formative process, that past and present do not connect, that either we have a past removed from and unavailable to self-understanding, or a present that is lived in terms of an overshadowing, dominating past. As Habermas states, the entire analytic procedure was, from the outset, 'subject to the general anticipation of the schema of disturbed self-formative processes' (ibid: 259).

Now this feature of psychoanalytic theory, its regarding of intractable mental items as rooted in a disturbed self-formative process, takes on epistemological prominence when it is placed into proximity with the role of acceptable belief in psychotherapy. What I have in mind here is this: we may think that our pre-theoretical comprehension of childhood experience itself and its role in the formation of the adult is so unregimented, diverse, and alterable on the one hand, and our present access to it so necessarily oblique, on the other, that they ill consort with the quite richly theoretical constructions of childhood necessary for giving substance to the idea of a disturbed self-formative process. We might, that is, think that there are features of childhood experience which make for more-than-methodological difficulties in providing evidence for a theory about it, and as a consequence there appears a more-than-ordinary gap between theory and evidence. Ironically, however, the interpretative character of theory and therapy inversely entails the utter inconsequentiality of that gap. Since in the last instance, if not the first, the acceptability of an interpretative suggestion guided by theory by fiat validates theory and interpretation together, assuming all other things are equal, then the representational function of the theory disappears with or in its application: it *becomes* the analysand's self-understanding which inaugurates his cure.

Our pre-theoretical sense of what aspects of childhood experience are or could be formative for later mental life is so complex, diverse and indeterminate that any number of explicit theoretical narrative schemes might be shown to be internally consistent enough, empirically accurate enough (where this is subject to independent confirmation), and conceptually close enough to it to become acceptable to analysands on rational grounds. Oral and anal stages, the depressive position and the paranoid-schizoid position, the mirror stage and the Oedipus complex all could, logically, possess the kind of combined pre-theoretical reference and theoretical pedigree that would permit them to serve for the redescription of childhood experience in an acceptable manner, so explaining the possibility of a type of disturbed self-formative process, and thus locating an acceptable significant cause of a disorder. So Freudian, Kleinian, Lacanian, and akin theories all could be equally true. But this, I want to say, is unlike empirically equivalent but incompatible theories, *for what these reflective theories are about becomes different as the theories are accepted and so become true.* If there is some idea of being 'equally true' here, it is more like the way in which different forms of life may be equally true.

'But surely', an objector might argue here, 'if there *is* a significant cause for a disorder, then while given the under-determination of theory by evidence there may be a difficulty in saying which of two or more competing theories is true, only one of them can be true. And untrue theories will be therapeutically effective because they are approximately true. To drop these realist intuitions would be to jeopardize our primitive understanding of how theory and therapy connect.' A purely epistemological answer to this might say that in the world of representation if two systems are empirically equivalent but incompatible, then they are both equally true; that it is only a picture of the relation between theory and world which leads us to think there can be but one true description of it.[8] If psychoanalysis were a descriptive theory, then this kind of reply to the metaphysical realist would be appropriate. Although what I want to argue is compatible with the neo-Kantian critique of realism, my fundamental suggestion has been that psycho-analytic theory is not descriptive even in the minimalist sense employed by the critics of realism. In order to see why this must be so, we must track down the connection between a significant cause and an acceptable belief. This will involve two steps: the first will show how the intentional component of a significant cause is necessarily unavailable for realist purposes; while the second will show how the affective aspects of therapy are internal to its constitution as a self-reflective enterprise.

When thinking about mental life it is important not to attribute to it more determinacy than it truly possesses; and this is more emphatically the case when dealing with 'unconscious' mental life. Consider the individual who has difficulties with authority figures. Note that it is only under some interpretations that we can collect the different persons with whom this disturbance manifests itself under the heading 'authority figures'. Different interpretive schemes might have suggested persons who are wilful or confident or aggressive or secure or masculine or domineering; and although there are manifest ways in which these concepts cluster, it is easy to conceive of regimentations of our ordinary usages which would produce different relations of inclusion and exclusion amongst these terms. Further, our individual's reaction might have been labelled as cowardly, angry, fearful, intimidated, passive, etc. In both cases the appropriate or correct description will be guided by the interpretive theory the therapist is employing. The point here is that implicit or unconscious beliefs, fears and desires *are* themselves vague and undisciplined. In interpreting them in one way rather than another we are giving them a 'shape and accent previously absent; to convince [the analysand] to whom they are attributed to accept the new formulation is partly to draw out what is already there and partly to change it and its role in his life'.[9] The mistake which naturalistic interpretations of attribution make is to suppose that, on the one hand, the appropriate description of an implicit intentional component of a present dispositional state is a matter of straightforward empirical discovery; and that, on the other hand, the correct description of the intentional component of the remote cause of the dispositional state is equally a matter for empirical discovery. The movement from implicit to explicit is not an empirical matter because what is implicit is not identical with what is explicit but for the fact of its being unconscious. In the first place, locating the correct description of the intentional component of a present dispositional state is not detachable from locating the correct intentional description of its remote cause. But the latter, we have seen, requires the employment of some generalized and theoretical narrative system of development. Secondly, however, while there are axes of development which are or might well be straightforwardly empirical in character (e.g. developmental cognitive psychology), psychosexual and moral-developmental schemes cannot be empirical in this way because they are determined by their terminus, their *picture* of maturity, autonomy, health, virtue, or the good life for man, which are not themselves subject to direct empirical questioning. Thirdly, then, accepting an interpretive suggestion, accepting, as in Habermas's account, a set of scenic equivalences, is an *act* of self-interpretation whereby one becomes, or attempts to become, the *kind* of person the theory normatively stipulates through acceding to its regimentation of our pre-understood self-understanding. So, finally, analytic suggestions unavoidably involve extending, refining, de-forming and re-forming our given conceptual apparatus.

To accept an analytic suggestion, then, is not like coming to believe, for good reasons, that one description of one's past is more accurate than another. Rather, accepting an analytic suggestion, and so redescribing one's past, involves accepting a regimented, refined and explicit version of our current conceptual scheme. But this involves more than agreeing to use a revised conceptual framework and apparatus (replacing one paradigm with another), for the framework in question is the one constitutive of our present self-understanding and so present self-identity (broadly conceived). Thus, within the boundaries of a constructivist or ontological hermeneutic, acceptable belief in cases of analytic suggestions must be assimilated into the horizon of identity projection, where one is being asked, is asking oneself, to project one's identity, one's understanding of who one is, along some new and different path. Hence the comprehension of what is involved in accepting an analytic suggestion itself becomes assimilated into the comprehension of what is involved in acts of self-reflection which have an ineliminable projective and constructive aspect. But since hermeneutic understanding itself is always, properly speaking, an act of extending, altering, de-forming and re-forming one's own horizon of understanding, then theory-mediated self-reflection looks to be but a specific and explicit account of what is always at issue in acts of understanding.

Now the necessity for this long detour might have been obviated if we had taken more seriously the thought that, at bottom, psychoanalytic self-transformation is a form of theory-mediated autobiography. It is a truism of our understanding of modern auto-biography, a truism about autobiography since Rousseau, that in autobiography the self narrated is a construction, not a representa-tion; and that in narrating a life the act of narration acts back upon the narrating self. Roughly, our intuition here is that the act of self-reflection which autobiography represents cannot be objective and representational not for lack of objectivity and honesty, or because of humanly endemic self-deception; but because the *retro-spective* construal of the significance of events, a construal constitutive of narrative sentences generally, entails a trans-cendence of the narrative emplotment of events beyond their original meaning. In a self-reflective narrative this transcendence folds back on the narrating self. The epistemological transcendence and productivity of narrative become ontological when the subject and object of the narrative are one and the same.

Of course, this feature of autobiographical discourse was unavailable prior to the development of secular autobiographies whose sole goal is the revelation – the producing and securing – of the identity of the narrated/narrating self. The common and consistent nervous reaction to this uncontrolled productivity has been to conclude that really autobiographies are not representations of a self in its travels through the world but art, creation, fiction. Psychoanalysis, theory-mediated autobiography, challenges this conclusion by revealing that the constitutively productive element of autobiography is but the consequence of the human temporal predicament when self-consciously realized in narrative praxis. Representational construals of narrative derive from regarding them as third-person, observer constructs, as forms for epistemically appropriating external events. When narrative turns self-reflective, the temporal and practical predicament of all narrative irredeemably surfaces.[10] Habermas's attempts to neutralize narrative productivity fail because self-narration is the excessive truth of narrative form; autobiographical excess reveals the self as twisting free from form and universality even as it appropriates it to itself.

What one might question in this schema is the fate of the 'other' narrated in autobiography. In autobiography the other is the id, the past, repressed need interpretations. Does this other suffer the same fate as the self appeared about to suffer from the scientistic self-misunderstanding of Freudian metapsychology? Is narrative's capacity to render *unique and particular* events and life-histories in their uniqueness and particularity, which, after all, is supposed to define the epistemic specificity of narrative, but another fable of the domination of the object by the subject? An answer to this question will require two steps: first, a more precise reconnoitring of the practical, as opposed to contemplative, features of self-reflection and self-knowing; and then a probing of the materials governing Habermas's interpretation of psychoanalysis.

A Passion for Critique

What is it to accept reflectively a radical interpretation of oneself and one's past? In order to answer this question we must necessarily ask: What might be involved in acts of self-reflection if not the mere discovery of some unnoticed mental item? On this question Freud himself supplies a valuable hint in a famous passage from his 'Observations on "wild" psychoanalysis'.[11]

It is a long superseded idea, and one derived from superficial appearances, that the patient suffers from a sort of ignorance, and that if one removes the ignorance by giving him information (about the causal connection of his illness with his life, about his experiences in childhood, and so on) he is bound to recover. The pathological factor is not his ignorance in itself, but the root of this ignorance in his inner resistances; it was they that first called this ignorance into being and they still maintain it now.

So long as we do not attempt to distinguish sharply what is repressed from the repression itself, thinking thereby of the repression and its object as two wholly different items, as Freud sometimes does, then this passage can guide us to an answer to the question posed above.

By construing the unconscious as a domain of ignorance a realist understanding of psychoanalysis naturally reads the therapeutic process in purely epistemological terms, as a movement from self-ignorance to self-knowledge. As a consequence, the realist reading of psychoanalysis is equally committed to a purely epistemic or contemplative account of self-knowledge; the activity of self-reflection is just the acquisition of significant items of information about oneself. Of course, with this conception of self-reflection go the beliefs that the effectivity of an unconscious item is a function of its exclusion from consciousness, and hence by bringing an item to consciousness its (dysfunctional) effectivity is eliminated. It is this automatic effectivity of knowledge which Freud is denying when he denies that the source of a disorder is located in simple self-ignorance.

What the contemplative reading of self-reflection obfuscates are the sources of resistance, and hence the sources of repression, which generate the particular kind of self-ignorance with which psychoanalysis deals. What is at issue in psychoanalytic self-reflection is not merely an unknown or unconscious item of mental life, but an item that has *become* unconscious, has been repressed, disavowed, disclaimed, and so excluded from consciousness. Conversely, then, for something to become conscious is for it to be avowed, recognized, assented to; its place in one's life must be thought through, its connections with other desires and emotions analysed and evaluated. The source, then, of self-ignorance is a certain set of attitudes toward oneself under the aegis of a particular evaluation and understanding of who one is. Correlatively, self-knowledge proceeds through the adoption of another framework of self-understanding which allows different attitudes toward oneself to be adopted.[12]

Analytic insights, to be effective, must have an affective basis; and the affective basis of a self-reflective therapy will be different from the affective bases of other therapeutic procedures. It is not sufficient in psychotherapy for the patient to desire relief from his misery or to be returned to full functionality. Such desires may promote a cure, but not an analytic cure. 'Critique would not have the power to break up false consciousness if it were not impelled by a passion for critique . . . analytic knowledge is impelled onward against motivational resistances by the interest in self-knowledge' (ibid: 234–5). The analysand's analytic insights are self-reflective not only because the understanding so happens to be an understanding of oneself, but also because the *need* for understanding arises in a context where some features of the patient's life are already inscribed as a practical issue: the significance for his life of 'these' feelings and acts is in question; they are yet to be resolved and require resolution. The self-questioning of self-reflection, then, is practical; to seek after 'the truth' about oneself and one's life is to seek after more than true beliefs about one's past, it is to grasp the significance of beliefs, desires, feelings and episodes as they determine one's relations to oneself and to others. The self-gathering of self-reflection is a praxis by means of which one might become who one (really) is; but, of course, who one really is is not something determinable external to the praxis of self-reflection.

The self-knowledge which analytic reflection brings is practical as well as epistemic. In analytic reflection it is the intelligibility and significance of the items composing one's mental life which are at issue; items must be scrutinized as to their connection and place within one's life as a whole; they must be evaluated and understood with respect to one's conception of oneself and one's fundamental aims and desires; and those fundamental aims and desires must be analysed as to their rightness with respect to one's fundamental norms and values, and so on. Analytic self-reflection, then, necessarily involves a willingness and a desire to make oneself different, to restructure and reconstruct one's life. And this, in its turn, requires a different conception of self-relatedness than that offered by the contemplative model of self-reflection, the image of turning one's mental eye inward upon the landscape of the psyche, sanctioned by realism. Let me quote Habermas at length on this.

> Because analysis expects the patient to undergo the experience of self-reflection, it demands 'moral responsibility for the content' of illness. For the insight to which analysis is to lead is indeed only this: that the ego of the patient recognize itself in its other, represented by the illness, as its own alienated self and identity with it. As in Hegel's dialectic of moral life, the criminal recognizes in his victim his own annihilated essence; in this self-reflection the abstractly divorced parties recognize the destroyed moral totality as their common basis and thereby return to it. Analytic knowledge is also moral insight, because in the movement of self-reflection the unity of theoretical and practical reason has not yet been undone.
>
> (ibid: 235-6)

Emotions can be disavowed or avowed, acknowledged or not acknowledged. To disavow what is your own is more like denying responsibility than being ignorant, for ignorance is still absence and may be undone through the providing of more information. What is disavowed is actively denied; one removes oneself from where one ought to be or needs to be. Avowal involves finding a place in one's life for a desire or emotion, and this is more than discovering it is there – it is doing something with that thought. Hence the undertaking of renarrating the events of one's life in accordance with the Freudian schema is a moral undertaking, and the insight it provides into one's character is inevitably and invariably a moral insight. In analysis one is being asked to take responsibility for one's feelings and actions; and the demonstration that responsibility has been taken is tokened by the progress of therapy, the capacity to write the narrative of one's life, and thereby to complete the disturbed self-formative process.

In all of this the self is conceived of as more than a body moving through space and time, or as a continuous series of overlapping mental events held together by habit and memory; the self here is a moral totality. As agents we can conceive of ourselves in terms of those fundamental purposes, goals, and values which orient the movements and directions of our life. As a consequence, the various parts of our life are not mere givens, but elements awaiting assignment within the whole. That whole, however, is ineliminably normatively structured; the whole of a life always has the sense of a good or bad life, a life well spent or frittered away, a life worth living or valueless. So the narrative of a life is always a moral narrative, a narrative whose general meaning is provided by some narrative schema, some proto-narrative whose intelligibility involves a mesh between normative and temporal terms. Individual narratives employ the terms of the proto-narrative in order to interpret, and reinterpret, the events of a life. As is always the case with stories, the intelligibility of the events being recounted only comes fully into view at the end of the tale.

To enter into psychoanalysis is like undertaking to write a serious novel or to engage in radical political activity. In each case one begins with implicit, unconscious doubts, fears, desires, needs, and thoughts; and in each case one presupposes that the source of the problem outruns available conceptual understanding: the narrative of the present is practically and cognitively inadequate. Self-knowledge requires preserving but going beyond self-understanding, producing a narrative which has the narrative of the present, one's false or partial self-understanding, as one of its moments. New and different meanings have to be attributed to past events. But since these events are partially constitutive of the self, their redescription entails a reconstitution of the self. The reconstituted self, the end of the story, provides the vantage point from which the adequacy of the narrative, both general and particular, can be judged -- although, of course, not the only or sole vantage point. Since the judgement of adequacy presupposes the validity of what is to be judged, then the judgement itself arrives too late. With self-knowledge at least, the owl of Minerva takes wing only at dusk.

The Causality of Fate and Tragedy

It is, or should be, evident that Habermas's reading of Freud is consistently governed by structures drawn from Hegel. He interprets repression and its overcoming in terms of the causality of fate and the dialectic of moral life. He concludes the 'when valid' passage discussed earlier by claiming: 'The subject cannot obtain knowledge of the object unless it becomes knowledge for the object -- and unless the latter thereby emancipates itself by becoming a subject' (ibid: 262). In short, pathology is the becoming substance of subject, and cure the return in which all that is substance is understood as subject. This movement is doubly mediated: the analyst can only have knowledge of the object (the analysand) if the analysand transforms him/herself into a subject; and the analysand can only do this if s/he recognizes in the analyst his/her suppressed life. General interpretation is not realized within itself; it is precluded from so doing because analytic anamnesis is the theory-mediated performance of the dialectic moral life. Hence, transference becomes the scene of the speculative recognition of self in otherness.

But the physician's constructions can be changed into actual recollection of the patient only to the degree that the latter, confronted with the results of his action in transference with its suspension of the pressure of life, sees himself through the eyes of another and learns to reflect on his symptoms as offshots of his own actions.

(ibid: 232)

When Habermas first essayed the dialectic moral life in 'Labour and interaction'[13] he did so as a refusal of Kantian moral theory, where the antagonism between universal law and particular desire is resolved by subsuming the latter under the former. This, Habermas avers, 'expels moral action from the very domain of morality',[14] reducing moral action to strategic action: 'The positive relation of the will to the will of others is withdrawn from possible communication, and a transcendentally necessary correspondence of isolated goal-directed activities under abstract universal laws is substituted.'[15]

Habermas turns to Hegel's model of communicative action as an alternative to the Kantian model. In Hegel love, fate, and recognition represent alternatives to law. The 'form of law (and the law's content) is the direct opposite of life because it signalizes the destruction of life'.[16] Fate, on the contrary, is the complex movement of life itself.

In the hostile power of fate, universal is not severed from particular in the way in which the law, as universal, is opposed to man or his inclination as the particular. Fate is just the enemy, and man stands over against it as a power fighting against it . . . . Only through a departure from that united life which is neither regulated by law nor at variance with law, only through the killing of life, is something alien produced. Destruction of life is not the nullification of life but is diremption, and the destruction consists in its transformation into an enemy.[17]

Habermas accurately presents the causality of fate in terms that should now strike us as familiar from his reading of Freud.

In the causality of destiny the power of suppressed life is at work, which can only be reconciled, when, out of the experience of the negativity of a sundered life, the longing for that which has been lost arises and necessitates identifying one's own denied identity in the alien existence one fights against. Then both parties recognize the hardened positions taken against each other to be the result of the separation, the abstraction from the common interconnection of their lives – and within this, in the dialogic relationship of recognizing oneself in the other, they experience the common basis of their existence.[18]

Love and recognition are, precisely, acknowledgements of separation and repression; such acknowledgements, however, are not dictated (by law), or logically required. They are acts of life, acceptances and acknowledgements. Recognition, acceptance, love and forgiveness (forgiveness as the act of love) are the opposite of autonomy and self-legislation; they are acts that cannot be commanded or demanded. On the contrary, they are excessive to what can be established by any subject independently of its others. What recognition recognizes is the heteronomous 'ground' of autonomy.

From 'The spirit of Christianity and its fate' and the 'Natural Law' essay to the *Phenomenology*, Hegel associates the temporal movement of the causality of fate, and hence ethical life as opposed to morality, with tragedy. In tragedy, as opposed to comedy, the ethical order is composed not by abstract law, but through the structured recognitions implicit in communal practices, practices in which a group possess a shared social and collective identity; and the individual accepts the moments of diremption, conflict, and antagonism, including incommensurable social obligations, as the movement of the totality, not something visited upon it from without.

Tragedy consists in this, that ethical nature segregates its inorganic nature (in order not to become embroiled in it), as a fate, and places it outside itself; and by acknowledging this fate in the struggle against it, ethical nature is reconciled with the Divine being as the unity of both.[19]

The recognition of self in absolute otherness that is the goal of Hegelian dialectic (itself, surely, just the movement of the causality of fate) is not the sublation or dissolving of otherness, but its acceptance as ground. Life is aporia; dialectic is fate and tragedy.

Psychoanalytic narration cannot escape the dictates of the subsumptive model merely through contextualization (ibid: 273); rather the passion for critique, realized in and through transference, must equally involve the work of love; the acceptance of conflict – of loving and feeling murderous toward the other; of desiring what can never be possessed – and the acceptance of the otherness of the other as constitutive of the moral totality of the analysand's life.

Habermas's reading of Freud was intended as the working out, for a critical theory of society, of the logic of the causality of fate he spied in the early Hegel. Very quickly, and very approximately, Habermas argues that Hegel came to abjure the model of the causality of fate as he came to recognize its attachment to the idealized form of certain historical communities, on the one hand; and, on the other, came to recognize specific features of modernity – above all the logic of self-consciousness and the new model of civil society developed by the political economists – as different from and incommensurable with those idealized forms of past historical communities. Habermas's strategy has been to insert the presupposition of constraint-free communication at work in all speech-acts into the place that the idealized forms of past historical communities had in the early Hegel.

This otiose move, otiose precisely because it attempts to replace historical reality by a transcendental or presuppositional structure, is unnecessary. What Habermas's reading of Freud shows is that our acceptance of the causality of fate and the writing of our tragic narrative must be theory-mediated. As he himself states, 'Only the metapsychology that is presupposed allows the systematic generalization of what would otherwise remain pure history' (ibid: 259). Pure history is not our history because the moral and social totality which we are and of which we are part are empirically unknown to us. We can come to ourselves only through the mediations of theory. *Capital*, just as much as the writings of Freud, offers a general interpretation (of capital) and not a representation. As such, it is neither true nor false in itself. It can become true only if we can, through it, come to tell the story of who we are and so continue our disturbed self-formative process. Such a story would, of course, be a tragedy.

To reiterate: what Habermas's deployment of the model of the causality of fate reveals is not the presupposition of communication free of constraints; but rather, that in our social practices an actual ethical totality is operative even in situations where the norms governing such practices and the structures reproducing them deny it. Habermas could avoid this point, and slip communication into its place, because at each moment where communication enters his argument another architectonic option is enunciated. Whenever communication is distorted, in Habermas's terms, the self, subject or ego necessarily 'deceives itself about its identity in the symbolic structures that it consciously produces' (ibid: 227). The force of unconstrained communication in Habermas is always parasitic on its being a transcendental marker for the 'we' which is the ground of each and any 'I'. In reality, however, this 'we', which is never just one, is constituted in and through practices which are 'neither regulated by law nor at variance with law'. No theory or set of theoretical presuppositions grounds or founds 'united life'. On the contrary, only the act that denies life reveals it. Our tragedy is that this revelation is not a direct empirical accompaniment of our acts. Because our tragedy has become unknown to us, so has our life.

From this vantage point it is not difficult to see why Habermas's notions of undisturbed communication and the ideal speech situation run into difficulty: they are linguistic reformulations of transcendental subjectivity. Undistorted communication, however partial, however remote as presupposed or yet to be achieved, has force only if it is necessary for the possibility of maintaining oneself as a subject; thus it functions as the Habermasian transcendental marker for the 'we' which is the ground of each and any 'I'. Habermas's own quasi-transcendental form of argumentation, however, tends to elide what is central to transcendental argumentation, namely, self-consciousness. If Habermas's claims for undistorted communication are unpacked, then it becomes evident that its necessity is conditional; it provides a necessary condition for the possibility of self-conscious agency. However, as in Kant's own transcendental presentations, what it is for anyone to be a self-conscious agent is left unspecified, or rather, in Habermas's theory, is made a function of the categorical determinations of undistorted communication itself. Thus the conditions for subjectivity come to displace subjectivity itself, and, as Habermas's procedures elegantly demonstrate, subjectivity can be read out of the argument altogether. But this strategy begs the question at issue: What is it to be a self-conscious agent? Like Kant's logical subject, Habermas's subject of an undistorted communication community is a logical fiction. Kant's argument wavers between according transcendental subjectivity its proper metaphysical status and leaving it an empty logical subject. Habermas attempts to rid himself of the problem of transcendental subjectivity altogether, but this he can manage only by an ellipsis in his argument which produces a rather evident *petitio*.

The direct result of making a science of self-reflection about the self is to displace emancipation from its position as being the sole object or goal of self-reflection. On the contrary, emancipation looks to be an effect or corollary of self-knowledge when it is comprehended as having an ineliminable practical dimension. In saying this I do not mean to deny the operations of the causality of fate, individually or collectively, upon us; but I do wish to insist that any such curtailment of our freedom is a constraint upon the self (upon ourself). What we become emancipated from in the production of a self-reflective narrative are false views about ourselves, about our goals and desires, about who we, really, are. The emancipatory power of self-reflection is hence inseparable from its cognitive aspects; but the cognitive aspects of self-reflection are themselves inseparable from the practical activity of the reconstitution of self-identity which is its controlling end. By separating action from knowledge, Enlightenment thought creates the illusion that *who the self is and its freedom can somehow be analytically distinguished.* But part of the force of the hermeneutic critique of Enlightenment ideology is to deny that questions of freedom and autonomy can be isolated from questions of self-knowledge and self-identity. In Kant this separation is pressed twice over: not only is the will separated from judgement, but moral goods, which belong to the will alone, are firmly isolated from non-moral goods, which belong to the body. Since any identity we might have is an empirical matter, then as moral agents we lack a continuing identity. Like Kant, Habermas uses the ideal of autonomy, written now in terms of undistorted communication, as the *form* in which particular formations of self-identity may be inscribed; so, as in Kant, the distinction between autonomy and identity provides the leverage for a distinction between a priori (transcendental) form and empirical content. When the dualism between freedom and identity is overcome, then with it goes the kind of form/content distinction which legitimates Habermas's transcendental strategy. And with that gone, critical theory becomes all it ever can be: a critical hermeneutics.

Now, if it is the case that the possibility of formally transcending our historical predicament is factitious, that the 'we' that conditions the possibility of self-consciousness and self-identity is always historically concrete through its immanence in social practices incapable of being wholly objectivized, then two important conclusions follow. First, and most evidently, individual acts of re-narration are never more than limit-cases of self-transformation. If individual subjectivity is but a weak precipitate of the 'we' that makes it possible, then substantial self-transformations require the re-formation of the practices conditioning individual subjectivity. And this may be another reason why apparently strong cases of re-narration, namely those found in modern autobiographies, not only appear as fictions but are fictions. No individual on their own can substantially remake themselves. Indeed, is this not the acknowledged pathos of Nietzsche's Zarathustra?

Second, if the conditions for self-consciousness are, as sedimentations of past collective subjectivities, incapable of ever being fully objectivized, then while our narrative predicament is in important ways historically specific, it is not historically unique. A tragic dimension of all collective identities and their narrative representations is that the moment of self-recognition must always be wrested from a social substantiality that remains submerged in darkness. But this is to say that the tragic pathos I have just attributed to Zarathustra must infect all narratives claiming insight into collective identity and collective fate. Absence of such tragic pathos is a sign of naïvety, not of better insight.

Narrative is the form of intelligible discourse proper to human life. Disturbed self-formative processes are, in reality, disturbances of identity – individual or collective; but disturbances in identity are, for us, always disturbances of the temporal ordering of existence; disturbances that can only be re-formed through (re-)narration.

Modernity involves the occlusion of the ethical totality of which we are nonetheless a part. And this means: the tragic conditions of life have, tragically, been occluded from everyday practice. Who we are, tragic insight into our fate, is now only possible via the mediations of theory. On this account, Freud and Marx are the tragedians of modernity; and the overcoming of modernity would be a kind of rebirth of tragedy.

Notes

1 All page references in the body of the text are to Jürgen Habermas, *Knowledge and Human Interests*, translated by Jeremy J. Shapiro (London: Heinemann, 1972). For a review of the inadequacies of psychoanalysis as a model for critical theory see Thomas McCarthy, *The Critical Theory of Jürgen Habermas* (London: Hutchinson, 1978) 205–13. On Habermas's repression of sexuality in Freud, see Rainer Nägele, *Reading After Freud* (New York: Columbia University Press, 1987) 67–90.

2 McCarthy, op.cit., 101–2, 182–92; and J.B. Thompson and D. Held (eds), *Habermas: Critical Debates* (London: Macmillan, 1982), essays 4, 7, 8. My contention will be that there is a uniform ground for these objections, viz., in Habermas's refusal of a fully hermeneutic theory of self-consciousness; but that because that ontologized conception of self-

consciousness is implicit in his reading of Freud, the idea of a depth hermeneutic, of a science of self-reflection, in fact overcomes the conservatism of hermeneutic theory, thus releasing the radicality of its conception of history.

3 On the relation between his reading of Freud and his critique of hermeneutics, see Jürgen Habermas, 'The hermeneutic claim to universality', in Josef Bleicher (ed.), *Contemporary Hermeneutics* (London: Routledge & Kegan Paul, 1982) 181–211.

4 Paul Ricoeur, 'Narrative time', *Critical Inquiry* 7 (Autumn 1980) 174. For considerations of narrative in relation to questions of action and self-identity directly pertinent to what follows see my *The Philosophy of the Novel: Lukacs, Marxism and The Dialectics of Form* (Brighton: Harvester Press, 1984).

5 Hans-Georg Gadamer, *Truth and Method*, translated by Garrett Barden and John Cumming (New York: Seabury Press, 1975) 273ff.

6 Amelie Rorty, 'Explaining emotions', in her (ed.) *Explaining Emotions* (London: University of California Press, 1980) 110.

7 See 'The hermeneutic claim to universality', op.cit., 192–4.

8 See Hilary Putnam, 'Realism and reason', in his *Meaning and the Moral Sciences* (London: Routledge & Kegan Paul, 1978) 123–37.

9 William Connolly, 'Appearance and reality in politics', *Political Theory* 7/4 (November 1979) 461.

10 Habermas reveals how the problem of narrative sentences entailing an ultimate end of history (a last historian) can be resolved if we move from a contemplative to a practical comprehension of historical teleology in his 'A review of Gadamer's *Truth and Method*', in P.R. Dallmayr and Th. McCarthy (eds), *Understanding and Social Inquiry* (London: University of Notre Dame Press, 1977) 349–52.

11 Philip Rieff (ed.), *Therapy and Technique* (New York: Collier Books, 1963) 93.

12 For two recent articles that present and defend this practical conception of self-knowledge as the one properly attributable to Freud, see Morris Eagle, 'Privileged access and the status of self-knowledge in Cartesian and Freudian conceptions of the mental', *Philosophy of the Social Sciences* 12 (1982) 349–73; and Bela Szabados, 'Freud, self-knowledge and psychoanalysis', *Canadian Journal of Philosophy* XII/4 (1982).

13 'Labour and interaction: remarks on Hegel's Iena *Philosophy of Mind*', in his *Theory and Practice*, translated by John Viertel (Boston: Elancon Press, 1973) 142–69.

14 ibid., 150.

15 ibid.

16 'The spirit of Christianity and its fate', in *On Christianity: Early Theological Writings*, translated by T.M. Knox (New York: Harper & Brothers, 1961) 225.

17 ibid., 229.

18 'Labour and interaction', op.cit., 148.

19 *Natural Law*, translated by T.M. Knox (Philadelphia: University of Pennsylvania Press, 1975) 105.

PHYSICAL SCIENCE

· 4 ·

Some Narrative Conventions of Scientific Discourse

ROM HARRÉ

Truth, Faith and Speech-acts

Since Fleck's pioneering analysis (1935) of scientific documents disclosed how far they are from unvarnished descriptions of uncontested facts, the way has been open for a radical rethinking of the nature of scientific discourse, both written and spoken. If it isn't a catalogue of truths, what is it? Popper's suggestion, that it is a stream of conjectures, is still framed within the old way of thinking. Factuality, both as a discipline (falsification) and as an ideal terminus (verisimilitude), still plays an essential role in his analysis. But stepping outside the discourse and its taken-for-granted rhetoric of factuality we come to another perspective altogether. (I shall use the term 'factuality' to refer to the idea of a known truth and 'facticity' to refer to whatever is presented as if it were a known truth.) We might ask what speech-acts scientific utterances and inscriptions typically are used to perform. Functionally the disinterested voice and the assertoric style seem to be aimed to get the interlocutor to see things from the point of view of the writer or speaker. Scientific discourse is marked by a peculiar rhetoric. The ostensible claim of scientific utterances is for agreement, since they are presented as knowledge. But suppose we did insert the ghostly performative operator, 'I (we) know . . .' before each such assertion: just what speech-act does it introduce? My proposal, upon which the analysis in this chapter is based, is that this operator should be read roughly as 'Trust me (us) . . .', or 'You can take my word for it . . .'. But why should such a speech-act be effective in generating trust? I suggest that it is because the speaker or writer is manifestly a member of an esoteric order, a 'community of saints' from membership in which the force of the claim descends.

If the illocutionary force of a scientific utterance is 'trust me . . .', its reciprocal, its perlocutionary effect, is belief. I owe to Marc Kucia the observation that that effect is possible only if the listener or reader has faith. As Popper reminded us, the role of citation of evidence in scientific discourse cannot be that of inductive proof. So the belief in question cannot be arrived at by rehearsal of a logical procedure. Given the importance of faith the scientific community must be seen as a moral order, a solidary whose internal structure is based upon a network of trust and faith. As Michael Polanyi put it, when one enters that community one commits oneself to it in a fiduciary act.

But something further must be said about the concept of trust. Trust appears in both symmetrical (friendship) and asymmetrical (child–parent) relationships. These relationships may be between people or they may be between people and things. For instance one may trust the rope one is using to climb the wall, but distrust one's inexperienced fellow climber. Then there is the rather special case of people trusting their eyes, their hunches, and so on.

Trust, then, is a relation, but can be grounded in the faith of only one of its terminal members. Trust belongs to the same category of personal attributes as beliefs, though trust is more like implicit belief than like opinions which are overtly expressed. It is what is taken for granted in a relationship, whether between people or between people and things. It is usually called into question only when it is violated.

Trust does not usually develop as the result of an empirical induction on past performances of the one in whom one trusts. It is very often role-related. It is because the trusted one is in the role of parent, guardian, policeman, research supervisor, and so on, that the trust is there until something happens to upset it. It is the role as much as, and in most cases much more than, the trusting 'look' of the other (say, one's dog) that induces the reciprocal obligation. This is why there is little room for an empirical induction in the development of trust, and why trust is often immediate and implicit. Introduced to their respective research supervisors, graduate students don't usually put them to the test to see if they are likely to plagiarize their pupils' research efforts. The role of supervisor carries obligations to care for and promote the welfare of the students.

The moral order of the scientific community is or appears to be élitist, at least in one sense of that term. The valuation of an opinion concerning some matter taken to be scientific is determined by resort to expertise, which is itself guaranteed by a combination of communal certification and personal demonstrations of mastery. Philosophers of science undertook to abstract a coherent set of rules of method from successful and unsuccessful practices as these are judged by the community itself. This style of philosophy of science reached its apotheosis in the beautiful studies by Whewell in the first half of the nineteenth century. The rules of method, which developed as the dimensions and depth of scientific research increased, were treated not only as moral imperatives by the community, but also as a theory which could account for the successes and failures of the enterprise as it was defined by the consensus of acknowledged scientists. Despite the protests of philosophers such as Hume, the aim seems to have been well understood as the improving of an imaginative representation of the natures of things as they existed independently of the limited resources of human perception and manipulation.

Trust is built up upon a basis of faith in the reliability of those who are trusted – and derivatively in what they write or say. Reliability with respect to what? Again we have to look from the outside into the community's activities. Scientists seem to be preoccupied with two concerns. Debating one against the other, scoring points and so on is clearly a favourite pastime. But also trying to make equipment work is another. Reliability obligations are related to both these activities. One trusts that making use of a claim to know originated by one of one's fellow scientists will not let one down in a debate, and that making use of someone's claim to have successfully manipulated something will help to make one's own techniques and equipment work in practical contexts. Reliability, it should be noted, is not truth. With this analysis of scientific discourse as background I turn to the task of trying to bring out the narrative conventions according to which discourses are produced by members of the community. What story lines do scientific discourses reveal?

Scientific Writing and Speaking as Narrative

The first narratological conclusion I wish to draw follows immediately from the considerations cited above. If trust and faith are the operative principles, so to speak, then the wherewithal for displays of character must be an important part of a scientist's repertoire. I mean 'character' in the moral sense. An upright character must be readable in the accounts. Nothing shifty or perverse, self-serving or self-deceiving must leak through the solid wall of integrity. If 'I know . . .' is to be read as 'Trust me that . . .', character becomes an epistemological variable, for on the assessment of character hangs one's readiness to give that trust, to have that faith. But in normal circumstances it comes without asking, so to speak, for it is created just by the presumption that the author of the performative utterances we call a scientific discourse is a bona fide member of the scientific community. Taken this way, that community reveals something of the character of religious orders, such as the Benedictines. The discourse must display the narrative contentions typical of the productions of members of the Order.

For the material of this section I am greatly indebted to a paper by K. Wales (1980). In scientific lecturing and more informal talk the pronoun 'we' is very prominent, to the virtual exclusion of 'I', even when the context makes it clear that the speaker could only be referring to his or her own individual activities or thoughts. Exophoric pronouns are those which are disambiguated for reference only if the hearer is fully apprised of the context of use, for instance by being present on the occasion of utterance. All indexical pronouns are exophoric. Third-person pronouns are examples of endophora since their sense can be grasped from the text alone. Wales distinguishes between specific exophora, in which the immediate context is relevant, and generalized exophora, in which a graph of what she calls the 'context of culture' is all that is required. So for example when a speaker uses 'we' to refer to the scientific community it is the context of culture rather than the specific context of that very utterance that is germane to a grasp of its referential force. In short it does not mean [+ego, +voc], that is, speaker plus addressee.

Wales offers an analysis of the peculiar use of pronouns in scientific discourse based on the principle that there is a tendency for *all* pronouns in English to acquire an egocentric force in both specific and generalized exophoric uses. The choice of 'we' rather than 'I' is a narrative convention which has the effect of a rhetorical distancing of the speaker from an overt self-reference to make the egocentricity of advice or knowledge or whatever it may be more palatable. The reason for calling this a narrative convention rather than a rhetorical device will be brought out in a later section. The editorial 'we', still to be found in journalism, excludes the addressee as a referent, that is it is not the 'nudge nudge' and cosy 'we' of complicity, but implies that ego is a member of and spokesman for a larger corporation.

The academic 'we' might seem at first glance to be just a version of the editorial 'we'. Like the latter it is mutedly egocentric but it is not mainly used to imply teamwork. Rather, it is used to draw the listener into complicity, to participate as something more than an audience. Wales cites the prevalence of this pronoun with verbs of saying, showing, thinking, anticipating, postponement, and return. The implication is that the audience is not only passively following what is going on but actively participating in the process of thought – and thereby committed to the results and conclusions of that process. A narrative structure is created within which the interlocutor is trapped, since the ephemeral special relationship created by the discourse prevents that addressee taking up a hostile or rejecting stance to what has been said. Trust in the other is induced through the device of combining it with trust in oneself. The force of the pluralizing of reference is even more marked with the alternative 'Let's . . .'. Thus as Wales put it,

the surface meaning of joint activity [+ego, +voc] frequently disguises only thinly the true agentive 'I' or (its target) 'you', and that, more generally, the authoritative persuasive voice of the ego will 'contaminate' the illusion of modesty. 'We' can acquire the very connotations its use has sought to avoid.

(ibid: 33)

At this point I can make good the claim that in the innocent use of 'we' a narrative convention rather than a purely rhetorical device is at work. One way of looking at the foregoing is as a sketch of a story line in which the plot of a human drama culminating in a scientific discovery is unfolded.

Who Are the Good Guys?

We have already seen in the first section ('Trust, Faith and Speech-acts') that the community is held together by a network of trust. Underlying this is the fact that the community is continuously recreated by the recruiting of new members through apprenticeship. In this way they are drawn into the moral order of the scientific community in a very deep way. But how do the members show that they belong? Obviously their behaviour does a good deal to illustrate their qualities of character. But there is another way, which is evident in the plots of their stories about their daily work and its triumphs. The good guys present themselves as the followers and even the friends of a saintly figure I shall call 'Big Ell' – logic. Accordingly their anecdotes are laid out in a quite definite and universal narrative form.

Each story has three phases. In the first the hero (though modesty prevents him ever using the egocentric pronoun 'I') presents a *hypothesis*. This is never presented as the result of an act of creative genius or even just plain guesswork, but is surrounded with a protective barrier of citations, culled from the published anecdotes of other good guys. It is worth remarking that it only makes sense to cite the writings of others if you have faith in them, and one can have that faith only if one believes that its recipients are trustworthy. We know they are trustworthy because they are members in good standing of the scientific community, and so on round the circle. In the second phase we have the presentation of the *results*. These are descriptions of the behaviour of pieces of trustworthy apparatus construed as tests of the hypothesis. Indeed the story line makes it clear that these practical activities were undertaken just as tests of the hypothesis. In the last phase the results are presented as *inductive support* for the hypothesis. Not only does this story encapsulate the right plot, but it displays the actors as followers of Big Ell himself. Those with a greater sensitivity to what logic actually demands may sometimes give the story a Popperian twist, and present the whole matter as a mere corroboration.

Anyone who has ever done any actual scientific research knows that this is a tale, a piece of fiction. The real-life unfolding of a piece of scientific research bears little resemblance to this bit of theatre. The first point to note about it, apart from its empirical falsity as a description of events, is that it is a 'smiling face' presentation. All has gone well. The apparatus has worked and/or the questionnaire has been fully understood and the answers properly encoded. No fuses have blown, and no one from the sample population has fallen ill, gone away, or inconveniently died. If anyone tried to publish a story more like real life, in which hypotheses were dropped for lack of support, apparatus couldn't be made to work within the parameters of the original experiment, and so on, it would be turned down. Journals do not publish inconclusive work. Articles devoted wholly to disproofs of hypotheses are rare. Science must present a smiling face both to itself and to the world. Again, this is not just a matter of adopting an optimistic rhetoric, but of a narrative convention: how a story is to be told. Of course the presentation of the author(s) as among the good guys is enhanced by an introductory section devoted to setting out the mistakes and erroneous beliefs of predecessors and rivals. The fact that articles, textbooks, and monographs are written within rather different narrative conventions cannot be explored in the space of this discussion but it is worth remarking that amongst other distinctions there are marked differences in the proportion of space given to the setting out and the demolishing of 'false' theories, results, and hypotheses.

To achieve the story line, events as experienced within the framework of common sense must be edited. In particular, those times when the apparatus did not work (or gave results contrary to those which were needed to support the hypothesis which had to stand at the end of the day) must be suppressed. The flexibility of the notion of 'working' allows this suppression to be achieved within the range of good actions permitted to the followers of Big Ell. Holton (1981) has provided us with a beautiful example of this. By carefully examining Millikan's experimental notebooks he was able to show how Millikan 'fiddled' his results to support the famous proof of the unitary charge on the electron. By a series of diverse and ingenious acts of special pleading Millikan persuaded himself that in all cases where he did not get the result he expected the apparatus had not 'worked properly'. It is again worth remarking that apprentice scientists spend a good deal of time learning how to apply the distinction between working and not working properly to their apparatus. Supervisors' reports on the work of graduate students are notable for the number of times that the difficulty that this or that tyro researcher had in making his or her technique or apparatus work is remarked upon. The notion of 'working' cannot be defined in the abstract. In practice it reduces to getting the kind of results that could have been expected. But that will be relative to whatever hypothesis one has in mind. A space for negotiation opens up just because an unexpected (and contrary) result can be used to support the claim that the apparatus was not working properly rather than as a reason for concluding that some amongst the hypotheses involved in the setting up of the experimental programme were mistaken.

Finally it is important to remember that the order of the scenes of the research drama as it is restaged in the narrative is determined by the Rule of Big Ell. For example, the genesis of hypotheses must be presented as prior to the gathering of results, otherwise we can hardly talk of testing the hypothesis. In this as in other scientific matters real life does not imitate art. In many cases the results are found first and a research programme is worked out after the event so that they will have a hypothesis or theory to test. This is so common a phenomenon as to be a commonplace. I can illustrate it with the famous case of Pasteur's discovery of the attenuation of viruses and so of a systematic technique for vaccination.

I set out for inspection and comparison two narratives, one told by myself in the role of 'impartial historian' (remembering that that *is* a role with its own narrative and rhetorical conventions) and the other told by Louis Pasteur. Here is my narrative, quoted from my study of experimentation (Harré 1981: 106).

In 1879 Pasteur went on a summer holiday to Arbois, his home town, from July to October. He left behind in the laboratory the last of the chicken broth cultures, recently infected with the [chicken] cholera microbe. When he returned in October (having postponed his intended date of departure from Arbois) the cultures were still there [in his laboratory]. So he immediately tried to restart the experiment by injecting some of these old cultures into fresh hens. Nothing happened . . . . [Disappointed] he decided to restart the programme from the very beginning with fresh virulent microbes. The hens (he had just impotently injected) did not develop the disease. Pasteur immediately drew the right conclusion. He had found a way of attenuating the 'virus' artificially.

Pasteur's narrative runs as follows, taken from the English translation of his original paper (Pasteur 1881: 179):

by simply changing the process of cultivation of the parasite; by merely placing a longer interval of time between successive seminations, we have obtained a method for decreasing virulence progressively, and finally get a vaccinal virus which gives rise to a mild disease and preserves from the deadly disease.

In this narrative the scientist is displayed in the active role. The process of cultivation is 'changed', the longer interval is 'placed', and so on. One should also note the strategic placing of the academic 'we'. In fact (that is, according to my narrative) there was no team of researchers, just Pasteur and various 'dogsbodies'. This 'we' is the 'we' of the scientific community, the general exophoric use, in the hearing of which the reader is invited to consider him or herself a member. It is fair to say that the subsequent research programme devoted to elucidating the mechanism of attenuation did follow, so far as I can judge, the prescriptions of the Rule of Big Ell, in that Pasteur manipulated the conditions according to what we would recognize as Mill's Canons.

Signs of Moral Corruption: the 'Bad Guys'

It should now be evident that to find accounts of the actual system of assessment in use in science one must bypass the study of printed scientific texts. These texts have been written within the conventions of a certain rhetoric and embody certain narrative conventions. I note in passing but will not discuss in any detail the fact that there has been a variety of such conventions since the Renaissance. Each 'secretes' its own favoured philosophy of science. For instance, a comparison between Gilbert's *De Magnete* of 1600 and Newton's *Opticks* of 1704 shows little difference in the structure of the respective research programmes but there is a striking difference in literary style and rhetoric. The *Opticks* is laid out with the organization and the terminology of the works of Euclid. It borrows the rhetorical force of those famous demonstrations, though the text reports nothing but a sequence of well-ordered and finely controlled experimental procedures, and their results. In this respect it is quite unlike the same author's *Principia*, in which the geometrical rhetoric reports a text structure that is indeed organized somewhat like the Euclidean *Elements*, that is by deductive chains.

Failing one's own research corpus gleaned by recording the conversations of everyday life in laboratory and common-room, and grubbing round for the remnants of early drafts of scientific papers, one must turn to the literature of the microsociology of science for detailed material evidence. One is on the look-out for examples of intermediate forms of scientific discourse between the incoherent chaos of nascent research programmes and the finely polished presentations of the relevant events in the framework of the narrative conventions of the 'good guys'. Only in this intermediate stage does the harsh life of the scientific jungle reveal itself. The literature of the microsociology of science is frequently enlivened with quotations in *oratio recta*. I shall illustrate something of the rhetoric of the intermediate phase of storytelling with descriptions of two main devices: the use of assessments of personal character in passing judgement on the reliability of the results of research, and the asymmetry in the way data are treated when they are used to support one's own ideas and when they have been quoted in support of the ideas of a rival.

Personal character is often quoted as an epistemic warrant. The most striking feature of the intermediate mode of storytelling is the extent to which assessment of a great variety of factual claims is rooted in judgements of persons rather than in the methodological quality of the experimental researches. These assessments include judgements as to which claims should be accorded the status of observational/experimental *results* (and this includes even quantitative data), and their deeper theoretical interpretation, for example what molecular structures such and such results indicate. 'Results' do not stand freely, so to speak, as the bench-mark against which reliability is routinely assessed, but are themselves judged for reliability pretty much on the basis of the character of the person who produced them. As Latour and Woolgar (1979) show, 'results' and 'interpretations' are not neutral decontextualized propositions, but come qualified by the name and so by the reputation of the person who obtained them (or under whose aegis they were obtained).

In a way qualification by name is a kind of 'epistemic equivalent' of assessments of truth and falsity, since citing some results as Green's means they can safely be accepted while citing others as Brown's means they should be treated with caution. Again to return to the opening argument, what is at issue in the citation of qualities of character is in the end the trustworthiness of the persons discussed. To illustrate, Collins (1981) quotes the following: '[Quest and his group] are so obnoxious, and so firm in their belief that their approach is the right one and that everyone else is wrong, that I immediately discount their veracity on the basis of self-delusion.' The moral status of persons determines the epistemic status of their results. This becomes entirely intelligible if we think in terms of trust rather than truth. Trust in someone's results depends very much on our faith in that person, whereas truth, so it seems to me, ought to be tied to trust in a methodology, regardless of who uses it, provided they use it competently. (This intuition will turn up again in the analysis of a second set of narrative conventions.) As Latour and Woolgar put it, 'this kind of reference to human agency involved in the production of statements is very common. Indeed it was clear from the participants' discussions that *who* made the claim was as important as the claim itself' (Latour and Woolgar 1979).

But is this any more than a specialized form of traditional inductive reasoning? Is the 'who' important as a ground for the assessment of these data as worthy of belief because that person's results have, in the past, turned out to be, in some traditional way, better than the results of others? In their discussion of these points Latour and Woolgar do seem to confuse the question of whether one would wish to collaborate with someone ('No – she's super-competitive!') with whether results, labelled as that person's, should be counted as reliable and thus be incorporated into the discourse as facts. Even the citation of psychological generalizations (ibid: 162–5) in unfavourable assessments, the principle that if people are too pushy and anxious they will tend to accept sloppy results or indulge in wishful thinking, is inductive. But the concept of 'sloppiness' seems to make sense only against the background of a quite traditional epistemic concept like 'accuracy'. Nevertheless it is striking that trustworthiness of colleagues and co-workers has displaced the truth of assertions as the touchstone of acceptance of something as worthy to be believed in the narrative conventions for the *telling* of the history of a research project.

The official rhetoric of the narrative of a research programme as it is published requires the author to present all this character-mongering as an inductive process from true (or false) singular statements to confirmed (or disconfirmed) hypotheses of greater generality. Induction is presented as if it existed as an impersonal schema, the value of which was independent of the person who used it or of their social position in the community of scientists. The actual system has no place for non-inductive singular true statements. The indexicality of the reliability of singular statements to the person who made them, or to the laboratory in which they are first represented as a discovery to the local community, or to the apparatus one or more of whose states such a statement describes, only makes sense as inductions from past performances of that person, laboratory, or apparatus. But these are *inductions from prior inductions*, for example that Green was a pupil of Black and Black's results were always trustworthy. I will call this 'inductive indexicality'.

But more can be said about the grounds for the personal reputations upon which 'inductive indexicality' depends. It is clear from the detailed studies made by Latour and Woolgar, and others, that in the realm of fact-stating discourse, raising the standards of experimentation played an important part in the grounding of reputations. This can be seen in the work of Berzelius, whose reputation depended on his developing standards of experimental work that transformed the accuracy of quantitative chemistry (see Harré 1981: 206).

This is quite a complex matter. Standards of experimentation are task-dependent. Set a new task and new, sometimes more but sometimes less stringent standards are called for. Latour and Woolgar (1979) note that one effect of adopting a new task definition and of raising the standards, whether by changing some intrinsic attribute of research such as the accuracy demanded of some physical measure, or by proposing a research programme that will cost large sums of money, is to eliminate some of the competition. Compare 'We have found a substance which does what is expected, that is it is biologically active' with 'We have discovered the structure of the substance which exhibits this level of biological activity'. According to Latour and Woolgar the shift from a research task defined in terms of attempts to substantiate the first claim to one intended to substantiate the second transformed the conditions under which the claims of the proponents of different points of view were readable as 'stating the facts'. They quote the following remark (ibid: 121):

'Everybody knowing the field could make deductions as to what TRF was . . . their conclusions were correct but it took ten years to prove it . . . . To this day I do not believe they had ever seen what they talked about . . . . There is no way you can postulate the amino-acid composition of an unknown substance.' (Quoted as a remark by Guillemin.) For the latter, much more stringently controlled chemical techniques are required and a much greater investment of time and money. The successful scientists in Latour and Woolgar's moral tale certainly seem to have thought that both the practical and the moral consequences of the shift of the task definition were relevant to their claim for hegemony.

Looking a little more closely at the actual discourse in which these claims are made, the moral element becomes very clear. The exertion of effort is claimed as a mark of moral virtue. For instance a Dr Schally is quoted by Latour and Woolgar (ibid: 118) as saying, 'the only way is to extract these compounds, isolate them . . . . Somebody had to have the guts . . . . now we have tons of it.' Of a colleague Schally remarks with a notable lack of charity, 'of course, he missed the boat, he never dared putting in what was required, brute force' (ibid: 119). Further studies of the social construction of 'reliability' and 'credibility', particularly in these curious personalized moral terms, can be found in Collins (1981).

In the actual system there is a marked asymmetry in the criteria by which one judges one's own hypotheses and those which are used to undermine the credibility of those of a rival. Gilbert and Mulkay (1982) show how 'experimental results' are used in a creatively equivocal way in discussions of the belief-worthiness of putative claims to knowledge. In supporting one's own ideas experimental results are cited as robust data, and a traditional inductive schema is invoked as the rationale of the claim. But when a scientist is discussing the ideas of an opponent 'experimental results' are treated as labile, and their supporting role as seen by the opposition appears as mere self-deception. Critics find little difficulty in coming up with an alternative interpretation of the results of their rivals. Once again narrative conventions must be invoked rather than reference to principles of logic or methodology. Of course the argument is *presented* in terms that would be agreeable to Big Ell, but the tale shifts from congratulating the good guys and denigrating the bad guys, and adjusting the citation of methodological principles in accordance with character-casting rather than impersonal justice. In this new guise the data no longer support and perhaps even undermine the rival's claim to knowledge. Critics show no inclination to do similar work on their own results. They treat them as if they were 'picked directly from nature'. One's own results are presented as capable of only one interpretation, that under which they support their author's claims. In the critical phase an epistemological doctrine rather like that of Whewell (1846) or Hanson (1958) is emphasized. Considerable weight is put on the way pre-existing beliefs and theories are involved in the creation of 'data' out of mere 'results'.

In neither of the cognitive practices I have described, that is inductive indexicality or the 'us and them' asymmetry, do the traditional concepts of 'truth' or 'falsity' seem to play any part. Instead we get phrases like 'confirmed as being correct over the entire range' (Gilbert and Mulkay 1982: 390); '*S* did beautiful experiments which were convincing to me mostly' (ibid: 391); 'it is very hard to get your hands on these things you are working on' (ibid: 393); 'these experiments demonstrate that . . . is real' (ibid: 397); 'see what certain molecular chains are doing' (ibid: 398); '*N*'s numbers agree with what *S* wants' (ibid: 399), and so on.

Strict Assessment and the Moral Order

The work of Knorr-Cetina (1981), Latour, and others has shown that there is a rhetorical use of the terminology of the official or strict system of epistemic concepts in the debates through which epistemic assessments of scientific claims are decided, pro tem. The 'logical' properties of discourse such as entailment or consistency (as the avoidance of contradiction) are used as part of the criteria by which scientific productions are assessed in the community's system of credit. They appear as essentially moral properties of an agonistic scientific discourse or debate. We can look upon it as one of the many language games that make up this form of life.

I propose in the light of these observations that we should reinterpret the activities of traditional philosophy of science.

When philosophers carry on their discussions of science in terms of the official or strict system they are not describing either the cognitive or the material practices of the scientific community, even in ideal form. They are describing a rhetoric and an associated set of narrative conventions for presenting a story in which rival teams of scientists appear as heroes and villains. In describing such narrative conventions, though obscurely and obliquely, they are touching on the moral order of the scientific community, the Order of St Isaac and St Albert.

If we read the realist manifesto, 'Scientific statements should be taken as true or false by virtue of the way the world is' as a moral principle it would run something like this: 'As scientists, that is members of a certain community, we should apportion our willingness or reluctance to accept a claim as worthy to be included in the corpus of scientific knowledge to the extent that we sincerely think it somehow reflects the way the world is.' Put this way the manifesto has *conduct-guiding force*. It encourages the good and the worthy to manifest their virtue in trying to find out how the world is. Seeking the truth is a hopeless epistemic project, but trying to live a life of virtue within the framework of a rule is a possible moral ambition. Those who promulgate their underground opinions as if they were proper contributions to the corpus of scientific knowledge are roundly condemned as immoral.

Moral principles are those maxims which would guide our conduct were we people of unimpeachable virtue. The moral version of the manifesto cited above would enjoin the carrying out of careful experiments, the avoidance of that kind of wishful thinking which leads to the fudging of results, and so on. The moral force of this kind of principle comes through very strongly in the discussions reported by Latour and Woolgar (1979) concerning the early work on TFH. The practice of science is what it is because the morality of the scientific community is strict. Looked at this way the study of the epistemology of science must begin with philosophical reflection on the actual practices of the community if as philosophers we wish to know what scientific knowledge *is*. Failing to follow this ordinance can lead us to confuse the demands of the moral order of the scientific community, the thought-collective, with the possibilities of the achievement of some ideal form of knowledge given the existing practices. Anthropologists have learned that when they ask a member of a community for an account of the local kinship system, they are as likely as not to receive an account of its moral order rather than a description of the vagaries of actual practice. Between the stringency of the moral order and the laxity of real life lies an idealization of the latter, made with an eye on the former. It is this third, middle way that is usually the guiding system for the decisions of everyday life. The concepts of the moral system appear in the rhetorical glosses on that life.

The effect of translating the work of a philosopher out of epistemology into morality can be illustrated with the case of Popper's 'fallibilism'. It can comfortably be reinterpreted as a cluster of moral principles, a 'rule' for the conduct of daily life in a community, a scientific community. As epistemology Popper's ideas have proved rather easy to criticize. For example, there is no way conclusively to falsify a universal hypothesis or the theory of which it forms a part. Even if there were, the rejection of a hypothesis just because it has been falsified by an instance would be irrational without some version of the principle of uniformity of nature as support for the decision to abandon it. But fallibilism can be a guide to 'good conduct'. The morality of the scientific community appears in principles such as 'However much personal investment one has in a theory one should not ignore contrary evidence', or 'One should seek harder for evidence that would count against a theory than for that which would support it', and so on.

But there is more yet to be drawn from looking at scientific writing and talk from this standpoint. Microsociologists, influenced by Erving Goffman (1959), have come to see how much our life activities are shaped by the need to present ourselves to those people who make up our human environment as persons of worth and virtue. So the telling of a scientific tale in accordance with the narrative conventions of the good-and-bad-guy rhetoric allows us to present ourselves as followers of Big Ell. It is not so much the acceptance by others of our results of the moment which is at issue, but their respect for us as members of the scientific community, the Order. And since this acceptance brings each of us, so installed, within the network of trust, we bring our results along with us. As good guys we must be trailing a cloud of good results.

Adherence to these and similar principles will help one to resist temptations, such as self-deception. But why is self-deception counted a vice in the moral order of the community of scientists? In the general morality of everyday life self-deception is perhaps a failing but hardly a sin. For an explanation we must return to the idea of a moral order based on trust, which I outlined in the first section ('Trust, Faith and Speech-acts'). Scientific knowledge is a public resource for action and for belief. To publish abroad a discovery couched in the rhetoric of science is to let it be known that the presumed fact can safely be used in debate, in practical projects, and so on. Knowledge claims are tacitly prefixed with a performative of trust. Interpreted within the moral order of the scientific community 'I know . . .' means something like 'You can trust me that . . .', 'You have my word for it'. If what one claims to know turns out to be spurious then on this reading one has committed a moral fault. One has let down those who trusted one. As an ethnomethodologist might put it, trustworthy knowledge is what is 'true for all practical purposes'. But the moral force of performatives of trust would be undermined if results were presented in this candid way.

This is connected with another moral distinction, that between pretending to have good reason for stating something when one has not, and being genuinely mistaken. Epistemologically they are on the same footing, but morally they could hardly be more distinct. Popperian fallibilism, if interpreted as a moral position, a kind of 'rule', would differentiate them clearly. In the first case I do not have contrary evidence because I have not bothered to look for it, or have not heeded it, while in the second I have just not happened to come upon it despite genuinely trying to find it. The trust that scientists claim from lay persons entails a commitment to intellectual honesty, to having made attempts to substantiate claims in the way that claims are substantiated in the community. It cannot possibly be based on a naïve claim to have the truth. The same argument which transforms epistemology into the communal 'rule' would apply to any intellectual community whatever, for instance the community of theologians.

What, then, should be the major concern of such studies as the philosophy of science or the philosophy of religion? From the considerations advanced in this paper it seems that a description of the moral orders of such communities must play an essential part in the philosophical project. But one can go further. If one could develop an idealized version of the actual system of assessment of candidates for belief, one might be able to explain why the use of the actual system does produce material that is valued in those moral orders, and why the strict system is an expression of that morality. The strict or official system of concepts is then the framework for the telling of stories, which not only fulfil the demands of the Rule of Big Ell but *inter alia* present the author in the most favourable moral light. We should be able not only to show why the claims of magicians should be taken as less trustworthy than those of engineers, but also why the moral order of the scientific community makes this kind of moral distinction. To accomplish the latter we would need to discuss the morality of science against the background of an idealized version of the cognitive and material practices of that community. There is no need to struggle with the impossible task of trying to prove that the actual practice of science truly realizes an epistemic state of affairs which is really nothing but the shadow cast on to philosophy of the conventions of a literary genre.

To my mind the importance of the narrative conventions of the official rhetoric lies not in epistemology, but in the fact that they represent the most perfect and generally sustained moral order ever created by mankind. Alongside the history of the moral force of the order within the scientific community the minimal success of 'Love thy neighbour' makes a regrettably ironic contrast. Philosophers of science set out to construct an idealized and abstract version of scientific cognition and its actual assessment modes. But would such a version be normative? Well, it would not be the whole story. It would bring out that part of the normative background of science that regulates it as a material practice – what someone who joins this community ought to do (just as the 'Rule of St Benedict' enjoined on the Benedictines certain daily observances). But one would have to look to the 'strict system' of 'epistemic' concepts for a guide to how to write up one's results as stories up for publication.

There is another kind of discourse, the theological, where terms from the strict system are cheerfully bandied about, and meet much the same fate, the encouragement of scepticism. No theological statement of which 'God' is the putative reference could be known to be true or to be false. But there is an obvious reading of the strict system in this context too as a cluster of moral maxims, part of the 'rule' that regulates the theological community, and provides it with the conventions of literary genre.

'Untouched by Human Hand'

So far I have concentrated on those narrative conventions by means of which a personal story is told so that the narrator appears in the guise of a modest but competent subscriber to the moral order of which he or she wishes to be seen to be a member. But scientific discourse is made complex from a narratological point of view by virtue of the interweaving of another story-line. It is a narrative of objectivity, of human indifference. Again I am indebted to Latour and Woolgar for drawing our attention to the phenomenon of 'deindexicalization', a sequence of grammatical transformations through which the claims of the discourse attain something like 'facticity'. By that I mean an epistemic standing as existing independently of any human matters, practical or conceptual.

According to Latour and Woolgar the results of research programmes first appear in the literature indexed with their date of discovery, the person, and often the apparatus or technique involved. As the result becomes absorbed into the corpus of 'fact' these indexical references are systematically deleted. The date of the work is the first to go, followed by the apparatus or technique employed and finally by the name of the person who published the result (unless they are of heroic stature). Now the fact exists not as something that is sustained by the personal guarantee and trustworthiness of the human author, but as a claim made on behalf of the community itself. And finally, as Fleck (1935) pointed out, even that reference is deleted so that the fact is presented as if it were wholly context-free, relative to nothing. Of course a putative fact can be 'rubbished' by reinsertion of indexical markers in the reverse order, particularly if the name of the scientist is discrediting in itself.

Complementary to this sequence of deletions is another stylistic device, the elimination of pronouns (even the academic 'we') and the adoption of the passive voice. Instead of 'We added some reagent to the solution' the preferred form would run 'Some reagent was added to the solution'. Students as apprentice scientists are trained in this rhetoric, from school days on. Everything that is personal is leached out of the discourse. Looked at as a narrative convention this choice of grammar enables the author to tell a story not, I think, in the person of Everyman, but of Big Ell himself. It is the impersonal engine of methodology and logic that has brought forth the snippet of truth. Start the machinery of science going and unfailingly, unless incompetently interfered with by a fallible human agent, it will bring forth the goods. Now trust has become generalized beyond the person-to-person commitment expressed in the first of our story-lines, to an impersonal relation between reader and technique. It is like trusting in the rope and pitons rather than in the mountaineer who handles them.

Bibliography

Collins, H.M. (1981) 'The son of seven sexes: the social destruction of a physical phenomenon', *Social Studies of Science* 11: 33–62.

Fleck, L. (1935) *Genesis and Development of a Scientific Fact*, Chicago: Chicago University Press.

Gilbert, G.N., and Mulkay, M. (1982) 'Warranting scientific beliefs', *Social Studies of Science* 12: 383–408.

Goffman, E. (1959) *The Presentation of Self in Everyday Life*, Harmondsworth: Penguin.

Hanson, N.R. (1958) *Patterns of Discovery*, Cambridge: Cambridge University Press.

Harré, R. (1981) *Great Scientific Experiments*, Oxford: Phaidon Press.

Holton, G. (1981) 'Thematic presupposition and the direction of scientific advance', in A. Heath (ed.) *Scientific Explanation*, Oxford: Oxford University Press.

Knorr-Cetina, K. (1981) *The Manufacture of Knowledge*, Oxford: Pergamon.

Latour, B., and Woolgar, S. (1979) *Laboratory Life*, Los Angeles: Sage.

Pasteur, L. (1881) 'Attenuation of the virus of chicken cholera', *Chemical News* 43: 179–80.

Polanyi, M. (1958) *Personal Knowledge*, Chicago: Chicago University Press.

Popper, K.R. (1959) *The Logic of Scientific Discovery*, New York: Basic Books.

Wales, K. (1980) 'Exophora reexamined', *UEA Papers in Linguistics* 12: 21–44.

Whewell, W. (1846, reprinted 1956) *The Philosophy of the Inductive Sciences*, New York: Cass Reprints.

· 5 ·

Making a Discovery: Narratives of Split Genes

GREG MYERS

In *The Double Helix*, James Watson's best-selling autobiographical account of the discovery in 1953 of the structure of DNA, the chapter describing how Watson and Francis Crick figured out the structure ends with a famous sentence in which the more cautious Watson is worried by his colleague's exuberance:

I felt slightly uneasy when at lunch Francis winged into the Eagle to tell everyone within thinking distance that we had found the secret of life.[1]

This is the popular view of discovery, the cry 'Eureka!', the lightbulb over the cartoon character's head that shows he has an idea; here is someone who has discovered something and, what is more, knows exactly what he has discovered.

Most studies of discovery have tried to define it as something intrinsic in a certain kind of psychological or historical event. But recently Augustine Brannigan and other sociologists of scientific knowledge have analysed discovery as a quality attributed to an event by the scientific community.[2] This attribution can be seen as a textual process; in effect, a way of telling the story. For instance, Steve Woolgar has analysed the opening of a Nobel Prize acceptance address to show how devices in the text situated the thing discovered – pulsars – as an object in the world and how they accounted for the fact that he – the speaker and Nobel Prize winner – was able to discover them.[3] I would like to extend (or perhaps distort) this line of inquiry to consider not one text, but the relations between one text and another.

I am going to argue that the attribution of discovery is made, not just in texts, but between texts, in the interpretation of one text by another, as a process of reading as well as writing. This process of interpretation is an essential part of the processes of recording, negotiating, selecting, arranging, and transforming statements, the processes that produce scientific knowledge. So if we want to find a discovery, we can't just go back to the original research articles or even earlier to the lab notebooks or recorded conversations or autoradiographs and electron micrographs.[4] We need to look at the interpretations of the articles as their stories are retold in news articles, review articles, textbooks, and popularizations.

In these retellings over time, I see two apparently contradictory processes going on. First, as is well known, textbooks and popularizations strip away all the narrative elements that make up a book like *The Double Helix*, the social contingencies and personal stories and historical time with its choices and chances, finally stripping away even the names of the researchers, until we are left, not with a narrative, but with a statement of fact: 'DNA is a double helix.'[5] On the other hand, other narrative elements are added in these texts that mark the making of such a statement as a discovery. These texts provide a new chronological framework that defines a singular event and gives it meaning as the transformation from one state – an unstable state of ignorance, overconfidence, or confusion – to another ordered state in which there is now knowledge. These texts also provide a new set of actors, including:

1 the discoverer, of course (often the conflation of several different research groups and findings), but also including
2 the thing discovered, as an entity or phenomenon in the world quite independent of the discoverers, and also
3 various agencies (new techniques, the progress of discipline, luck) that make the discovery possible, and
4 perhaps most important, the audience.

In the quotation I started with, the unsuspecting drinkers of bitter at the Eagle are essential to the morning's work being a discovery.

I am not going to write about the discovery of DNA, which has certainly been analysed well enough,[6] but about a more recent set of texts in the same field that describe the discovery of split genes. The texts that I will examine include the first published reports in *Proceedings of the National Academy of Sciences* (*PNAS*) and *Cell*, the versions presented at the annual molecular genetics symposium at Cold Spring Harbor in June 1977, and some texts that refer to them: some news articles that came out in the scientific press in the next few months, some review articles that came out in the next few years, a recent textbook, and some popularizations (see Bibliography). I will argue that the process of discovery cannot be located in the papers to which it is usually traced. I am not saying that the authors of these papers do not deserve credit for the discovery; these papers do indeed contain the techniques and claims with which their authors are credited. But they are not organized to show the development of the techniques and the formulation of the claims *as an event*. The news articles (not in newspapers but in *Nature, Science* and *New Scientist*) retell the story of these papers in a way that makes them an event. The review articles, some of them huge compilations referring to hundreds of articles, integrate this discovery event into larger narratives, human narratives such as the progress of the field, or natural narratives such as the processes of transcription, the regulation of gene expression, or the course of evolution. The textbooks tell an exemplary narrative of techniques and experimental method, with all the personal and historical elements removed so that it can be symbolically repeated by the student. Popularizations, on the other hand, tend to leave out these processes and present the discovery as the personal and historic encounter of researcher and waiting object.

I will compare the transformation of the account of split genes through the reports, news articles, reviews and textbooks by asking what actors each narrative involves, and how each sequences events into a beginning, middle and end. Then I will turn to see how these narrative techniques work in the popularizations.

Normally, at this point in a sociology of science paper, I would tell you what split genes are. But to do that would only add one more of these accounts, and not a very good one. Instead, I refer you to an account that recently appeared in *Scientific American*, in the course of Thomas Cech's explanation of his own more recent discovery (Appendix). At this point in the article, he has just finished explaining that DNA is a very long double-stranded molecule that carries all the information needed to put together the organism encoded in its sequence of bases; messenger RNA (or mRNA) is a single-strand molecule that takes this coded information by binding to the DNA; that is called *transcription*. It then breaks away and carries the information to where the code is *translated* into a sequence of amino acids that makes up a particular protein. For now, I am using this passage only as an introduction; I will come back to it later to discuss what about it is characteristic of the popularizations on this topic, and to note how words and images are reused or transformed through the chain of interpretation.

The First Reports

I am arguing that we cannot find the original version of this discovery narrative by looking up the articles published in 1977 by the two groups Cech mentions, hoping to find one that begins, 'We have discovered split genes in higher organisms'. It's not that the original papers are hard to find. Everyone agrees that the discovery was announced at the Cold Spring Harbor symposium in 1977; the proceedings of that conference have been published, and the same reports also appear, in a different form, in *PNAS* and *Cell* articles written before the symposium but published after it.[7] And this was not one of those cases, so common in scientific history, where an important discovery was not recognized on its first announcement. James Watson, the director of the Cold Spring Harbor lab, says in his 'Foreword' to the proceedings:

Even more surprisingly, a number of experimental approaches gave us the bombshell that functional RNA molecules can derive from physically quite separate sections along a DNA molecule. At the end we were both overwhelmed and dazzled, and many participants left feeling they had been part of an historic occasion.[8]

And the problem in locating the discovery is not, as it is in some cases, in the lack of an explicit claim in the texts. Though the term *split genes* was not used, the MIT group coined the term *spliced segments* and the abstract of their *PNAS* article ends with a claim that sounds like the discovery Cech describes:

Thus, four segments of viral DNA may be joined together during the synthesis of mature hexon mRNA. A model is presented for adenovirus late mRNA synthesis that involves multiple splicing during maturation of a larger precursor nuclear RNA.

The abstract of one of the articles by the group at Cold Spring Harbor starts with a sentence that seems similar:

The 5' terminal sequences of several adenovirus 2 (Ad2) mRNAs, isolated late in infection, are complementary to sequences within the Ad2 genome which are remote from the DNA from which the main coding sequence of each mRNA is transcribed.

The problem with our search for the discovery narrative in these texts begins if we ask what these groups did that counts as a discovery. The two groups use quite different methods, and, where they use similar methods, study different molecules and hybrids. Of course they phrase their claims differently. In fact, I was able to find the two sentences that make the articles a discovery only by working backwards, looking for sentences that sounded like those in later accounts. There are many other sentences that could be taken as the claims of the articles. Indeed, they were both later cited for several different claims. The consensus judgement of later accounts that these two somewhat different texts say 'the same thing' is the first step in the reduction of their narratives to knowledge.

It doesn't worry me here that all research reports are idealized versions of what went on in the lab. The methodological point is not that we can't find what actually happened, though we can't,[9] but that the earliest reports don't give a sense of any happening at all, don't give a narrative that could be considered a discovery. The problem is that the features necessary for a discovery narrative are just those conventionally excluded from research reports – historical chronology, human actors, and an audience. In the rest of the chapter I will look at how actors and historical time enter into some retellings and how they are removed in other retellings.

Actors

It has often been pointed out that the conventions of scientific texts, with their impersonal constructions and passive verbs, imply a narrative in which the object studied, not the researcher, is the main actor. Indeed, a list of the subjects of sentences in the abstracts of the first two articles would suggest that these narratives are driven by the molecules.

(MIT)	(CSH)
An mRNA fraction	The 5′ terminal sequences
The mRNA sequences	This
hybrids of . . . RNA and	The 5′ terminal sequences
. . . DNA	The structures visualized
DNA sequences	A late mRNA
four segments	It
A model	These findings

Here the process and models used in the research come in only at the end of the story.

As rewritten for the Cold Spring Harbor symposium proceedings, these papers have subjects referring more often to the technical work, rather than just to the entities being studied. For instance, in the passage in the MIT article describing the discovery, the molecules, or parts of them, are the subjects of most of the sentences. But there are some crucial sentences that have, instead, subjects that refer to the design of the experiment:

A function for the synthesis and rapid turnover of hnRNA . . . (1)
A variety of mounting conditions . . . (7)
An example of the type of hybrids . . . (10)
The presence of three loops . . . (15)

As we will see in analysing the sequence of the passage, the points at which the subjects refer to the experiment rather than to the molecules are crucial in our reading. My point here is just that such formulations, as we would expect, carefully avoid any reference to the researchers themselves as actors.

But even if the symposium reports include both an (explicit) entity and an (implicit) researcher, we still don't have the actors of a discovery narrative. For that we need another actor, which is provided in the news reports in the scientific press. These reports allow the implicit researcher of the reports to come out, to have a name, and to be the subject of sentences and observe, demonstrate, announce. But they also add the research community of other scientists as an active participant. For instance, the first report in *Nature*, a month after the conference and before the papers had been published, has the title, 'Adenovirus amazes at Cold Spring

Harbor'.[10] And in the key sentence that announces the discovery, it is the audience, not the researchers or the genes, that is the subject:

The audience at the symposium was amazed, fascinated, and not a little bewildered to learn that the late adenovirus mRNAs are mosaic molecules consisting of sequences complementary to several non-contiguous segments of the viral genome.

(Sambrook 1977: 101)

The same sort of transformation is apparent in the opening sentences of the later news articles in *Science* and *New Scientist*.

A recent discovery about the synthesis of some of the messenger RNAs of two unrelated animal viruses has excited molecular biologists.

(Marx 1977: 853)

There is an air of bewilderment bordering on incredulity in molecular biology labs at the moment.

(Rogers 1978: 18)

It is the presence of an audience, like that of the people of Rome in Browning's *The Ring and the Book*, that places the event in human history, shows it is important, makes it an event.

In reviews, a new actor enters: the discipline as a whole. The discipline is not the same thing as the audiences of the news articles, for this actor replaces the researchers, the discoverers. We can see this in the title of Chambon's 'Summary' of the Cold Spring Harbor symposium: 'The molecular biology of the eukaryotic genome is coming of age'. A paragraph from the introduction to John Abelson's review article in the *Annual Review of Biochemistry* for 1979 also shows how the researchers disappear into footnotes and seem (but only seem) to leave the credit for their work to the field as a whole:

There have been tremendous advances in this field in the three years since Perry reviewed the subject (1). They have been mostly due to the rapid acquisition of information about the structure of genes and their initial transcription products, and have come mainly through the application of recombinant DNA technology and the development of rapid DNA sequencing techniques (2,3). The most important result is that the genes of eukaryotes are not necessarily colinear with their products – instead they contain interruptions in the coding sequence which have been called intervening sequences or introns (4).

(Abelson 1979: 1036)

Note that the agency also becomes an important actor in these narratives: here the field acquires information *through* recombinant DNA techniques and rapid sequencing, and the *result* is that genes are split. (Many reviews credit recombinant DNA techniques; this was at a time when the controversy over the safety of such techniques was at its height.)[11] The conclusion, 206 references later, also suggests a new actor:

This field is obviously in a state of rapid flux and it will be fascinating to see where it goes.

(ibid: 1069)

In the textbooks, the RNA, DNA, and the methods for displaying them are the only actors. Experiments seem to take place without researchers. The form of this sentence is typical:

Through direct nucleotide sequencing and other methods, it soon became clear that the gene in eukaryotes is composed of coding and non-coding segments interspersed between the beginning and the end of the genetic message.

(Avers 1986: 119)

Such a sentence highlights the agency of the sequencing methods. The account seems to return to the subjectlessness of the research reports. But in this text there is not even an implicit researcher suggesting possible artifacts, or proposing alternative interpretations, or deciding what to do next. An experiment like that on ovalbumin moves forward with a sort of inevitability, for the result is already known and the account is just illustrating the result. I will try to explain this odd kind of narrative later. One clue is that there seems to be another implied actor here, the student who then reads on to learn the Maxam and Gilbert sequencing method.

So in the course of the interpretation and reinterpretation of the texts, actors are added – the ideal researcher, the research community as audience, the discipline as the ultimate discoverer – and then actors are removed, so that the researcher disappears again, and we are left with molecules and techniques.

Sequences

All narratives imply a beginning and an ending; in a discovery narrative the transforming event is the revelation of a previously concealed truth. But in the research articles there is no event, just a logical sequence of experiments. In the results section of the MIT group's *PNAS* article, the sequence moves from information on the infection cycle of the virus, to purification techniques, to a hybridization experiment with one DNA fragment, showing the tails, through experiments with fragments made with another fragment, through three control experiments, and finally to the crucial (in retrospect) hybridization of the tail with the *Eco*RI A fragment, showing the leader hybridizing with several loops left out of the hybrid. The same movement can be seen in compressed form in the symposium paper (so that, for instance, four paragraphs and four different experiments are summarized as, 'A variety of mounting conditions for observation with the electron microscope were tested . . .').

The Cold Spring Harbor *Cell* article moves in the same way, but starts with the crucial hybridization instead of ending with it, and then follows it with the control experiments. In both cases, the order of telling is a reconstruction of the logic of argument, not the story of experimentation. The typical form of transition in the articles by both groups is a statement of a logical alternative – usually a possible artifact – followed by the action necessary to exclude it. For instance, the MIT group's symposium article has:

To investigate whether these sequences were of viral origin, purified hexon (II) mRNA was hybridized to single-stranded *Eco*RI A DNA and the resultant hybrids were visualized in the electron microscope.

Each step is apparently dictated by the previous results; the first surprising tail of the hybrids sends the researchers down a series of experiments, each checking on the last. In this narrative, the phenomenon tries repeatedly to trick the researchers, but they block off one line of escape after another, and finally corner it and get its secret.

A closer look at the passage shows how the sequence is marked by verb tense shifts. Just as the content of the passage falls into three parts, presenting old knowledge, following the narrative of experiments, and representing new knowledge, so the verb tenses divide the passage into three parts.

1 At the beginning, the claim is made in the present perfect, so that all this narrative is viewed as leading up to the present hypothesis, and then sentences 2–5 are in the present tense, suggesting that the statements in them are permanently valid descriptions of nature.

2 Then in the sixth sentence of the passage the tense shifts to the past tense of an account of particular historical events, not 'what happens during hybridization', but 'what happened when we observed this particular hybridization'. So this is a crucial shift, but note that it does not exactly coincide with the shift at the level of apparent content, for sentence 5 is in the present and sentence 6 in the past when they both describe the same electron micrograph. I would explain this by seeing the tense shift as the signal of new information, after the description of what was expected, marking an apparent anomaly that sets off the string of events that follows. The reasoning and response too are in the past tense, as is the decision to try another hybridization.

3 But the results of the new experiment and all the interpretation are in the present tense, marking a shift to a third part of the paragraph and also suggesting some sort of parallel status between this newly produced but atemporal knowledge and the accepted background knowledge in statements at the beginning of the paragraph. So while the analysis of what was being said suggested a sequence of several experimental steps, the verb analysis suggests a historical narrative of events linking two similar present-tense states.

This analysis applies to the Cold Spring Harbor group's *Cell* articles as well, but their paper in the symposium is interesting in following a chronological rather than a logical sequence; it reads like a scientific history, but one written days after the discovery. They say, 'In this paper we provide an account of when various pieces of the puzzle emerged, and how they all led to the conclusion that . . .'. The pieces of the puzzle include chromatography to show that the RNAs have the same cap, restriction enzyme mapping to show that the cap is separated from the genes, hybridization of Ad2 and DV40 that shows secondary sites of hybridization, and finally the R-loop mapping of various hybrids with an electron microscope. The links between parts in this article tend to be references to narrative time: 'As our research proceeded on these and other topics during the next year, certain results emerged which, at the time, seemed puzzling or anomalous.' So as the article moves towards a conclusion, it builds a sense of confusion and apparent error that can only be resolved with the assertion that the genes are split. This kind of narrative is essentially comic, in the sense that it introduces incongruities and tensions that will be resolved as it all comes together in the end.

What neither the first articles nor the symposium papers do is clearly fix a moment of discovery, a moment when they could leave the lab, go to the nearest pub, and announce that they had found the secret of eukaryotic life. I have already noted that the news articles introduce the audience as an actor; they also introduce the discovery as an event. To do this they define the research field in a first state of weariness, blockage, or tension, as in Sambrook's opening:

If success were exactly proportionate to effort invested, our understanding of the mechanism of gene expression in eukaryotes would be virtually complete. Unfortunately, despite intensive investigations for a number of years, our ignorance remains almost total.

(Sambrook 1977: 101)

The narrative ends with a vision of a field now on the move:

Perhaps it is not too optimistic to hope that what has been so clearly shown for adenovirus 2 may also help to explain how host cells regulate their own genes.

(ibid: 104)

The other news articles all follow this pattern; some sense of rigidity or of confusion in the opening state implies that a break will come.

But each of the news articles puts the various reports they are describing in a different narrative order. So Sambrook, in *Nature*, uses Darnell's results to present one kind of regulation, and parallels them with the results of the MIT group. It was not obvious, a month after the conference, that the split genes work must be foregrounded; at this stage it is just half the story. Then the Cold Spring Harbor findings are used only as extensions of the MIT results, and the work of the other virus groups is just mentioned as confirmation.

Jean Marx, writing in *Science* a couple of months later, also presents the MIT group's work first, and restructures the Cold Spring Harbor account in the symposium article so that the electron micrography, the parallel to the MIT group's work, is mentioned first, rather than last. Darnell's findings now enter just because they suggest which of the four possible splicing mechanisms operates. In John Rogers' account in *New Scientist* (Rogers 1978), after further findings on eukaryotic genes had been published, the MIT group's work is again first, and the Cold Spring Harbor researchers are just 'the other groups who reported the same thing'. Rogers sharpens the moment of discovery even more by building up a mystery (sentence 4) and then presenting the MIT group's electron micrograph as the answer, without giving any explanation of the previous kinds of experiments leading to it. The interpretation is here in the audience's response; it is they who see the extra segments (sentence 8). This narrative leads from the late adenovirus mRNAs (MIT and CSH) to the early Ad2 mRNAs studied by Westphal's group, and then this discovery – all one discovery – has an effect on the groups working on SV40: 'The news about Adenovirus 2 immediately solved a puzzle for Sherman Weissman's group at Yale.' The transition in Rogers' article to the research reported after the Cold Spring Harbor symposium shows that the creation of the discovery as an event implies a placement on a historical scale:

But these bizarre discoveries were only half the story. On their own, they would be comparable with the discovery of reverse transcriptase enzyme in 1970; they imply new manipulations of RNA that had been believed impossible, but coming from viruses they needn't interfere with our view of the normal cell. What has really opened the Pandora's box are data showing that normal genes too are discontinuous . . .

(Rogers 1978: 19)

Rogers can compare the significance of quite distinct discoveries in almost quantitative terms by keeping the narrative framework (knowledge after, minus knowledge before, equals size of discovery) but taking the events out of their particular contexts in the history of the discipline.

In reviews, this discovery event can be worked into other narratives. Review articles, unlike research reports, do not have a standard narrative pattern; part of what makes them so difficult to write (as well as to read), besides the weight of 200 or 300 references, is that the parts are usually arranged by dividing up recent knowledge into more or less logical chunks, rather than by presenting a chronological sequence. But there is always an underlying narrative – of the progress of the field, as in Chambon's summary of the Cold Spring Harbor symposium, or of the processing of RNA, as in Abelson's review, or of molecular evolution, as in Gilbert's, Darnell's, and Crick's, so articles on the same research can present surprisingly different stories, with different agencies at work.[12]

In the textbook the discovery is frozen into a fact without a narrative of its own. The section introducing split genes in Charlotte Avers' text starts with a reference to history – 'Until the mid 1970s' – and the second paragraph remarks that the discovery was an event, that 'The existence of split genes . . . came as a complete surprise' (Avers 1986: 119–20). In Ursula Goodenough's textbook it is 'certainly the most unexpected discovery to emerge from recombinant DNA and sequencing technology . . .' (Goodenough 1984: 272). But just as there are no names in Avers' book, so there is no chronology. Instead of starting with adenovirus, Avers offers ovalbumin as typical (Goodenough takes beta-globin), and there is no mention of the way research took an insight gained from virus models and applied it to eukaryotic cells. Terms like *introns*, *exons*, and *split genes* are given in both textbooks, but it is as if they were always waiting in the dictionary, not as if they were coined by particular researchers for particular reasons. But then, the whole principle of organization of a textbook makes difficult the kind of storytelling that is crucial to many popularizations. The main problem of the textbook, as of the reviews, is parcelling out the field of knowledge into sections. The cross-references, for instance, suggest the way the information is to be taken as all existing at once, and as arranged in an array, like a table. In its choice of sections, the textbook follows the sections of most of the reviews, but without their linking narrative, their outstanding problem of, say, RNA processing or evolution. Each section of the textbook does then have a narrative of its own, built around an exemplary experiment, but this experiment or technique may or may not be linked to a researcher, to a historically unique performance.[13]

The transformation of the actors in the textual processing and reprocessing of the first reports is paralleled by a retelling of the story.

1 The research reports order a sequence of actions.
2 The news articles transform this sequence into an event.
3 The reviews insert this discovery event into other narratives.
4 The textbooks remove these narratives, leaving the discovery fixed in the spatial, atemporal array of the ordered presentation of information.

Popularizations

Now we can reread the passage from *Scientific American* (Cech 1986) with which I began, looking for some of the patterns we have noticed in other articles. First, we see now that it is constructed as a narrative, beginning with an unstable first state of deceptive knowledge (sentences 1–2, which are the 'once upon a time' of this story), and ending with a second state, a 'happily ever after', in which molecular geneticists are given lots of work to do in three areas (sentences 12–14).

The subheading '"Split" Genes' introduces the phenomenon as an entity in itself, as something that existed and was discovered, rather than as one way of describing other, real entities, such as molecules. It is significant that the two groups are said here to have discovered 'split genes in higher organisms', when they were in fact working with viruses, not higher organisms, and that they are said to have found interruptions in 'the DNA encoding a protein' when they found them in the leader, a part of the molecule that does not code. These comments may seem picky. It was realized at the time that the work showed the possibility of interruptions in eukaryotic genes, and in coding sequences, but in the first reports and news articles these are still suggestions, and when interruptions in beta-globin, immunoglobin, and ovalbumin were announced a few months after the symposium, these announcements were treated then as separate discoveries. Now, ten years later, the discoveries are conflated, following the pattern of compression we have seen, and the earlier reports are credited with the findings of later reports (or the later with the earlier).[14]

The other actors in the narrative besides the split genes themselves are the researchers (sentence 3) and, less obviously, 'the rest of the scientific world' who are 'amazed' (sentence 3), the 'everyone' who had expected (sentence 4), the learners who did not take long (sentence 7). As we have seen, they are crucial to making the event a discovery. Finally there is Thomas Cech himself, who enters the story in sentence 14, and on whom this discovery had its effect.

There are two kinds of statements in the passage, past-tense statements of events and present-tense statements of facts (sentences 4, 5, 7):

It *did not take long* to learn the fate of the introns: after the RNA is transcribed from the DNA, the introns *are snipped out* and the exons are spliced to form a continuous molecule.

(Cech 1986: 78)

Besides these present-tense statements of what is discovered, there are present-tense statements of general biological knowledge, against which horizon the event is a discovery (sentences 10–11). The naming in sentence 6 is a crucial past-tense event that makes the introns an object that is part of the present-tense world.

Our sense of this discovery as a narrative construction is supported by the sentence openings that guide the reader by giving time expressions:

By the late 1970s . . .
In 1977 . . .
It did not take long . . .
In the late 1970s . . .

Note that most of the rest of the sentence openings refer either to the researchers (sentences 3–4) or to their actions (sentences 2, 8, 9, 12, 13). Only three of the sentences actually open with the things studied, and all three are general definitions, what we might call insertion sequences necessary to promote processing of the text by its popular audience.

This passage shows in compressed form the essential features of the discovery narrative:

1 A change of state.
2 A chronological sequence.
3 Actors, including the entity, the researchers, and the audience.
4 A statement of background knowledge against which the new knowledge can be defined as a discovery.

Different levels of narratives, following research protocols, researchers' careers, the changes in the discipline, the evolution of molecules, or the process of transcription itself, are interwoven to show the intrusion of the contingent stories of humans into the timeless processes of biology.

A brief look at one other, less typical popularization will bring out some of the other features that link accounts of the discovery. *DNA for Beginners* (Rosenfield, Ziff, Van Loon 1983) is a 'documentary comic book' by a science writer, a well-known molecular biologist, and a cartoonist that, like others on Marx or Darwin in the series from the Writers and Readers Cooperative, provides a primer explaining quite abstract concepts in words and pictures. It is, then, explicitly narrative, and the molecules and researchers both talk in the exclamation-mark-laden prose of comics. The molecules are shown with a set of caricature conventions throughout the book; in the split genes section we see trucks for the bases, phosphate wheels, a pennant streaming form the 5' end to show the direction of transcription, and little tractors for the enzymes, here DNA polymerase. Before the split genes are described, the text describes the hybridization experiments, showing a simple schematic drawing of 'what they expected to see'. In turning the page we turn from the overly simple model to an obviously complex image, the schematic diagram of an electron micrograph. Then, from this image, the text gives an account of transcription, with the images getting more schematic and metaphorical.

We have seen several of the features of this text in other accounts. First, what were once several discovery events are conflated, so that the first schematic diagram of a split gene, though it doesn't say so, is ovalbumin, the second is beta-globin, and the text then tells us the discovery 'was made with mRNA from Adenovirus, and it was soon confirmed with cellular genes'. So here, as in the Cech account, the events that seemed separate in 1977, so that there were several discoveries, can now be seen as the same thing. All the popularizations start with a picture like the one in *DNA for Beginners*, usually an electron micrograph, just one, and nearly always one of those from the first discovery reports. This similarity in presentation tells us several things:

1 that the historical status of these images makes them preferable

to any that might be made later, even if the later ones had some technical advantages,

2 that the images of ovalbumin, beta-globin, and adenovirus hybrids are equivalent for the purposes of popularization, and

3 that it is important to have a realistic image to start with, before the more symbolic representations. In this case, the ovalbumin picture may have been chosen both because ovalbumin is the most complex of the earlier genes to be studied, with seven introns, and because this particular electron micrograph is remarkably easy to read, with all strands clear, no loops crossing, and all the introns showing, arranged in order so that it is easy to transform into a map.

But there is an irony in the reuse today of these images. They are not, strictly speaking, pictures of split genes, but pictures of the result of a complex hybridization experiment that is interpreted as showing which sequences are complementary and which are not. As an experimental method, 'its resolving power is low', as Francis Crick has said in his review (Crick 1979: 268), and it was soon superseded by sequencing of the amino acids using what were then new techniques. I have seen no electron micrographs in the report literature since the first articles; what one sees now are the autoradiographs recording the sequences, or perhaps just a diagram showing the sequence represented by a code of letters. The electron micrographs may have had the effect of showing, more convincingly than other methods (such as autoradiographs of the gels with the hybrids complementary to various fragments separated out), that the phenomenon was really there. But, in the constant reuse of these images, they become pictures *of* split genes; the image becomes an icon for a concept. This reuse affects the popular reader's retrospective view of the research, so that, for instance, one of the four transcription methods first discussed at Cold Spring Harbor now seems to be self-evidently right; since we see the strands of DNA looping out in the pictures, we incorrectly transfer this image from the hybridization experiment to the *in vivo* transcription process.

I have argued that a discovery narrative needs not only a researcher, and an entity, treated as an actor independent of the researcher, but also the scientific community to give its response. In the image of discovery in *DNA for Beginners*, the phenomenon and the community are brought together in one picture, with a little Kirby-like cartoon observer peering over the hill formed by a squiggle of DNA. This is a visualization of the effect we saw in the Rogers account, in which the audience looks directly at the image and sees the new knowledge. The cartoon character here is saying, 'AMAZING!' This same word pops up in a number of texts on the discovery, for instance in the title of Chow and Broker's article in *Cell*, and in Sambrook's *Nature* news article, Chambon's 'Summary' in the conference proceedings, and Rogers' *New Scientist* article. The recurrence of this one word shows, first of all, the need the authors felt to register the audience's response. It may also show that molecular geneticists have a fondness for alliteration; perhaps if the discovery had been made with another gene at another lab we would see 'Beta-globin bewilders' or 'Ovation for ovalbumin'. But it also supports an important assumption of my argument, one I haven't really justified, that these texts are not all variant treatments of the same original happenings, but that one author reads another, so we are seeing a retelling of a retelling of a retelling of the story, even when, as is usually the case here, the later writers in this line of interpreters were there for the first reports.

DNA for Beginners explains the relation of split genes to the genetic message with a clever illustration in which the text of the explanation is itself split up by nonsense letters that must be deleted to make it readable. While none of the other popularizations is reflexive in this way, many use an analogy to text to explain the basic principles of information transfer from DNA to RNA to protein. This metaphor goes back even before the structure of DNA was known. Chambon draws on it when he chooses an epigraph for his Cold Spring Harbor 'Summary' from a passage by Malraux on the immortality of reproduction of forms in art (Chambon 1977).

What makes the *DNA for Beginners* example different is that it uses the illustration reflexively, causing the reader to think of his or her own reception of a code in reading the book. This raises further questions for those of us who analyse texts. The metaphor treats texts as vehicles of information transfer, a model of texts I reject in this paper, while I am treating texts as constructing reality, a model that makes no sense in terms of molecular genetics. The 'central dogma' underlying nucleic acid research since the 1950s holds that the information all goes one way; as the title of one collection has it, 'DNA makes RNA makes protein'. I am suggesting that with written texts, the information can go backwards as well, so that the first texts observing loops in the leaders of Ad2 are now read as 'the discovery of split genes in higher animals'. The change from the first article to the reviews and popularizations is like the processing of RNA in that some parts are taken out and others are brought together. But it is unlike the processing of RNA in that the original message can now only be read as saying what the later, transformed message says, as if the protein at the end were our only guide to the DNA at the beginning.

Molecular geneticists are certainly aware of the shaping power of narrative; Abelson, for instance, refers in his review to the telling of 'the adenovirus story'. But when they talk about different ways of telling the story, it is always with the assumption that one way of telling it is the right way; they assume the truth will out.[15] We must acknowledge this assumption in any account of the inter- pretation of scientific texts. To say that these scientific texts are stories is not to say that they are *just* stories, that they are like all other stories, and that therefore the literary and anthropological specialists in stories can understand them on a deeper level than the understanding of the scientists themselves. Scientific texts are different from literary texts; Berget, Berk, Harrison, and Sharp's 'Spliced segments at the 5' termini of adenovirus-2 late mRNA' is different from Poe's 'The purloined letter'. It does not help us understand this difference to say that one kind of text refers to things that really exist, and the other does not, that one is a story about molecules and the other a story about adultery, blackmail, and a detective. Instead, we can see the difference as the result of two different methods of interpretation, of retelling the story, in two different disciplines. It is often noted how the readings of literary texts, and the readings of readings of readings of literary texts, proliferate in a bewildering way, so that as time goes on there are more and more versions of Poe's 'The purloined letter'. As we have seen, scientific texts seem to have as many different versions at the beginning, but as the process of interpretation within the discipline and in public proceeds, one version is used for practical purposes, for placing one's claim in historical context, for drawing lessons for the research community, for explaining one's research to the public, for training students to be researchers. We end up with just one standardized story of the discovery of split genes, one 'adenovirus story'.[16]

Appendix

Thomas Cech, 'RNA as an enzyme', *Scientific American*, November 1986

1 By the late 1970s the roles of mRNA, rRNA and tRNA had long since been worked out, and it appeared that RNA was no longer a source of
2 mystery. But the appearance was deceptive.

'Split' Genes

3 In 1977 two groups of research workers – Philip A. Sharp and his colleagues at the Massachusetts Institute of Technology and a group at the Cold Spring Harbor Laboratory – amazed themselves and the rest of the scientific world when they discovered 'split' genes in higher
4 organisms. The two groups found that the sequence of nucleotides in the DNA encoding a protein is not arranged continuously, as everyone
5 had expected. Instead the coding sequences are interrupted by large
6 stretches of noncoding DNA. The interrupting stretches were dubbed introns, or intervening sequences; the divided coding sequences were
7 called exons. It did not take long to learn the fate of the introns: after the RNA is transcribed from the DNA, the introns are snipped out and the exons are spliced to form a continuous molecule.
8 The discovery of RNA splicing was tremendously exciting for several
9 reasons. One reason was that splicing was found to take place in eukaryotes but not in prokaryotes, at least not in one well-studied
10 prokaryote, the bacterium *Escherichia coli*. Eukaryotes are organisms –
11 ranging from yeasts to human beings – that have nucleated cells. The prokaryotes – bacteria and certain algae – have cells that are not
12 nucleated. It seemed plausible that the study of RNA splicing would illuminate the novel evolutionary potential of the eukaryotes, including their capacity for evolving specialized cells organized in multicellular
13 organisms. It also seemed reasonable to suppose that RNA splicing would provide an important new form of regulation of gene expression.
14 In the late 1970s the problem of gene expression was being worked on in many laboratories, including my own.

Notes

1 James Watson (1980) *The Double Helix: A Personal Account of the Discovery of DNA*, 2nd edition (1968), ed. Gunther Stent, New York: Norton, 115.

2 Augustine Brannigan (1981) *The Social Basis of Scientific Discoveries*, Cambridge: Cambridge University Press. Also see Simon Schaffer (1986) 'Scientific discoveries and the end of natural philosophy', *Social Studies of Science* 16: 3.

3 Steve Woolgar (1980) 'Discovery: logic and sequence in a scientific text', in *The Social Process of Scientific Investigation, Sociology of the Sciences Yearbook* vol. 4, ed. Karin Knorr, Roger Krohn, and Richard Whitley, Dordrecht: D. Reidel, 239–68. See also Steve Woolgar (1976) 'Writing an intellectual history of scientific development: the use of discovery accounts', *Social Studies of Science* 6: 395–422.

4 Michael Lynch (1985) *Art and Artefact in Laboratory Science: A Study of Shop Work and Shop Talk in a Research Laboratory*, London and Boston: Routledge & Kegan Paul.

5 Bruno Latour and Steve Woolgar (1986) *Laboratory Life: The Construction of Scientific Facts*, 2nd edition, Princeton: Princeton University Press. See also Greg Myers (1986) *Writing Biology: Texts in the Social Construction of Science*, Madison: University of Wisconsin Press.

6 Robert Olby (1974) *The Path to the Double Helix*, London: Macmillan; Franklin S. Portugal and Jack S. Cohen (1977) *A Century of DNA: A History of the Discovery of the Structure and Function of the Genetic Substance*, Cambridge: MIT Press; Pnina Abir-Abn (1985) 'Themes, genres, and orders of legitimation in the consolidation of new scientific disciplines: deconstructing the history of molecular biology', *History of Science* 23: 73–117; and Edward Yoxen (1985) 'Speaking out about competition: an essay on *The Double Helix* as popularisation', in Terry Shinn and Richard Whitley (eds) *Expository Science: Forms and Functions of Popularisation*, Dordrecht: D. Reidel. Also see the articles collected in the Norton Critical Edition of *The Double Helix*, op.cit., note 1.

7 The first public announcement of the research was made at the symposium at Cold Spring Harbor in June, which took place before the papers were published in *PNAS* and *Cell* in August and September. But the papers were received by the journals before the symposium, and Phillip Sharp, senior author of the MIT paper, comments, 'The primary article describing the discovery of splicing was the PNAS article in 1977. This article was drafted and accepted for publication before the C.S.H. symposium and was more carefully considered. The C.S.H. paper was drafted, in large part, from the PNAS article'. But I often refer to the C.S.H. article because the passage in it summarizing the complex experiments is relatively short.

8 James Watson (1977) 'Foreword', *Cold Spring Harbor Symposium on Quantitative Biology* 42: xv.

9   See, for instance, Mike Lynch, op.cit., note 4, and G. Nigel Gilbert (1976) 'The transformation of research findings into scientific knowledge', *Social Studies of Science* 6: 281–306.

10 Professor Sambrook points out that his account of the conference for *Nature* was submitted just days after the conference, so that in the chronology of texts it probably comes after the writing of the *PNAS* and *Cell* papers and before final writing of the papers in the symposium proceedings. His article was the first news of the discovery to appear in print.

11 Susan Wright (1986) 'Molecular biology or molecular politics? The production of scientific consensus on the hazards of recombinant DNA technology', *Social Studies of Science* 16, 4: 593–620.

12 The larger story in which one views research results is not just a way or organizing the mass of citations in a review article; the interpretation of results is determined by the context in which one puts them. Pierre Chambon points out, in both his 'Summary' of the Cold Spring Harbor symposium and his *Scientific American* article, that he and other researchers came to the symposium with results they had been trying to interpret in various ways, which they could then reinterpret in the light of the findings with adenovirus 2. 'In retrospect, it is amusing to note again that the way we interpret an experiment is strongly influenced by what we already know. For instance, at the meeting, Leder *et al.* interpreted their R-loop data as indicating the juxtaposition of two nonallelic beta-globin genes' rather than as evidence for split genes (Chambon 1977: 1211). Similarly, Chambon says that before the Cold Spring Harbor symposium, when his own group presented their results (showing that the complementary DNA from ovalbumin messenger RNA hybridized with several different fragments of the cellular DNA), 'The most frequent suggestion was that we were seeing an artifact of blotting or hybridization' (Chambon 1981: 51).

13 This sort of arrangement and the sense of science as a lab exercise are typical of textbooks, though not universal. Gunther Stent and Richard Calendar, the authors of one of the two main molecular genetics textbooks of the 1970s, *Molecular Genetics: An Introductory Narrative*, compare its 'organic (rather than logical) manner' to the 'sovereign didactics' of James Watson's *Molecular Biology of the Gene*. And the two recent textbooks I refer to differ in their format, with Goodenough giving more of the background and personalities, usually in a separate box.

14 Phillip Sharp has commented that there was uncertainty even at the time about whether the discoveries with adenovirus and with cellular genes like those for ovalbumin, immunoglobin, and beta-globin were the same or separate events. 'Immediately after the discovery of splicing [in adenovirus], it was not clear to the community at large whether splicing and split cellular genes should be considered one single discovery. Clearly, the equating of splicing as an explanation for the role of hnRNA in mRNA synthesis implied the existence of split

cellular genes. This was the purpose of both coining the term "splicing" and including the term "hnRNA" in the title of our [Cold Spring Harbor] paper'.

15 G. Nigel Gilbert and Michael Mulkay (1984) *Opening Pandora's Box: A Sociological Analysis of Scientists' Discourse*, Cambridge: Cambridge University Press, 90–111.

16 Professor Sambrook criticizes my analysis for not taking the complexity of social interactions within the research community into account. His comment is worth quoting because it makes an important point that I meant this study to support, not to contradict.

> You assume that these publications were independent of one another. They were not. These people did not live in a vacuum: all of the major figures were talking actively and intensely about their work to one another and to many common colleagues during that exciting time. Their written ideas and statements, therefore, tend to represent a consensus view rather than free-standing opinions, individually held. It is simply not possible to attach much significance to the contrasts and comparisons you attempt to draw between the statements of different scientists. Accurate attribution of ideas and even experimental conclusions in these circumstances is almost impossible.

He also points out that all the papers were read and criticized by a number of people who may or may not be listed among the authors, and that further revisions were made by editors, including changes in features I analyse, such as the order of statements. Though I have avoided the question of authorship in this chapter, I would not want to be taken as implying that either the words or the views of these articles are attributable to individual authors of the sort imagined in some literary studies. But I would still want to hold that two different texts, such as those in the Cold Spring Harbor symposium volume, can present two different views of discovery, even if neither the texts nor the views are directly attributable to the people whose names appear on the articles. I have tried to be more cautious about such attribution in this version of the paper. It is interesting that I addressed my paper to an audience interested in the theory of literary criticism, but the critical theory questions were raised by a biologist.

Bibliography

Research Reports

Susan M. Berget, Claire Moore, and Phillip A. Sharp (1977) 'Spliced segments at the 5' termini of adenovirus-2 late mRNA', *Proceedings of the National Academy of Sciences* 74, 8: 3171–5.

S.M. Berget, A.J. Berk, T. Harrison, and P.A. Sharp (1977) 'Spliced segments at the 5' termini of adenovirus-2 late mRNA: a role for heterogenous nuclear RNA in mammalian cells', *Cold Spring Harbor Symposium* 42: 523-9.

T.R. Broker, L.T. Chow, A.R. Dunn, R.E. Gelinas, J.A. Hassell, D.F. Klessig, J.B. Lewis, R.J. Roberts, and B.S. Zain (1977) 'Adenovirus-2 messengers – an example of baroque molecular architecture', *Cold Spring Harbor Symposium* 42: 531-53.

Louise T. Chow, Richard E. Gelinas, Thomas R. Broker, and Richard J. Roberts (1977) 'An amazing sequence arrangement at the 5' ends of adenovirus-2 messenger RNA', *Cell* 12: 1-8.

News Articles

Jean L. Marx (1977) 'Viral messenger structure: some surprising new developments', *Science* 197: 853-6.

John Rogers (1978) 'Genes in pieces', *New Scientist* 5 January, 18-20.

Joe Sambrook (1977) 'Adenovirus amazes at Cold Spring Harbor', *Nature* 268: 101-4.

Review Articles

John Abelson (1979) 'RNA processing and the intervening sequence problem', *Annual Review of Biochemistry* 48: 1035-69.

Pierre Chambon (1977) 'The molecular biology of the eukaryotic genome is coming of age', *Cold Spring Harbor Symposium Proceedings* 42: 1209-34.

Francis Crick (1979) 'Split genes and RNA splicing', *Science* 204: 264-71.

Walter Gilbert (1978) 'Why genes in pieces?', *Nature* 271: 501.

Textbooks

Charlotte J. Avers (1986) *Molecular Cell Biology*, Reading, Mass.: Addison-Wesley.

Ursula Goodenough (1984) *Genetics*, 3rd edn, Philadelphia: Saunders.

Gunther S. Stent and Richard Calendar (1978) *Molecular Genetics: An Introductory Narrative*, 2nd edn, San Francisco: W.H. Freeman.

J.D. Watson (1975) *The Molecular Biology of the Gene*, 2nd edn, Menlo Park: W.A. Benjamin.

Popularizations

Marcel Blanc (1979) 'Une mini-révolution en génétique moléculaire', *La Recherche* 103, September, 896-8.

Thomas Cech (1986) 'RNA as an enzyme', *Scientific American*, November, 76-84.

Pierre Chambon (1981) 'Split genes', *Scientific American*, April, 48-59.

Antoine Danchin and Piotr P. Slonimski (1984) 'Les gènes en morceaux', *La Recherche* 155, May, 616–26.

John Gribbin (1985) *The Search for the Double Helix: Quantum Physics and Life*, London: Corgi, 313–20.

Israel Rosenfield, Edward Ziff, and Borin Van Loon (1983) *DNA for Beginners*, London: Writers and Readers.

NARRATIVE
AND 'FICTION'

PHILOSOPHY AND LITERATURE

· 6 ·

Narrative and Invention:
The Limits of Fictionality

PETER LAMARQUE

Preliminaries

In the most general terms, to narrate is to tell a story. My concern
is with fictional narration – the telling of stories that are 'made up',
'invented', 'products of the imagination'. There are other kinds of
stories, or narratives, of course. Historians, biographers, journalists,
psychoanalysts are all involved in narration, as are, at least some of
the time, lawyers, scientists, sports commentators, and people in
pubs. One of my aims is to keep some basic distinctions intact, to
resist the tendency to collapse all storytelling into a single category.

A brief word, first, about what I take to be common to all
narrative. Narration of any kind involves the recounting and shaping of events. Description is not enough. A mere catalogue of
descriptive sentences does not make a narrative. For one thing,
there must be *events* described, not just things. Narration has an
essential temporal dimension. The descriptions in botanical
taxonomy, for example, do not comprise a narrative. Furthermore,
the events must be shaped or ordered. Narrative imposes structure;
it connects as well as records. In some cases it even defines the
events it connects (The Hundred Years War and The Middle Ages,
for example, owe their identity to historical narrative). Finally, for
every narrative there is a narrator, real or implied or both. Stories
don't just exist, they are told, and not just told but told from some
perspective or other. Already we have four basic dimensions of all
narrative: time, structure, voice, and point of view. Under 'structure' I include the idea of 'plot'; a plot is a structured concatenation
of events.

Narrative *per se* is a formal feature of a text. It is indifferent to subject matter and to discursive ends. Narratives might amuse or instruct, philosophize or theologize. Some philosophical works, but not all, are in narrative form: Descartes's *Discourse* is, Spinoza's *Ethics* is not. Nor is narrative identical with literature. For one thing, 'literature' is an evaluative term, while 'narrative' is not. Furthermore, some literary works, like much lyric poetry, lack the narrative form; and some narration, like much sports commentary, lacks literary merit. Above all, narrative *per se* is indifferent to truth and reference. The appearance of a sentence or a name in a narrative has no implications for the truth-value of the sentence or the denotation of the name. Narratives can be about real people or fictional characters and their descriptive content can be true or false.

The relation between narrative and fictionality is complex. There is a strong temptation to conflate the two concepts, or at least to suppose that in talking about narrative one is talking about fiction. For example, to focus exclusively on the narrative features of a text involves laying aside questions about referentiality. Yet the latter is also a characteristic of our attitude to fiction. At a deeper level, it is clear that we are not going to be able to distinguish fictional narratives from other kinds merely, as I suggested earlier, in terms of what is 'made up', 'invented', or 'a product of the imagination'. After all, we have seen that all narration involves making or structuring and it would be hard to deny a prominent role for the imagination in the narratives of science, history, or philosophy.

The distinctness of fictionality from narrative is open to challenge from different directions: from literary narrative as well as from issues deep within metaphysics and literary theory. Let us begin with these challenges.

A Literary Example

A recent literary example nicely brings home the difficulties we face. I have chosen the novel by the Peruvian writer Mario Vargas Llosa, entitled *The Real Life of Alejandro Mayta*.[1] In fact its original Spanish title is more teasingly ambiguous, *La Historia de Mayta*. *Historia* covers both 'history' and 'story'. One striking feature of the book, reflected in the title, is that few readers will have any clear idea as to how many (if any) of the events narrated actually took place and how many (if any) of the characters are real. It is offered as a novel and we read it as 'fiction'. The crucial question is: what does that mean?

The narrative tells of a writer (maybe Llosa, maybe not) trying to piece together the life of an obscure would-be revolutionary, a Trotskyist, who was at the centre of an abortive, even ludicrous, insurrection twenty-five years earlier in the Peruvian mountains. The narrator, intrigued by the thought that he'd been at school with the revolutionary, painstakingly delves into the records, examines old newspaper cuttings, and interviews anyone who had any connection with the event. Inevitably what emerges is a fragmented, partial, often contradictory, account. The participants interviewed are either wilfully forgetful or resentfully deceitful. Seemingly, the facts behind this pathetic débâcle of history are unrecoverable. 'One thing you learn', the narrator remarks, 'when you try to reconstruct an event from eyewitness accounts, is that each version is just someone's story, and that all stories mix truth and lies' (Llosa 1986: 118).

An added twist is that the narrator admits to us, and to his interviewees, that he is not trying to write a history but only a kind of fiction: '[n]ot a biography, but a novel. A very free history of the period, Mayta's world, the things that happened in those years' (ibid: 15). The clear and serious suggestion is made that only a novelistic or literary narrative is possible for recounting events in a country like Peru, full of deception, turmoil, and incompatible perspectives.

The complex time-frame of the narration reflects the fragmentation of history. There is a narrative present and a narrative past bounded, as it were, by the real (or external) present and the real (or external) past. The narrative present sees the narrator cross-examining the participants (even, finally, Mayta himself). But the dialogue is indissolubly interwoven with dialogue from the narrative past, twenty-five years earlier. Twenty-five years might separate the facts from the distorted recollections but fact and report simply blur into one. The narrative 'I', the investigator, even merges, momentarily, into the persona of Mayta, the investigated. Meanwhile, this narrative time-frame is located in the wider frame of real time. The real past of Peru is obliquely evoked, part mirror, part explanation: a visit to the Museum of the Inquisition reveals cruelty and corruption as somehow integral to the country's history. The real present is evoked in the slums and garbage of present-day Lima. To round it off, this present embodies a nostalgia for a more naïve past and a gloomy prognosis for the future.

The novel revels in the complexity of its formal features – time, structure, voice, and perspective – and it plays unceasingly with the ambiguity of history and fiction. Using all the artifice of literary form, it gives us a sharply focused, pessimistic insight not just into the turmoil of modern Peru but into the revolutionary sensibility.

Do novels like *Mayta*, either in formal structure or in theme, give us reason for blurring fact and fiction, truth and invention, fictive and historical narrative? In the end, I think not. But this calls for philosophical investigation.

Some Aims Outlined

As the discussion which follows has many strands, let me briefly outline the direction I want to take. Much of the focus of the chapter will be on fictionality. Through the identification of different kinds of fiction – notably logical, epistemological and 'make-believe' fiction – the central purpose is to establish constraints on the tendency to 'fictionalize' our narratives or to see the world as 'invented' rather than 'discovered'. From the metaphysical point of view, my intuitions are realist. I believe that objects exist independently of what we think about them. I do not believe, to use Goodman's expression, that the world is 'man-made'. I will not be defending these intuitions as such but I will try to keep my conclusion consistent with them.

When it comes to distinguishing kinds of narrative I hold a pragmatic view. Fictional narrative *is* distinct from historical (or scientific or philosophical) narrative but the distinctness, I will argue, does not reside either in formal features – time, structure, voice, perspective – or in semantic features – truth, correspondence with the facts, or reference. A narrative like *Mayta*, which I will show is 'fictional' in the 'make-believe' sense, can contain true sentences and even references to real objects. It can convey truths of both a particular and a universal kind. Its fictionality, I will argue, lies elsewhere: in pragmatic, conventional features, such as context, attitude, intention, response. In the relevant sense, fictionality resides in a special kind of institutional and rule-governed relation between writer, text and reader.

A common mistake, which I will try to combat, is to suppose that what we say about narrative must affect our metaphysics, i.e. what we say about the world, and that our metaphysics must inform our view about narrative.

The Challenge from Metaphysics and Literary Theory

It is easy to see how discussions of metaphysics get drawn into discussions of narrative. The starting point is the reasonable-sounding attempt to distinguish fictional from non-fictional narratives in terms of what they are about. A fictional narrative, so the thought goes, creates an imaginary world with imaginary characters, while a non-fictional narrative is about the real world and the real things in it. To find out which is which is just a matter of checking for 'correspondence with the facts'.

It is precisely the implied link with contentious metaphysical conceptions that I want to sever, not by proposing an alternative view of truth or the world, but by producing a much sharper account of narrative and fictionality.

Let us, however, briefly recall the issues, both metaphysical and literary-theoretical, which make the simple picture problematic. At the heart of the matter is the distinction between a world constructed (by the imagination, by the mind) as against a world discovered ('out there', independent of the mind).

Any undergraduate can rehearse Descartes's seductive sceptical challenge: what we call the real world might be just a massive illusion, just a figment of the imagination. Although we can perhaps shrug off talk of illusions and demons, we should take seriously Descartes's challenge when stated in terms of belief. In effect, Descartes tries to convince us of the thought that we could have beliefs indistinguishable from those we now have about the world even though each one is false, either because the world is quite different from how we believe it to be or (in the extreme case) because there is no world at all. This sceptical challenge is still an issue for philosophers examining the nature and content of belief.[2]

The analogue with narrative might be this: if it is impossible to tell with any logical certainty which, if any, of our beliefs correspond with a world 'out there', why should one suppose that narratives will reveal their referential commitments with any greater conviction? Narrative-content is as susceptible as belief-content to 'methodological solipsism'.[3] Maybe all our narratives are, as it were, Cartesian narratives describing different aspects of an inner world. No intrinsic features, if Descartes is right, can guarantee correspondence.

Doubts about the distinction between what is 'made up' and what is 'out there' are only compounded if we take the Kantian route out of Cartesian scepticism. Kant showed, or purported to show, how you could be an 'empirical realist', holding on to an objective world independent of the mind, and at the same time a 'transcendental idealist', insisting on the ultimate ideality of objects. Objects, he thought, can be 'out there' empirically yet 'made up' transcendentally. Ordinary things can be mind-independent from the empirical point of view, in contrast to illusions and fantasies, while at the same time mind-dependent from the transcendental point of view, in contrast to unknowable things-in-themselves. From the transcendental viewpoint, we have knowledge only of appearances; from the empirical viewpoint, we can readily distinguish how things appear from how they really are.

Kant's Copernican Revolution, with its complex equivocating on the ideas of 'object', 'appearance', 'reality', 'inner', 'outer', and so on, encourages a conception of the world as a 'product of the mind' or a 'construction'. More than that, Kant seems to have identified something like a narrative process, the temporal structuring of experience unified by a 'transcendental' subject, at the heart of epistemology. Against this background, along with subsequent refinements of idealism, we at least become wary of trying to distinguish narratives in terms of 'worlds'.

Then there is the contribution from literary theory. Many modern literary theorists automatically put quotation marks (or scare quotes) round such words as 'reality', 'existence', 'the world', 'objective', even 'truth'. They view as naïve philosophers who still retain the old hankerings for a world 'out there', independent, something to ground and validate our thoughts, something to make our true propositions true and our false ones false. In their own terms, in the literary context, I am sure these theorists are right. One of the enduring insights in twentieth-century literary theory is that realism so-called in literature is a convention, a genre: a kind of writing, not a kind of relation (think of Barthes's 'reality effect'[4]). The realistic novel, contrary to the claims of its early French proponents, has no privileged status in representing the world 'as it really is'. Indeed, and this is the point of all those inverted commas, the very idea of representing the world either better or worse has virtually no useful role to play in literary criticism.

The whole modernist movement in art amounted to a challenge at a fundamental level to the idea of representing reality. At its best modernism exhibited the plurality of worlds, private and public, in contrast to some single 'objective' world given in experience. Once representation itself had been exposed as a kind of artifice it was natural for artists to highlight the artifice of their own media. In the literary case this became an obsession with drawing attention to the fictionality of literary writing: an obsession clearly manifested in Mario Vargas Llosa.

In response to modernism, there arose various attempts by literary theorists to generalize the lessons learned from literary fiction. The generalizations are far from implausible. All writing involves some degree of artifice; there is no pure unmediated representation of extra-linguistic fact; there are other purposes served by words than merely describing how things are in the world. It is a short step, so it seems, from these modest claims to stronger, more anti-realist conclusions. Just as the idea of a single objective reality seems to crumble away in the literary case, perhaps it crumbles away in any case. Perhaps there is a lesson to be learned from literary realism about realism *tout court*.

Out of all this an argument might be mounted, though I haven't yet seen one, from the conventionality of literary realism to metaphysical anti-realism.[5] By 'anti-realism' here I mean the view, which takes many forms, that the world itself is in some way or other dependent on the mind (or language, or concepts, or theories, or verification-procedures).

My interest is with an argument of a slightly different kind, going in the other direction. This is the appeal to varieties of anti-realism, drawing on the metaphysical and literary-theoretical challenges just outlined, to try to run together different kinds of narrative, that of the novelist, the historian, the scientist, and so on. Such a move, which I will criticize, partly explains the not uncommon inclination among literary theorists to see all discourse as a kind of fiction.[6]

Schematic Arguments Towards the 'Fictionalizing' of Narrative

I suggest there are two arguments, with particular appeal to literary theorists, which evoke versions of anti-realism in the service of 'fictionalizing' narratives. The following are abstract and schematic renderings. Although the arguments are stated in general terms they can be applied directly to narrative. The first goes like this:

(A) 1 The distinction between fictional and factual discourse (or narrative) ultimately depends on a correspondence conception of reference and truth. Factual discourse makes reference to, and corresponds with, what is 'out there' (objects and facts) while fictional discourse concerns only what is 'made up'.

2 But the correspondence conception of reference and truth is untenable. Anti-realist and pragmatist arguments in philosophy of language show this, not to speak of Kantian-type arguments in metaphysics.

3 Therefore, there is no ultimate ground for the distinction between fictional and factual discourse (or narrative).

The second argument goes like this:

(B) 1 Fiction is whatever is man-made (conceptually or linguistically).

2 Truth is man-made (conceptually or linguistically).[7]

3 Therefore, truth is just a species of fiction.[8]

Although I think the conclusions follow from the premises, I don't think the premises are true. I have doubts about the second premise in each argument but I will be concentrating only on the two first premises. I think by identifying different conceptions of fictionality, along with the different kinds of 'making' involved, with different referential commitments, we will see that no widespread 'fictionalization' is going to be licensed along these lines.

Fictionality in Object and Description

One difficulty with our discussion is the looseness with which terms like 'fiction' and 'narrative' are often used. In literary contexts, 'fiction' can simply mean 'novel', or even 'story', and in that way become virtually synonymous with 'narrative'. If we are to distinguish fictional narratives from other kinds we will need finer discriminations. The etymology of 'fiction' reveals it roots in the idea of making or fabricating but on closer inspection we will see different kinds of making connected with different conceptions of fiction.

First of all, we need to note an ambiguity between the object and the description sense of 'fiction'. We speak of fictions sometimes as *things* – Pickwick, average families – sometimes as kinds of descriptions – *Pickwick Papers*, John's statement to the police. To say of a thing that it is fictional is to suggest that it doesn't exist. To say of a description that it is fictional is to suggest that it isn't true. The object sense of fiction gives us the contrast between what is fictional and what is real, the description sense the contrast between what is fictional and what is true.

An ontological enquiry will show whether we can retain a distinction between an invention of the mind and a real object. A semantic enquiry will show whether we can retain a distinction between the truth of a description and the fictionality of a description. I hope to lay the groundwork for retaining both distinctions in the discussion which follows.

The second ambiguity, if that is the right word, is between positive and negative connotations of 'fiction'. On the positive side, fiction is constructed or imagined. On the negative side, it is false, fabricated, contrary to fact, non-existent.

The two ambiguities cut across one another. A fictional object may be praised as a product of the imagination, or denigrated as non-existent. Likewise a fictional description can elicit favour for being imaginative, e.g. *Pickwick Papers*, or invite censure for being false, e.g. John's statement.

The term 'narrative' carries clear connotations of making, or structuring, but without the ontological implications of 'making up' or 'fabricating'. Within narratives there can be fictions both in the object and the description senses. But narratives are not limited to fictions in either sense. Also narratives, fictive or otherwise, can be subject to praise or blame. Yet when we praise a narrative for its imaginativeness we make no assumptions about its truth-values and when we denigrate it for unreliability with regard to the facts we might nonetheless applaud its inventiveness. As earlier stated, narrative in itself is indifferent to both semantic and ontological constraints. Only further classification of narratives, relating to genre, intent, convention, and so on, will reveal the criteria appropriate for other forms of assessment.

Fictions in Philosophy

It is time to pursue some of the different kinds of fictions that arise in philosophy. The acknowledgement by philosophers of fictions deep within our ordinary descriptions of the world as well as in our knowledge of the world might seem a further irresistible argument for the blurring of distinctions among narratives. Logical fictions, on the one hand, have a venerable place in semantic theory, as do epistemological fictions, on the other hand, in ontology and epistemology. It is worth giving some attention to these conceptions before returning to narrative *per se* so we can see exactly what support there might be here for the schematic arguments given earlier.

Logical Fictions

The concept of a logical fiction connects with naming and analysis. The core idea is this: a logical fiction is the purported referent of an eliminable syntactic name. Such a conception probably originated with Bentham. It found its fullest expression in Russell's logical atomism. I will say a bit about both.

Bentham thought that our ordinary language was unavoidably committed to what he called fictitious entities. He didn't think that mattered, indeed he thought if often advantageous, as long as confused inferences weren't drawn about what is real. Bentham argued, for example, that all of the following were fictitious entities: motion, relation, faculty, power, quantity, form, matter, and, more notoriously, duties, obligations, and rights.

While his contemporaries in the French and American Revolutions used the existence of rights as their rallying-cry, Bentham kept insisting that rights were mere fictions. What did he mean? After all, he saw the danger that denying the existence of rights would appear to give *'carte blanche* to tyranny'.[9] He meant two things: first, that the word 'right' as a noun doesn't stand for any real entity; second, that sentences containing 'right' as a noun can be paraphrased into sentences containing only nouns that do stand for real entities.

So Bentham's theory of fiction has two parts: a theory about what is real and a theory about paraphrase. The first is a thoroughgoing empiricism: a real entity is an 'object the existence of which is made known to us by one or more of our five senses' (Ogden 1951: 114). The theory of paraphrase is more interesting, though it of course connects with the theory of the real. It has been hailed, notably by C.K. Ogden and John Wisdom (and more recently by Ross Harrison), as a clear forerunner of twentieth-century logical analysis. Bentham's breakthrough was to move from the level of the single term to that of the sentence. Locke had offered a compositional view of complex ideas and mixed modes in terms of the concatenation of simple ideas. Vestiges of the Lockean view remain in Bentham (as I suppose they do in Russell) but the step to the level of sentences allows for a much richer analysis of a concept. For example, Bentham wants to explain rights and duties in terms of the omissions for which someone is liable to be punished in law; in turn, punishment is explained in terms of pain. Bentham is not claiming that rights and duties are somehow constructed out of pains, like Lockean complex ideas. He is rather explaining the conditions under which someone can correctly be said to have a right or a duty.

The connection of logical fictions with names, sentences and analysis by paraphrase also appears in Russell. Russell's theory of logical fictions is more complex than Bentham's (not least because it changed) but like Bentham's it presupposes a conception of what is real and a mechanism of analysis. It also involves a theory of meaning. Russell conceived of what is real as what we are acquainted with. This idea connects with the theory of meaning, which has two parts: first a realist view of meaning itself, i.e. the meaning of an expression is the entity for which the expression stands, and second, the principle of acquaintance, i.e. the view that understanding the meaning of an expression involves acquaintance with the entity which is its meaning. The atoms of logical atomism are precisely the entities which, according to the realist view, are meanings and, according to the principle of acquaintance, are the basis of our understanding. Russell held that only these entities, simple sense-data, for example, are 'genuine entities'; everything else is a 'fiction' or 'construction'. That leaves all material objects as fictions.

Logical analysis, for Russell, is the process that takes us from ordinary sentences to sentences conforming to the principle of acquaintance, i.e. those that are immediately understandable. But it also has ontological implications. Russell says that if you analyse the statement 'Piccadilly is a pleasant street', 'you will find that the fact corresponding to your statement does not contain any constituent corresponding to the word "Piccadilly"'.[10] The theory of descriptions provides the paradigm of analysis. But its connection with what is real and fictional was perhaps originally misunderstood by Russell. Russell seems to have thought that because he could eliminate descriptions by translation into propositional functions this was equivalent to showing that there was nothing real, or no 'genuine entity', answering to the description. He called descriptions 'incomplete symbols', a term with just that connotation according to the realist theory of meaning. But in fact of course that conclusion requires further premises from logical atomism. The theory of descriptions itself remains neutral as to whether any object is designated by a description. All it shows is that the syntactic form of a sentence containing a definite description doesn't require the existence of a designated object for it to be meaningful.

Quine went on to argue that the theory of descriptions, or any elimination of singular terms, shows not what exists or is real but only what a person is committed to accepting as real in what he says. Logical paraphrase, in both Bentham and Russell, cannot in itself give a direct answer to the question of what is real. It shows only how we can avoid apparent (syntactically based) commitments to types of entities. In both cases to say that something is a logical fiction is to say that its existence need not be assumed in order to make sense of a particular sentence. The fact that objects for Russell and rights for Bentham turn out to be logical fictions is a product of other features of their theory.

Even with these qualifications, it still might seem that logical fictions offer support for the conclusions of both the literary theorists' arguments: in effect blurring fact and fiction. After all, the suggestion is that quite ordinary descriptive sentences, by means of which we convey factual beliefs, turn out to be shot through with talk about fictions. Logical fictions also seem to offer some confirmation of the first premises of argument (A), which grounds the distinction between fact and fiction in correspondence. Both Bentham and Russell see meaning itself in referential and correspondence terms.

But I don't think there is much to be gained here for the literary theorists, at least not for their general ambition of running together different kinds of writing, literary fictional, philosophical, scientific, etc. For one thing, logical fictions belong in the object, not the description, category; they concern reference rather than truth. It is not a sentence or narrative that is fictional in the logical sense, only a kind of name, even though the removal of the fiction takes place at a sentential level.

Furthermore, the dichotomy between what is 'made up' and what is 'out there' is not obviously applicable to logical fictions. For Russell, what is real is not what is 'out there' but what is 'in here' (i.e. sense-data). Yet this affords no blurring of the distinction between what is real and what is 'made up' (sense-data are not 'made' but 'given'). The positive connotations of construction or imagination are also absent from logical fictions. The focus is on eliminability, not creativity. Finally, as I will go on to show, there is a marked difference between logical fictions, defined in terms of elimination by paraphrase, and literary or 'make-believe' fictions.

Epistemological Fictions

Whereas logical fictions relate to naming and paraphrase, the central idea being the elimination of reference, epistemological fictions emphasize not elimination but construction. Perhaps the term 'fiction' is tendentious here; but only so if we stress the negative connotations. Constructivist theories of knowledge with which I am concerned see objects, indeed the empirical world itself, not as *given* in experience but as constructed out of it. The theories, which take many forms, stress the active role of the mind in the construction of an ordered and unified world.

Epistemological fictions arise from two kinds of constructivist theory: foundationalist and anti-foundationalist. Locke, Kant, and

Russell were foundationalists in the sense that they distinguished between a 'given' and a 'construction'; what is constructed in knowledge is constructed out of a given that is not itself constructed. It would be wrong, though, even for foundationalist theories, to associate the given exclusively with the real. Although Locke had reservations about the reality of things corresponding to at least some complex ideas, Kant was in no doubt that the synthetic world of objects was real; that's the point of empirical realism. Russell, in contrast, did associate the given exclusively with the real. 'All the ordinary objects of daily life', he wrote, 'are extruded from the world of what there is.'[11] And he spoke of 'the unreality of the things we think real' (Russell 1956: 274). It is far from clear why Russell couldn't admit his logical constructions to be real or genuine entities. Part of the answer is that he thought of objects as classes or series and he held an anti-realist view of classes. But part also rests on the doctrine of logical fictions and the mistaken belief that to eliminate a syntactic name is to eliminate any entity named.

Epistemological fictions also appear in anti-foundationalist theories of knowledge. I would put Quine's idea of objects as posits into this category. The overt connection with fiction is made in Quine's famous comparison of physical objects with the gods of Homer. He spoke of the 'conceptual scheme of physical objects' as 'a convenient myth'.[12] Quine, of course, in relativizing ontology, wouldn't hesitate to accept his posits as real. Reality too is relativized. Quine agrees enough with Carnap to reject so-called 'external' questions of existence. There is no contrast for Quine between what is real and what is posited nor ultimately between what is posited and what is given.

Such too is the position of Nelson Goodman, another anti-foundationalist. In his view we make worlds by making world-versions. There is no single world but a plurality of worlds. And we make a world-version not out of an experiential given but out of other world-versions. Goodman describes his view as 'irrealism' partly to pour scorn on the very idea of a real world. Yet although he thinks the world is man-made, and he rejects the idea of truth as correspondence, he insists in the end on quite strict rules for good and bad makings. Not all versions are right versions. To be right is to be deductively and inductively valid and to consist only of 'right categorizations'. Inductive reasoning must be based on 'all the available genuine evidence'.[13]

Goodman is happy to appropriate the idea of 'making' for both facts and fictions but he offers no consolation for those who would in other ways weaken that distinction. Indeed, he takes a remarkably restrictive view of imaginative fiction, identifying such fictions as literal falsehoods.[14] At best he allows literary fictions only metaphorical truth.

Although he is to be commended for keeping apart his meta-physical theory – the world is man-made – and his literary theory – fictional narratives are false – Goodman, I believe, has not made out his case on either side. We need not pursue the matter directly. For our purposes certain general conclusions are already emerging. For example, epistemological fictions, or constructions, in their many forms from Locke to Goodman, provide no sharp line between what is made and what is real. Objects and truths them-selves are viewed as products of human makings, even though the makings, Kantian synthesis, Russellian logical construction, Quinean positing, are of different kinds.

All this might seem congenial to the literary theorist. But our two schematic arguments, (A) and (B), don't automatically go through even for epistemological fictions. Makings there might be but, as even Goodman admits, we can still distinguish true and false makings. They also occur at what Kant would call the transcendental, rather than the empirical, level. They do not occur at the level at which we distinguish between, say, a real person and a fictional character. In spite of superficial similarities, the creation of epistemological fictions and that of literary fictions are radically different. Premises about epistemological fictions will give little support for the literary theorists' scepticism about distinguishing imaginative from truth-stating discourse.

Before we return finally to literary fictions, I should offer some brief remarks on Richard Rorty's pragmatism, for Rorty purports to make a connection between what we say about truth and what we say about imaginative fiction. Rorty doesn't go as far as Good-man in speaking of making worlds but he does believe that truth is 'made' rather than 'found'. All this idea amounts to, though, is the reaffirmation of the long-established doctrine that truth is a property of sentences, i.e. linguistic entities, along with the further premise that 'languages are made rather than found'. Nearer the heart of Rorty's position is the rejection of the correspondence theory of truth and, more generally, of what he calls the 'picture picture' of language. He identifies the resistance to the idea of language as a 'game' rather than a 'picture' (of reality) with the anxiety, characteristic of the Western philosophical tradition, that we might lose the distinction between 'responsible' and 'irresponsible' discourse, 'that need to distinguish sharply between science and poetry which makes us distinctively Western'.[15] Rorty insists that this anxiety is unwarranted. We need constraints, certainly, on our claims to truth but these need only be what he calls 'conversational' constraints; there are 'no wholesale constraints derived from the nature of the objects, or of the mind, or of language, but only those retail constraints provided by the remarks of our fellow-inquirers'.[16]

However, it turns out for Rorty, as we might expect, that these 'retail constraints' are all that the metaphysical realist might hope them to be, barring only the idea of a transcendent mind-independent world. It is not as if Rorty proposes a different kind of scientific research, different methods of experimentation, or different standards of proof. Nor does he propose, in the literary fictional case, that we somehow overlook the obvious differences between a work of fiction and a work of science or philosophy. For Rorty, the world of the realist is a world 'well lost', but in effect all that is lost is Descartes's thought-experiment about massive illusion. Otherwise the same familiar world remains. It is as much a question for Rorty as for the realist whether Alejandro Mayta really exists and what he is like. At the level at which these questions are raised, Rorty's view, like that of the realist, *leaves everything as it is*.

So what are the distinctions between fictional and non-fictional narratives that I have suggested are independent of ontological or epistemological theories about the real world? Rorty rejects the idea that there is a 'problem' about fictional discourse on the ground that the perceived 'problem' rests on the 'picture picture' of language.[17] As I see it, on the contrary, all the interesting problems remain, regardless of our view about correspondence theories of truth. We need to identify the special kind of 'making' involved in fictional narratives, the purposes, the methods of assessment, and indeed the relations that the narrative can bear with how things are in the world.

Make-believe Fictions

As a rough sketch as to how these questions might be answered, let me introduce the idea of a 'make-believe' fiction, in contrast to both logical and epistemological fictions. There is an object and a description sense of make-believe fiction. A make-believe object is a fictional character. A make-believe description is, or is part of, what I will call a fictive utterance. Some fictive utterances comprise fictional narratives. When I speak of a fictional narrative it is make-believe fiction that I have in mind.

Just as narratives in themselves are indifferent to reference or truth so fictive utterances have no semantic prerequisites. *Pace* Goodman, not all predications in fictive utterances are literally false. There is no reason why make-believe descriptions should not describe (truly) actual states of affairs. It is in virtue of other features, as we will see, that they are make-believe. Likewise, not all proper names occurring in fictive utterances are names of make-believe objects. Fictive utterances could contain the names of real objects. Finally, not all make-believe fictions are literary. Literariness, as we saw, is an evaluative property while fictionality, in the make-believe sense, is simply a mode of utterance.

The defining feature of a make-believe fictive utterance, which includes fictional narrative, does not rest on a contrast between what is 'made up' and what is 'out there', nor does it presuppose a correspondence view of either reference or truth. Instead it lies in a network of institutionally-based relations at the centre of which is a set of attitudes I will label the 'fictive stance'. The fictive stance is not a property of sentences or utterances but is an attitude taken towards them by participants in the 'game' of fiction. The fictive stance is made possible only within a complex conventional practice which determines storytellers' intentions and readers' responses. We could conceive of a society with a language indistinguishable from ours, in vocabulary, syntax and semantics, but which lacked the practice of fictive utterance. We could even suppose that this society had textually identical narratives to ours. But without the conventions of the fictive stance we could not classify these narratives as fictional in the make-believe sense. We would have to suppose that they performed quite different pragmatic functions.

How is the fictive stance to be characterized? Most attempts to define fictionality in pragmatic terms appeal either to speech-acts or to the idea of pretence.[18] Neither, I believe, is necessary. We do not need to postulate a special speech-act of fiction nor do we need to suppose that writers of fiction necessarily pretend anything.

First of all, the fictive stance, as I define it, involves a disengagement from certain conventional commitments of utterance. For example, many (though probably not all)[19] inferences are blocked from a fictive utterance back to the speaker or writer, notably inferences about the speaker's or writer's beliefs. This feature underlies the postulation of a narrator separate from the real author. The characterization of a narrative voice, or narrative attitude, although invoking a psychological vocabulary, can proceed to a large extent autonomously from any individual's psychological states.

Second, the fictive stance involves an invitation to a particular response. An audience is invited by a storyteller not so much to *believe* the propositions presented in a narrative as to *make-believe* them.[20] To make-believe a proposition is to play a kind of game with it.[21] Part of the game is to act as if the standard speech-act commitments of the utterance were present, including referential commitments, while knowing that they are not. Here we must be careful. Strictly speaking, it is not propositions (or sentences) that are make-believe, only the attitude taken to them. The propositions themselves might have determinate truth-values and denotations. The make-believe attitude, even in cases where there are no make-believe objects, is one of 'distancing' (hence the familiar notions of disinterestedness, suspension of disbelief, etc.). Just as inferences to an author's beliefs are blocked or suspended under the fictive stance so too are inferences about speech-act commitments under the response of make-believe.

The fictive stance is an invitation, contextually determined, for a reader to make-believe, to adopt a cognitive distance from the propositional content. All this of course needs to be spelt out in much more detail. My purpose here, though, is primarily to make the connection with narrative and to show the ways in which a narrative offered under the fictive stance is distinctive. The crucial link with narrative comes in the focus of attention that the make-believe attitude demands, a focus away from external relations of reference and truth towards internal relations of sense and form.

We have seen that narrative is defined purely in terms of form or structure. That does not mean of course that our interest in a narrative must be confined to its formal features. On the contrary, a characteristic of our interest in historical or philosophical narratives is a concern with wider matters, not least regard for evidence in the case of history and logical soundness in the case of philosophy. However, with fictional narratives, in the make-believe sense, there is a close connection between the formal features of the narrative and the attitudes definitive of fiction.

In this discussion, it is important to retain the distinction between fiction *per se* and literary fiction; the responses are not identical. Make-believe fiction *per se*, presented under the fictive stance, invites a reader to give primary attention to propositional content and internal connectedness (and hence set aside external connections of reference, verification, and so on). Where make-believe objects and make-believe events are described there is nothing more than this content and connectedness. The objects and events owe their very existence to the descriptive predicates in the narrative sentences.[22] Here the formal features of narrative play an integral part in determining the nature and content of the make-believe response. For example, the predication which characterizes a make-believe object not only defines the object but does so through a particular point of view which will inform a reader's response. The foregrounding of propositional content entailed by the fictive stance finds its clearest realization in the foregrounding of the formal features of narrative.

With literary make-believe fiction, a reader's interest in the internal connectedness of propositional content embraces further literary notions such as thematic interpretation. Here attention is directed towards more universal features of the content. Returning to *The Real Life of Alejandro Mayta*, we recall the narrator invoking 'Mayta's world'; it is a 'world', not an individual, which we are invited to consider. In Aristotle's terms, the universality of poetry not the particularity of history shapes our response to the narrative. To make sense of Mayta's world and the complex narration through which it is presented we need certain universal thematic concepts: time, the fragmentation of history, memory, nostalgia. A literary reading gives prominence to such themes.

None of this proves of course that *Mayta* is either a literary work or a fictional one. Maybe a word-for-word identical text could be offered and read as an exclusively historical or biographical narrative.[23] A great deal of contextual and institutional stage-setting would be required to make sense of this possibility. But that is just the point. It is not part of my thesis that a narrative is *intrinsically* fictional or historical or philosophical. I offer only a pragmatic, externalist, account of the differences. Intention, fictive stance, invited response, make-believe; in these lie the distinctiveness of the fictional. It is thus that make-believe fictions are radically different from logical and epistemological fictions. It is neither the semantic eliminability of names that explains their fictionality nor the ideas of logical construction or posit. Make-believe fictionality is not an inherent property of a narrative in any respect.

Nevertheless, I do believe that an author can signal a fictive stance through conventional, albeit defeasible, means. The narrative devices employed in *Mayta* – the complex time-frame, the contrived symmetries in dialogue, the fragmented characterization – draw attention to themselves in such a way as to encourage and reward both the make-believe response (fictionality) and the quest for universal themes (literariness).

No doubt we could read any narrative as fictional, in the make-believe sense. We could direct our attention to narrative form, adopt the appropriate distance from truth-telling or assertive commitments, and reflect only on the sense and inner connectedness of the propositional content. But nothing follows from this about the 'fictionality' of all narratives. It merely shows that we as readers can also adopt the fictive stance. We are not required to do so, nor are we always invited to do so. Above all, there are no metaphysical implications in doing so. Questions about reference and truth-value will still remain open.

Conclusion

My theme has been the juxtaposition of narrative and fictionality. The presence of narrative structure and technique in history, philosophy, and science, as well as literary fiction, attests to the power of the narrative form as a mode of cognition. It is a commonplace that 'telling stories' helps us to make sense of the world. If we inject into this commonplace even the modest claims of classical empiricist epistemology we can give respectability to the altogether more daring idea that we have no access to the world beyond the stories we tell. The centrality of narrative in our cognitive processes is further enhanced by Kant's epistemology which gives primacy to temporal and causal organization in the very conception of an 'objective world'. The first glimmer of the mind- or even narrative-dependence of the world comes in Kant's Copernican Revolution which defends the 'transcendental' subjectivity of both time and cause (crudely, they are both 'in the mind').

Once storytelling and mind-dependence become established in epistemology, it is a short step to far more radical conclusions, for example that there is no difference in principle between modes of storytelling and that there are no special privileges accorded to any one kind of storyteller, historian, philosopher, scientist or novelist, with regard to the 'representation of reality'. Add to this an anti-realism that discards the correspondence theory of truth and we are well on the way towards 'fictionalizing' all stories or narrative, at least in the sense that what is fictional is what is 'made up' or 'invented'. The final destination of this line of thought, with its comforting egalitarianism, is the claim there is nothing *more* fictional about the novelist's narratives than those of the historian, the philosopher, or the scientist.

My aim has been to put a damper on this euphoric progression. I have sought to show that what we say about narrative must be kept apart from what we say about metaphysics. Questions of ontology and truth are strictly independent of the formal features of narrative in the sense that it is always open to ask of any narrative what its referential commitments are. I have also offered a detailed examination of the idea of fictionality, identifying logical, epistemological, and make-believe fictions. In none of these do we find support for a general 'fictionalizing' of narratives. The novelist and the historian might both be storytellers but nothing is gained by blurring their different ways of telling.

Notes

1 Page references that follow are to: Mario Vargas Llosa (1986) *The Real Life of Alejandro Mayta*, London: Faber and Faber.

2 See, for example, Andrew Woodfield (ed.) (1982) *Thought and Object*, Oxford: Oxford University Press.

3 The term comes from Putnam: 'the assumption that no psychological state, properly so-called, presupposes the existence of any individual other than the subject to whom that state is ascribed'. Hilary Putnam (1975) *Philosophical Papers Vol. II: Mind, Language and Reality*, Cambridge: Cambridge University Press, p. 220.

4 Roland Barthes (1986) 'The reality effect', in *The Rustle of Language*, trans. R. Howard, Oxford: Basil Blackwell.

5 But note the slide towards anti-realism in the following, not uncharacteristic, passage from a book on literary structuralism: 'A wholly objective perception of individual entities is therefore not possible: any observer is bound to *create* something of what he observes. Accordingly, the *relationship* between observer and observed achieves a kind of primacy. It becomes the only thing that *can* be observed. It becomes the stuff of reality itself . . . . In consequence, the true nature of things may be said to lie not in things themselves, but in the relationships which we construct . . . *between* them.' Terence Hawkes (1975) *Structuralism and Semiotics*, London: Methuen, p. 17 (italics in the original).

6 For example, Christopher Norris (1985) *The Contest of Faculties*, London: Methuen, particularly chs. 4 and 6.

7 For a defence of his view, see Richard Rorty (1986) 'The contingency of language', *London Review of Books*, 8, 7, April 17, p. 3.

8 It is common to find independent support for this conclusion in Nietzsche's famous aphorism: 'truths are illusions of which one has forgotten that they *are* illusions'. See Friedrich Nietzsche (1911) 'On truth and falsity in their ultramoral sense', in vol. II of *Collected Works*, ed. Oscar Levy, London and Edinburgh: T.N. Foulis, p. 180.

9 C.K. Ogden (1951) *Bentham's Theory of Fictions*, London: Routledge & Kegan Paul, 2nd edition, p. 121.

10 Bertrand Russell (1956) *Logic and Knowledge*, ed. R.C. Marsh, London: George Allen & Unwin Ltd, p. 191.

11 Bertrand Russell (1956) *Logic and Knowledge*, ed. R.C. Marsh, London: George Allen & Unwin Ltd, p. 273.

12 W.V.O. Quine (1961) 'On what there is', in *From a Logical Point of View*, New York: Harper Torchbooks, p. 18.

13 Nelson Goodman (1978) *Ways of Worldmaking*, Hassocks, Sussex: The Harvester Press, p. 126.

14 Nelson Goodman (1984) *Of Mind and Other Matters*, Cambridge, Mass.: Harvard University Press, p. 124.

15 R. Rorty (1982) *Consequences of Pragmatism*, Brighton: The Harvester Press, p. 132.

16 R. Rorty (1982) *Consequences of Pragmatism*, Brighton: The Harvester Press, p. 165.

17 See R. Rorty (1982) 'Is there a problem about fictional discourse?', in *Consequences of Pragmatism*, Brighton: The Harvester Press.

18 The seminal work is John Searle (1975) 'The logical status of fictional

discourse', *New Literary History*, VI, 2.

19　See, for example, Colin Lyas (1983) 'The relevance of the author's sincerity', in Peter Lamarque (ed.) *Philosophy and Fiction: Essays in Literary Aesthetics*, Aberdeen: Aberdeen University Press.

20　Here I am indebted to Gregory Currie (1985) 'What is fiction?', *Journal of Aesthetics and Art Criticism*, XLIII, 4, though I disagree with Currie's postulation of an illocutionary act of fiction.

21　The relation between fiction and games of make-believe is developed by Kendall Walton, e.g. in 'Fearing fictions', *Journal of Philosophy*, LXXV, 1, 1978. Walton, however, denies that there can be *propositions* containing the names of fictional characters: see 'Do we need fictional entities? Notes toward a theory', *Aesthetics*, Proceedings of the 8th International Wittgenstein Symposium, Kirchberg, Part I, Vienna: Holder-Pichler-Tempsky, 1984, p. 182.

22　I give a fuller account of the ontology in 'Fiction and reality', in Lamarque (ed.) (1983) *Philosophy and Fiction: Essays in Literary Aesthetics*, Aberdeen: Aberdeen University Press.

23　The implications of such a thought-experiment are explored in Arthur C. Danto (1987) 'Philosophy as/and/of literature', in Anthony J. Cascardi (ed.) *Literature and the Question of Philosophy*, Baltimore and London: The Johns Hopkins University Press, pp. 16ff.

· 7 ·

Ill Locutions

CHRISTINE BROOKE-ROSE

This century seems to have relived, with greater intensity and sophistication, all the ancient quarrels, and none more than the quarrel between literature and philosophy. For although this has often taken the form of a quarrel between literature and science, basically it's the same quarrel, since ancient philosophy included science, both being searches for the truth, whereas poets, as everyone knows, told lies.

Today, however, we have been brought curiously back to that age in antiquity when philosophy could embrace not only science but politics and metaphysics and literature, even if poets lied and writing was a threat to pure thought. We seem, at any rate, much closer to those times, and notably to pre-Socratic times, than we did earlier this century, when science and poetry were still deeply opposed in a two-truths theory (one for poetry and one for science), which was only a refurbished version, refurbished by the New Criticism in various guises, of the nineteenth-century two-truths theory, one for religion (a 'higher' truth) and one for science.

Today we have apparently come out of our entrenchment and in various ways have stopped hiding behind the notion of a higher truth. Nevertheless we have done this by opening out on to other disciplines which are often considered scientific, or which at least claim to use scientific methods, such as psychoanalysis, sociology, linguistics, different kinds of logic, or even mathematics. And all these, like philosophy, mostly still claim to seek truth. We thus have a curious double situation.

On the one hand, the movement which led Plato to exclude poets from his Republic, and writing from his notion of the truth, is, according to Derrida, regularly repeated in the logocentric tradition to which we belong. It recurs for example in the work of J.L. Austin and that of his disciple John Searle, whose texts, as Derrida has shown, deconstruct themselves exactly in the same way as do those of Plato or Rousseau or Saussure or Heidegger, or even, as others have shown, those of Derrida himself, in the sense that the author repeats the very gesture which he has criticized in his predecessors.

On the other hand, and largely thanks to this deconstructive activity, philosophy and literature have moved closer and closer together in the work of many scholars, who have come round to proclaim, or to admit, sometimes regretfully, that the language of all the human sciences without exception, and indeed all language, is literary through and through, rather as one might say, rotten through and through.

There is an ingenious reading of J.L. Austin for instance, by Shoshana Felman (1980: 99–210), who tries to turn Austin into Derrida, partly in order to show that Derrida has misread him. His famous act of exclusion of the 'non-serious' or literary from his performative (such as promises uttered by actors in a play, or jokes, or poetry, in other words literature) is read as itself non-serious. His sentence defining the performative, which says 'I must not be joking, for example, or writing a poem', is read as itself a joke, on the well-demonstrated and delightful grounds that Austin has such fun with language, takes such pleasure in it, and transforms his whole performance into a performative, which in the end, through his vocabulary of desire and excitement, itself represents promise, while the constative represents constancy and the difficulty of remaining faithful to a text.

But Jonathan Culler comments:

Still, to treat the exclusion of jokes as a joke prevents one from explaining the logical economy of Austin's project, which can admit infelicities and exploit them so profitably only by excluding the fictional and the non-serious. This logic is what is at stake, not Austin's attitude or his liking for what Felman calls 'le fun'.

(Culler 1983: 118n)

I shall not enter here into the quarrel between Derrida and speech-act theory. What I want to do is to look at some of

Austin's examples in *How To Do Things With Words*, and relate them to narrative technique, or rather, to one very particular aspect of narrative technique, namely a type of sentence which represents the two different kinds of perception – reflective and non-reflective. Most philosophers have recognized these two different kinds of perception, even if they seem to have had some difficulty in representing reflective consciousness OR non-reflective, except in long-winded descriptions about someone automatically side-stepping puddles (Russell) or counting cigarettes (Sartre), and becoming conscious of this only if asked about it afterwards. The type of literary sentence which does this much better is a pure invention of narrative and cannot occur outside narrative. It is usually referred to as 'free indirect discourse', but I wish to avoid the word 'discourse' and follow Ann Banfield (*Unspeakable Sentences*, 1982), whom I shall be discussing in some detail and who calls it 'represented speech and thought', precisely because she opposes this type of 'unspeakable' sentence to 'discourse' in a much more specific sense, as speech-act in the communications model. This opposition between *histoire* (history, not story, best translated as 'narration') and *discours* (the communications model or 'system of person', with deictics, etc.) is that established by Benveniste (1966), and it will become clear below. It is not to be confused with the more familiar narratological opposition *histoire* (story) vs *discours* (treatment) established by Genette (1972), which derives from the opposition *fabula/sjuzhet* of the Russian Formalists.

As a non-philosopher I am often surprised at the sentences that philosophers think up to make their points. With Austin in particular, it is amusing to see how many of his examples are cast in narrative form – which is odd for someone who claims to exclude fiction as non-serious. At any rate, linguistic philosophy is full of fictional suppositions such as this one:

Suppose that before Australia is discovered X says 'All swans are white'. If you later find a black swan in Australia, is X refuted? Is his statement false now? Not necessarily: he will take it back, but he could say 'I wasn't talking about swans absolutely everywhere: for example, I was not making a statement about possible swans on Mars'.

(Austin 1955 (1971): 143)

Under our eyes, X has become a peculiarly complex fictional character. A novelist might want to continue the dialogue to see how X could develop.

In Lecture VIII we get the odd distinction between phonetic, phatic, and rhetic acts – the first not illustrated since 'it is merely the act of uttering certain noises'. The phatic act, however, turns out to be our old friend 'direct speech' or *oratio recta* (now called 'direct discourse', but I am avoiding that word):

He said 'I shall be there'
He said 'Get out'
He said 'Is it in Oxford or Cambridge?'

(ibid: 95)

While the rhetic act turns out to be our equally familiar friend *oratio obliqua* or 'indirect speech':

He said he would be there
He told me to get out
He asked whether it was in Oxford or Cambridge

(loc. cit.)

Now indirect speech is always summary: we are not given the words uttered, and this can even lead to ambiguity, as in the sentence analysed by Quine (1976: 185–96), 'Oedipus said that his mother was beautiful', which can be read in two ways (see Banfield 1982: 17).

Austin later drops these terms, which have not survived, and calls the phatic act ('direct speech' for literary critics) *locution*, and gives more examples (ibid: 101–2):

He said to me 'Shoot her!'
He said to me 'You can't do that'

While the rhetic act (indirect speech) can be either *illocution*:

He urged (advised, ordered . . .) me to shoot her
He protested against my doing it

Or *perlocution* (effect incorporated, two degrees):

(a)   He persuaded me to shoot her
        He pulled me up, checked me . . .
(b)   He got me to (made me) shoot her
        He stopped me, brought me to my senses, etc.

The philosophical reasons for these distinctions are not in question here, but formally the three types correspond to the traditional narrative distinctions that Genette (1972) classifies under *distance* (distance between what he calls the narrator's voice and the character's actual words): direct being the least distant, indirect more so (the character's words summarized or even interpreted), and 'narrativized' (a new refinement) being the most distant, the character's words transformed into an action (*stopped*, *brought me to my senses*) and thus even more irrecoverable than in indirect speech, as in for instance 'I informed him of my decision to leave'.

Clearly language has developed these different registers for specific reasons that have to do with distancing of the speaker's perception from that of the person whose words he is reporting, and hence with the indirect manipulation of his interlocutor.

But what *don't* we find in Austin's examples? Obviously, since he excludes fiction as non-serious, what is missing is the type of sentence specific to narrative, invented by narrative and impossible in discourse, that is, in the speech situation as opposed to that of narration. What is missing is the sentence of represented speech and thought (traditionally called free indirect discourse, *discours indirect libre*, *erlebte Rede* . . .). This is the type of sentence which gives the vocabulary and idiom characteristic of direct speech, expressive elements such as exclamations and questions, as well as the deictics of the character in his situation (*now*, for instance, although in a narrative past); but it retains the shift of tense and the change of person from first to third which are characteristic of indirect speech. It is like indirect speech but without the impression of summary, since we get the words and expressions of the character. Here is an invented example:

(1) He was walking down the street. Would he find the courage to tell his father? Yesterday there had been nothing but trust. But now, yes, oh God, he was afraid.

Note that the presence of the thinking or perceiving character is given. We get the tense-shift and change of person of indirect speech rather than those of direct speech (Shall I find the courage to tell dad . . .), but we also get the deictics and personal vocabulary and often the characteristic syntax of direct speech (question-form, exclamation, the deictics *yesterday* and *now*, although we are in the narrative past).

Because of these dual characteristics this type of sentence – which appears spontaneously in all European narrative with the rise of the novel, but which was not formally recognized or analysed until the end of the last century – has been regarded as 'mixed', and the traditional view has been and still is that the character's thought or speech is given in his own words but that the 'narrator's voice' is also heard, in the narrational tenses and in the distancing third person, thus creating an ironic distance and indirect comment.

This is certainly the way most people have come to read this type of sentence, which is often used for comic effects, and these are automatically attributed to an ironic over-voice. The first example below, from George Eliot, is represented thought, the second, from Zola, is represented speech:

(2)   A wild idea shot through Mr Chubb's brain: could this grand visitor be Harold Transome? Excuse him: he had been given to understand by his cousin that . . .

(Eliot, *Felix Holt*)

(3)   En tout cas, Monsieur était prévenu, elle préférait flanquer son dîner au feu, si elle ratait, à cause de la révolution.

(Zola, *Germinal*)

But we can get a represented letter or a represented conversation, as in these two examples from Forster's *A Room With A View*:

(4)   Of course Miss Bartlett accepted. And, equally of course, she felt sure that she would prove a nuisance, and begged to be given an inferior spare room – something with no view, anything. Her love to Lucy.

(5)   A conversation then ensued, not on unfamiliar lines. Miss Bartlett was, after all, a wee bit tired, and thought they had better spend the morning settling in; unless Lucy would rather like to go out? Lucy would rather like to go out, as it was her first day in Florence, but, of course she could go alone. Miss Bartlett could not allow this. Of course she would accompany Lucy everywhere. Oh, certainly not: Lucy would stop with her cousin. Oh no! that would never do! Oh yes!

By the time we get to Virginia Woolf and Joyce we have this changing viewpoint highlighted, and the supposed ironic voice seems a little louder and more intrusive, indeed in Joyce the device is already part of the parody of narrative styles displayed in *Ulysses*:

(6)   'I met Clarissa in the Park this morning', said Hugh Whitbread,

diving into the casserole, anxious to pay himself this little tribute, for he had only to come to London and he met everybody at once; but greedy, one of the greediest men she had known, Milly Brush thought, who observed men with unflinching rectitude. . .

(Woolf, *Mrs Dalloway*)

(7) Cissy Caffrey caught the two twins and she was itching to give them a ringing good clip on the ear but she didn't because she thought he might be watching her but she never made a bigger mistake in all her life because Gerty could see without looking that he never took his eyes off her.

(Joyce, *Ulysses*)

Despite the traditionally clear 'said' and 'thought' in (6), there is a blurring of represented thought and what Banfield calls narration *per se*, or narrative sentence, which *can* carry authorial comment (e.g. 'who observed men with unflinching rectitude' could be narrator-comment or still part of Milly Brush's consciousness). And in (7), what looks here like a changing viewpoint from Cissy to Gerty is not so in context, but we do have to reread. The main ambiguity I shall be discussing, however, is that between represented thought and narrative sentence.

In practice both stylistics and linguistics treat a narrative sentence as represented thought as long as a character is clearly present as perceiver:

(8) Emma mit un châle sur ses épaules, ouvrit la fenêtre et s'accouda. La nuit était noire. Quelques gouttes de pluie tombaient.

(Flaubert, *Madame Bovary*)

Formally there is no distinction here between a narrative sentence in the progressive, that tells us that the night was dark, and a sentence of represented thought that represents what Emma was passively perceiving (as opposed to consciously thinking). One test (apart from the presence of a perceiving character) is to see whether one can insert deictics such as *now* into that past: 'the night was dark now', where a narrative sentence would have (unnecessarily) 'the night was then dark'.

This is Benveniste's famous distinction between *discours* (or speech as part of a communications model, which he calls 'the system of person') and *histoire* (narration), which he clearly envisaged as both historical and fictional (history and story). For the difference between so-called truth and fiction is not

linguistically marked (a 'lie' uses the same syntax), any more, in
fact, than is irony, since irony is saying a sentence and meaning
more, or something else, even the opposite, or letting a character
say a sentence that has a clear meaning for him while another interpretation is also possible for the reader. But it is made possible
contextually and culturally. Parody, too, is culturally determined.

I have on purpose given examples from Banfield's book, because
it created quite a rumpus among literary critics, as her earlier
articles had done. The debate continues. I cannot go into the detail
of it here, but I do want to take up its main thesis as something
that clearly interests philosophy, something that should convince
literary critics more than it has so far succeeded in doing, and
something that ought to make writers think.

For the spontaneous development of this device, which she calls
represented speech and thought because it *represents* (as opposed to
imitating, as does direct speech) the words or perceptions of
characters, has had two consequences: one in the way the device
has been perceived by analysts of it, which is what I shall mostly
deal with here; another in the way it has come to be used by
writers, and this I shall touch on at the end of this chapter.

Literary critics, then, have persisted in seeing a dual-voiced device,
and this is because they remain in a communications model of
addresser–addressee.

Certain linguists, however, make a distinction, like Benveniste,
between the 'discourse' of the communications model (the 'system
of person') and the language of narration (*histoire*), which is,
literally, unspeakable: 'No-one speaks here, the events seem to
narrate themselves', says Benveniste (1966: 241; trans. 1970: 206).
This language of narration cannot use the pronouns *I/you* (without
passing into the discourse situation), or the deictics that go with
these (*here, now, tomorrow, last week,* etc.), and it has its own
tenses. It cannot use the present tense, for instance, or the present
perfect, or the future, which belong to discourse.

The tense-system of narrative is particularly clear in French,
where the *passé simple* or aorist is wholly restricted to literary
narrative and unusable in speech except in mock-quotes. Contrary
to what some may think, it is still very much alive in narrative and
necessary to it, though not, interestingly, in the second person, for
the narrative sentence does not belong to the communications

model and thus excludes the second person as well as its deictics. The prescriptive exclusion of the *passé simple* from discourse can be dated very precisely in the sixteenth century, says Banfield, and it is not by chance that represented speech and thought, which is based on the narrative sentence but allows certain deictics, can first be found in La Fontaine (poetic narratives) and develops with the novel, a form specifically associated with writing, as opposed to the taking down of essentially oral narratives (Banfield 1982: ch. 6).

Benveniste's theory, as well as Käte Hamburger's work on 'the epic preterite' and *erlebte Rede* (*Die Logik der Dichtung*, 1957), are used by Banfield to analyse these two types of unspeakable sentences that are narration and represented speech and thought. She takes as her cue Kuroda's discovery of a literary style in Japanese that 'transcends the paradigm of linguistic performance in terms of speaker and hearer' (Banfield 1982: 11) and involves an epistemological distinction between two forms of language, one used to indicate fact, the other to express the speaker's state – thus even an emotive adjective like *sad* can indicate a fact or express a state. This distinction seems roughly equivalent to that between *énoncé* and *énonciation*, sometimes translated as 'statement' versus 'utterance' (utterance not in the philosophical sense but understood here as that containing the subjective elements such as 'I think', 'surely', etc.). But Kuroda also distinguishes between reflective and non-reflective consciousness. These elements enable Banfield to develop several hypotheses in a way that accounts linguistically for the types of sentence in question.

Let us go back for instance to example (4), Miss Bartlett's letter. Banfield stops the quotation at 'Her love to Lucy'. But the text goes on:

(4a) Of course Miss Bartlett accepted. And, equally of course, she felt sure that she would prove a nuisance, and begged to be given an inferior spare room – something with no view, anything. Her love to Lucy. And, equally of course, George Emerson could come to tennis on the Sunday week.

Clearly the last sentence cannot represent Miss Bartlett's letter, since she is away and quite unaware of the arrangements at the Honeychurches. We have passed from represented speech (or writing) in the mind of the letter's reader (the hostess) to represented thought, which takes over the 'and equally of course' of Miss Bartlett. The traditional view would be that the 'of course' and the 'and, equally of course' come from the narrator. In Banfield's theory, however, both these would 'represent' Miss Bartlett's way of writing and talking (cp. example (5)), as reflected in the mind of the letter's reader. Another of Banfield's examples, from Jane Austen, is even more revealing, since it can in itself be read as narration on first reading, but must be read as represented thought on second reading:

(9) He [Frank Churchill] stopped and rose again, and seemed quite embarrassed. He was more in love with her than Emma had supposed.

(Austen, *Emma*)

Banfield discusses this, and other examples that contain the proper name or kinship names like *dad* or *papa* (see my example (1)), or even title and surname (*Miss Bartlett*), under what she calls non-reflective consciousness. It would be too complicated here to rehearse the details of this essential chapter in her book, but obviously the sentence from *Emma* must be read as character's perception second time round, since we know by then that Emma was wrong, and a narrative sentence by convention cannot lie (in the sense that it must be coherent with the rest of that fictional world).

Banfield's theory has been attacked, not by linguists but by literary critics who cling to various versions of the dual-voiced theory, and above all to the notion of a narrative *voice*. Banfield on the other hand insists that the word 'narrator' has become a holdall substitute for the evacuated and taboo word 'author', so that we now have

two competing theories about the text's unity, one which assigns all the sentences of the text to a single narrating voice and another which sees author and narrator as distinct constructs of literary theory, restricting the latter to [here she cites Hamburger 1976: 140] 'cases where the narrating poet actually does "create" a narrator, namely the first person narrator of the first person narrative'.

(Banfield 1982: 185)

And she adds that 'since the thesis of the author's silence ultimately touches the language of the text it is fair to ask whether linguistic argumentation can enable us to decide between these two theories'. Clearly she defends the second (narrator and author as literary constructs, narrator referring only to an explicitly present I-narrator, not to the author behind the narration).

On the mere question of constructs and terminology we would have to ask what useful function is fulfilled by simply substituting 'narrator' where critics used to say 'author', which then forces further distinctions between explicit/implicit, reliable/unreliable, and all the other terms inherited from Booth (1961). But beyond the terminology, Banfield seems to have hit somewhere below the belt of reflective consciousness, at the question of 'authority' – at least judging by the acidity of the debate. Her theory essentially draws a distinction between 'optionally narratorless sentences of pure narration and sentences of represented speech and thought', both 'unspeakable' but representing two poles of narrative style (narration and representation of consciousness) (Banfield 1982: 17, 18). And in chapter 5 she deals with the type of 'ambiguous' sentence I have just been talking about, which can be read either at one pole or at the other (but, like Wittgenstein's duck-rabbit, not both at the same time). It is this type of sentence which has become the centre of the controversy, precisely because 'it seems to combine features of both narration and represented speech and thought', and has been used as 'counter-evidence' for a supposed 'merging' of two voices, and as proof of 'the constantly shifting data of literary style' (ibid: 12) or the mysterious inaccessibility of literature to scientific analysis, in the kind of argument which, like religion before the onslaught of science, attacks the very attempt to define narrative style linguistically.

Banfield's thesis is presented through extremely rigorous linguistic argumentation, that shows (for example) why indirect speech cannot be derived from direct (ibid: 28ff.), and, more generally, that extends Chomsky's grammar to account for these 'unspeakable' sentences of narration and represented speech and thought, by adding a top node E (expression) to Chomsky's $\bar{S}$, from which expressive elements such as exclamations descend directly and announce subjectivity, rather in the same way as Ross (1970) posited an introductory performative to all declaratory sentences; whereas deictics and evaluative words are embeddable within the $\bar{S}$ which wholly represents the announced subjectivity or character's point of view. She does not invent examples the way philosophers and linguists do, but goes through, element by element and literary example by literary example, all the formal differences between sentences that are uttered in a context of the communication model (first and second person, addressee-oriented adverbs, subject/object inversion in parentheticals, echo-questions, etc.), and shows that direct speech in a narrative naturally belongs to this system of person, since it imitates communication, whereas narrative sentences and sentences of represented speech and thought (reflective and non-reflective) do not imitate but represent, in words, what does not occur in words (actions, gestures, expressions, objects, landscapes, etc. in the case of narrative sentences) or what does not necessarily occur in words (consciousness in the case of represented speech and thought).

For this she posits a formula with both a *speaker* and an *addressee/hearer*, and a *present* for the communication model (the *speaker* being one with the E of expression); but a *self* for the unspeakable sentences, a *self* who is separated from the *speaker*. Her formula, which has naturally received the brunt of the attacks, is 1E/1*self* (and of course there can be many Es, and hence *selfs*, in one *text*, however short, as we have seen from the Forster and Woolf examples). That *self* perceives in its own *present* which is past in the narrative (*now* = *past* is her second rule).

In discourse, the speaker's telling cannot be separated from his expression. But in narration, a sentence exists whose sole function is to tell. Alongside this sentence is another whose sole function is to represent subjectivity. When a NOW is invoked in narration, language no longer recounts: it represents. This is as true for first person narration as for third person narration.

(ibid: 178)

The language of narration, she goes on to show, has no 'voice', no accent, no dialect (otherwise it becomes discourse, as in, say, *Huckleberry Finn*, or Russian *skaz*).

If narration contains a narrator, this 'I' is not speaking, quoted by an author; he is narrating. If it does not [contain a narrator], then the story 'tells itself', as Benveniste has it. Rather, it is of its nature to be totally ignorant of an audience, and this fact is reflected in its very language.

(ibid: 179)

She goes on to say that it is the language of narrative that 'realises most fully in its form and not only in its intent the essence of the literary which has for so long been taken to be the achievement of poetry', and she quotes J.S. Mill's contrast between poetry and eloquence, likening it to that between narration and discourse.

So far I have seen no convincing reply to Banfield's arguments. Literary critics tend to think that the mere producing of supposed counter-examples (assuming they are properly understood and do not prove Banfield's case) can demolish a linguistic argument, whereas, as in science, only a better linguistic argument can do so. As Banfield puts it:

For a sentence to qualify as a syntactic counter-evidence to 1E/1SELF, it must be either (i) a single E containing both a first person and a third person SELF, or (ii) a single E containing more than one expressive construction, where all are not interpreted as the expression of the same SELF.

(ibid: 188)

For instance, I myself thought I had found counter-examples from Jane Austen, but they do not fulfil these conditions and therefore can illustrate Banfield's thesis. Emma is imagining Jane Fairfax married to Knightley, and she wickedly imitates Jane Fairfax's companion Miss Bates:

(10) If it would be good to her, I am sure it would be evil to himself; a very shameful and degrading connection. How would he bear to have Miss Bates belonging to him? – To have her haunting the Abbey, and thanking him all day long for his great kindness in marrying Jane? – 'So very kind and obliging! But he always had been such a very kind neighbour!' And then fly off, through half a sentence, to her mother's old petticoat. 'Not that it was such a very old petticoat either – for still it would last a great while – and indeed, she must thankfully say that their petticoats were all very strong.'
  For shame, Emma! Do not mimic her!

I quote Mrs Weston's reproach to show that we are in dialogue (direct speech). Of course we hear another voice here, which assumes responsibility for the represented speech of Miss Bates exactly as an *author* does, but it is Emma's voice, and the represented speech, which 'represents' only Miss Bates's speech, has been embedded in the direct speech, exactly as the 'narrativized' speech of 'thanking him all day long' or 'flying to her mother's old petticoat' are embedded. For represented speech, although 'unspeakable' (and this Banfield does not say), can be used inside direct speech, even in 'real life', but only in narration, when we are telling a story and unconsciously using literary devices. And I suspect (with no 'evidence') that this only occurs

among fairly literate speaker-narrators, whereas non-literate ones
tend to retell with direct speech ('And I sez to 'im I sez, Well, I
never . . . And Ow, he sez . . .', etc., to use an extreme example).
But this is only an unresearched impression.

Or Mrs Bennett bidding farewell to Mr Bingley in *Pride and
Prejudice*:

(11)   'Next time you call', said she, 'I hope we shall be more lucky'.
       He should be particularly happy at any time, &c &c; and if she
       would give him leave, would take an early opportunity of waiting on
       them.
       'Can you come tomorrow?'
       Yes, he had no engagement at all for tomorrow; and her invitation
       was accepted with alacrity.

Who says '&c &c'? It is very easy to hear 'narrator' irony about
polite formulas. But in Banfield's theory, the '&c &c' would represent the character's own awareness of them, though at a non-
verbalized, semi-conscious level (formulas he could add but does
not, or formulas he is adding and still uttering but which we are
not given). We thus have a passage from represented speech to
represented thought (perhaps non-reflective). Such passages are
swift in Jane Austen: even here we pass from direct speech to
represented speech to represented thought, back to represented
speech, then to direct speech and back again to represented
speech, ending with a narrative sentence that names the acceptance
without giving the words ('narrativized discourse' in Genette's
system).

We have a situation, then, in which a linguist has shown the
grammatical evidence for one point of view only, the character's,
in represented speech and thought, while non-linguists cling to a
narrator's point of view as well, to which certain bits and pieces of
the sentence are attributed on the ground that the character would
be incapable of 'thinking' those words. Thus the whole subtlety of
the device, which represents the complexity of non-verbalized
consciousness – and even the flashes of self-awareness a character
may have about himself – this subtlety is lost, with value-
judgements parcelled out to a narrator (often *also* confused with the
author, despite the 'taboo', e.g. 'Flaubert' or 'James'). 'But what
grammatical evidence of a narrator's point of view do we find?',
Banfield asks. 'This is what is problematic in the dual voice claim.

The second voice of the dual voice position is always the narrator's, never another character's [e.g. Emma of (10)]. The logic behind the claim [. . .] is a case of *petitio principii*.' Certain words of narration in a sentence of represented speech and thought cannot, it is said, represent the character's point of view, therefore they represent the narrator's. 'But the missing premise is none other than the conclusion' (ibid: 189).

The incapacity to argue in rigorous linguistic terms is understandable, if regrettable, in literary critics who attack a linguist. But what is so strange (and this will be my small contribution to that debate) is their self-deconstruction, their insistence, by way of the supposed richness and unaccountability of literature in scientific terms, on pushing narrative into discourse, on pushing the type of sentence that is unspeakable and thus absolutely specific to the novel, into the merely speakable; on pushing the type of sentence that uniquely represents two levels of perception that have long fascinated philosophers, into a banal narrator/character dichotomy that merely replaces the author/character dichotomy and harks back to the author as God, present and authoritative and omniscient in his text. And of course, the pushing of such sentences, which uniquely result from the achievement of writing, back into a communications model, repeats the very gesture that Derrida has revealed as phonocentric and logocentric, from Plato to Austin and Searle, as privileging voice and speech over what he calls *l'écriture*, that 'writing in general' of which writing and speech are but particular cases. *L'écriture*, or differentiation and deferral, is once again rejected here.

That's for the critics, and ultimately unimportant, although it has necessarily received the most space in this type of chapter. What is sadder has been the misunderstanding of represented speech and thought by writers. Invented spontaneously, almost unconsciously, unreflectively, then developed very reflectively indeed, represented speech and thought, like most artistic devices, eventually became unconscious again, that is, it was not only used as a cliché (already parodied in Joyce), its subtlety wasted on trivia, but it was also misused because misunderstood.

Formally, as we have seen, the sentence of represented speech and thought is similar to the narrative sentence – indeed, identical with it when deictics and other signs of E are not linguistically present, but only the presence of a perceiving character. This formal similarity led, inevitably, to these two distinct poles being fused, and the sentence of represented speech and thought being used as narration, to tell, to give narrative information – whole summaries of a situation for instance, or analepses of a whole past, which are clearly there to inform the reader and not to represent a character's perceptions, save at the cost of making them rather gross. This can go on for pages. Such misuse is extremely frequent in the average modern neo-realist novel, including most classical science fiction that imitated the already worn techniques of the realist novel in an attempt to be respectable. This misuse is a direct result not only of the post-Jamesian condemnation of 'telling' in favour of 'showing', but also of the concomitant attempt to eliminate the author: and since narrative information must be given, the easy solution was to 'filter' it through a character's mind, however implausibly, thus thoroughly weakening the device into its opposite.

Consequently – and writers on the topic never seem to say this – the device at its best belongs wholly to the classical novel. A reaction to its weakening had to come, and it came with Camus's *L'Etranger*, written in the present perfect, and especially with Beckett, who used direct speech as narrative, and with the *nouveau roman* in the 'fifties. Robbe-Grillet loudly dismissed the *passé simple* as *the* mark of the traditional novel, and adopted (after Dujardin and Joyce) the present tense, which he used in a brilliantly unsettling manner (since time-shifts are necessarily unmarked), though this was soon more weakly imitated. What he did not mention as a sign of the traditional novel was represented speech and thought (which he would call *discours indirect libre*), but its jettisoning was implicit in his rejection of the past, as in his rejection of *le mythe de la profondeur* (psychological exploration in depth, and so on). At any rate, the device disappeared, together with the traditional narrative sentence in the past tense. The novel passed for a while into discourse, a voice speaking (but not two) in Beckett, or, in Sarraute, many voices (but one at a time) speaking, thinking, perceiving, but in direct speech, or what Voloshinov (Bakhtin) has called 'free direct speech'. In Robbe-Grillet it was less a voice speaking than a consciousness perceiving, but in present-tense deictics. And in Butor we even got the second-person plural as central consciousness.

It was a necessary purge, and parallel in a way to the critics' rejection of the 'unspeakable', as a concept, for the 'speakable', except that the critics remain in the old dispensation of the dual-voice theory which merely replaces the old author/character dichotomy, with the 'narrator' as ironic God; whereas the modern novel truly dispenses with both narrator and irony and lets the character speak direct, in 'free direct speech'. As Sontag said long ago (1969: 34), irony, after Nietzsche, is no longer possible, has exhausted itself, and similarly Barthes (1970), for more political reasons, insists that classical irony is merely the power of one discourse over another, merely another bit of the referential code. None of the critics writing on represented speech and thought cites many examples after Woolf and Joyce.

It was a necessary purge, and certainly brought new ways of perceiving. Some postmodern writers have adopted this free direct mode, others play with all literary devices, but to explode or undermine them. And represented speech and thought has not been renewed: perhaps because, according to Derrida (1967: 335), representation is death. If so it would have to be renewed through some other development.

We can, however, understand why Austin and other speech-act theorists after him do not deal with this kind of sentence. First, it is fictitious and therefore non-serious – though that also applies to Austin's swan story (which, however, and I can say it now, is in direct speech and so not in a traditional narrative mode); but second, and more important, the sentences of both narration and represented speech and thought are too literary, a by-product of writing, unspeakable, ill locutions.

Bibliography

Austin, J.L. (1955) *How To Do Things With Words*, Oxford: Oxford University Press; Oxford Paperback 1971.

Banfield, Ann (1982) *Unspeakable Sentences*, London: Routledge & Kegan Paul.

Barthes, Roland (1970) *S/Z*, Paris: Seuil; trans. (1975) Richard Howard, New York: Hill & Wang.

Benveniste, Emile (1966) *Problèmes de Linguistique Générale*, Paris: Gallimard; trans. Elizabeth Meek, (1970) *Problems in General Linguistics*, Coral Gables, Fla: University of Miami Press.

Booth, W.C. (1961) *The Rhetoric of Fiction*, Chicago: University Press.

Culler, Jonathan (1983) *On Deconstruction – Theory and Criticism after Structuralism*, London: Routledge & Kegan Paul.

Derrida, Jacques (1967) *L'Ecriture et la Différence*, Paris: Seuil.

Felman, Shoshana (1980) *Le Scandale du Corps Parlant*, Paris: Seuil.

Genette, Gérard (1972) 'Discours du récit', in *Figures III*, Paris: Seuil.

Hamburger, Käte (1957) *Die Logik der Dichtung*, Stuttgart; trans. Marilynn Rose (1976) *The Logic of Literature*, Bloomington and London: Indiana University Press.

Kuroda, S.-Y. (1973) 'Where epistemology, style and grammar meet: a case study from the Japanese', in P. Kiparsky and S. Anderson, *A Festschrift for Morris Halle*, New York: Holt, Rinehart & Winston, 377–91; cited Banfield (1982), 11.

—— (1976) 'Reflections on the foundations of narrative theory from a linguistic point-of-view', in T. Van Dijk, *Pragmatics of Language and Literature*, Amsterdam and New York: North-Holland, 108–40; cited Banfield (1982) 196.

Quine, W.V. (1976) 'Quantifiers and propositional attitudes', in *The Ways of Paradox and Other Essays*, Cambridge, Mass: Harvard University Press.

Ross, John (1970) 'On declarative sentences', in R. Jacobs and P. Rosenbaum, *Readings in Transformational Grammar*, Waltham, Mass: Ginn & Co, 222–72.

Sontag, Susan (1969) 'The aesthetics of silence', *Aspen* 5 and 6, 1967, repr. in *Styles of Radical Will*, London: Secker & Warburg.

· 8 ·

How Primordial is Narrative?

MICHAEL BELL

The nature of narrative has for several decades now aroused
speculation extending beyond the literary realm into a variety of
disciplines concerned with the fundamental construction of meaning. The shaping of experience by narrative, indeed the very
impulse to tell stories, may suggest primordial, but subliminal,
processes underlying even the apparently independent planes of
reason or evidence. As a professional student of narrative fiction I
have found such speculation illuminating. However, the best
contribution of literary history in this debate may now be of a principally negative, or corrective, kind. For the term 'narrative', with
its rich charge of suggestiveness, evidently does not require selling.
What it does require is careful handling so that, for example,
incompatible meanings are not treated as identical, or tautological
conclusions taken for speculative novelty.

The nub of the difficulty here lies in the shifting use of the term
'narrative' partly as an illustrative analogy and partly as a literal
definition. Hence persuasive arguments on significant topics will
use the idea of narrative in an essentially illustrative way such that
the references to narrative could in fact be removed without
damage to the substantive case. Yet it is often the professed
purpose of such arguments to demonstrate that narrative is a
necessary, rather than a simply illustrative, category for the case
being made. In this way, the importing of the term 'narrative' into
other disciplines may create an obfuscatory penumbra around the
very object it seeks to illuminate. But my present purpose is not
to dwell on individuals' uses of this term. I wish rather to spell out
in a more general way how its positive value has to be understood

through its corresponding limitations.

It is relevant to note first that 'narrative' has assumed in the latter part of this century some of the functions of the word 'myth' in the pre-war decades of modernism. In a purely literary-historical context this reflects differences between modernist and postmodernist fiction. But one can see broader reasons for preferring the term 'narrative' to 'myth'. Apart from the dubious company this latter word has kept in twentieth-century history, the new focus on narrative proposes a more technically definable entity whose claims are at once more modest and more testable. It is an analytic gain to shed the metaphysical nimbus of myth. But the advantage of the word 'myth' is that it insists, sometimes embarrassingly, on its problematic status and large claims. 'Narrative', on the other hand, may give a misleading impression of avoiding such problems while effectively sneaking myth in through the back door.

Myth is characteristically a point of intersection between lived time and a timeless order. This double order of time is most clearly expressed in ritual and may cast its shadow on certain kinds of narrative such as folklore. In identifying the mythic we recognize a vertical axis of timeless significance intersecting with, and imparting its meaning to, the horizontal axis of temporality. I take it that the preoccupation with narrative is, by contrast, an attempt to generate adequate significance from within the experience of lived time itself. Narrative, by this argument, does not merely reflect or embody significance, it may self-sufficiently create it. And if this is so then narrative provides a fundamental model for the creation of human meaning at large.

This is the point at which the precise claims of such arguments have to be scrutinized since, as it seems to me, many narratives quite properly rest on already given orders of significance while seeking to generate a fresh awareness of such significance in apparently intrinsic terms within the narrative itself. Narrative can explain or celebrate what we already know. Hence we must be careful not to confuse the dramatic action with the process, and premises, of its creation. Narrative after all presupposes language and it is the relation of narrative to this prior order of meaning that I wish to consider. If narrative is implicitly dependent on a prior order of meaning then there will be something circular and illusory about its claims to a primordial function in this regard.

The immediate point of reference for much recent discussion of narrative along the kind of lines I have sketched is Alisdair MacIntyre's *After Virtue*.[1] I should say at once that, in so far as I am qualified to judge, his argument about the nature of virtue seems to me impressive and persuasive. In seeking to counter the reductively abstract or atomistic conceptions of virtue that have grown up since the Enlightenment in some schools of moral philosophy, psychology, and the social sciences, MacIntyre appeals to narrative as a model for the complexly rounded and communal form of life within which virtue has is meaning. But in saying this I take his use of the term narrative to be essentially metaphorical. The imperative of virtue can be understood 'as if' it were conduct governed by the teleology of a communal narrative. There is a strongly Nietzschean dimension to this as is suggested by the title of Hans Vaihinger's *The Philosophy of 'As If'*.[2] But MacIntyre does not wish to espouse the personal mythopoeia of Nietzsche. Virtue, for MacIntyre, is naturalized within a communal form of life. He wishes as far as possible, therefore, to elide the implicit 'as if' and identify the narrative order with a given way of experiencing lived temporality. Within the community for which such a conception of virtue is active it will not be experienced as an 'as if'.

MacIntyre's use of narrative as a model of the moral life seems to me to be justified for his purposes. But the need for this metaphor to be so deep and subliminal as not to appear metaphorical at all leaves it with a slippery and potentially misleading value when extrapolated from its context. The essential problem here is that narrative has to be a different kind of a thing from lived temporality or there is no point in drawing any analogy between them. The meaningfulness of the comparison depends on an implicit recognition of this difference even while it is being denied. Yet it is as if the very obviousness of this cardinal point makes it subject to being overlooked. In a narrative everything is put there by the real or implied author. Hence the elements of narrative are intrinsically meaningful. Even in a modern anti-narrative in which meaningfulness is being subverted the same fundamental principle still applies. In life, elements and events do not have this intrinsic meaningfulness. Of course, we may accord meaning to events in life and we can dispute the interpretation of events in a narrative but these internal qualifications that have to be made in respect of both narrative and lived time do not affect their fundamental difference in kind. Narrative is an implicit contract even if the contract in many given instances is lost, indecipherable, or deliberately enigmatic. Life, on the other hand, has no contract.

Some of the consequences of eliding this distinction may in fact be indicated from MacIntyre's passing treatment of two earlier essays on this theme. He first quotes, approvingly, some introductory remarks from an essay by Barbara Hardy: '. . . we dream in narrative, day-dream in narrative, remember, anticipate, hope, despair, believe, doubt, plan, revise, criticize, construct, gossip, learn, hate and love by narrative' (*After Virtue*, 1985: 211). I am not myself convinced that, as a general proposition, this is usefully or significantly true. The plenitude of example here obfuscates the precise claim being made for narrative. Much would depend, at the least, on how the term is developed or used. And as it happens the principal burden of Barbara Hardy's subsequent argument is actually to show how the Victorian novelists she discusses, even when committed to showing in their fictions the dangers of imposing imaginary narratives on life, are often guilty of imposing such imaginary structures themselves. Hence although her opening remarks affirm, in an apparently celebratory spirit, the continuity between narrative structuring and the primordial processes of lived temporality, the critical burden is largely a caveat with respect to that very continuity. To the extent that there is such a continuity, it is a dangerous one.

MacIntyre then adduces, for purposes of disagreement, a reply to Barbara Hardy by Louis Mink (ibid: 211–13). Mink would presumably not deny that the various impulses listed by Hardy have some relation to the creation of narratives. But he insists that the construction of the narrative is a transformative act. It brings these varied potentialities into a particular order. Of course, this order may in itself be problematic both critically and interpretatively. The point at stake here bears simply on the frame of reference, the implicit contract, within which the narrative invites such scrutiny. In the course of his argument he emphasizes the 'configurational' meaning which we perceive in a narrative as we come to see it spatially rather than just temporally. He goes so far as to declare that 'time is not of the essence of narrative'. Although the point Mink is making, or reaffirming, here is a traditional one it has a special interest in the present context if we relate it to the significance accorded to the spatial dimension of narrative in modernist writers such as Joyce, Mann, and Proust. The formal foregrounding of the spatial in their work frequently invests it with the timeless and numinous value of myth. This can be seen as a willed and artistic imposition on their part. But it can also be seen as their recognition that there are always implicit orderings underlying the apparently positivistic creation of meaning in temporal terms such as we find, for example, in naturalism. This indicates that the spatial 'configuration' is crucially ambiguous. It may represent an order won from the experience or it may be the opening, implicitly or explicitly, on to a plane of significance antedating the narrative. This ambiguity is not Mink's immediate concern but when adduced as the counter-point to Hardy his argument completes the analytic purchase required to appreciate the fundamental ambivalence of narrative in this regard.

When taken in combination, Hardy and Mink represent the logical problematic of using narrative as a model of meaningfulness in life. Hardy, who affirms the continuity of narrative and life, produces a largely negative conclusion from it. Mink, who insists on the qualitative difference between narrative and life, is able to affirm the positive value of narrative as a creation of meaning. There is nothing surprising about this. The kind of meaning offered by narrative is contingent upon the discrimination Mink points out. Yet this meaningfulness will always itself be judged by reference to those primordial potentialities of meaning to which Hardy refers. The significance of narrative lies in the tension between the two orders. If the gap were closed the significance of the relationship would disappear. Of course, the gap can never actually be closed and rhetorical attempts to close it are to that extent harmless. The intellectual capital represented by the term 'narrative' cannot really be squandered in this way but the corollary of that is that speculation based upon it may prove to be an unsound investment.

Yet the collapsing of this distinction between narrative and life is precisely what MacIntyre encourages. Hence, although he shows an impressive ability in the reading of literary narrative including Homer, even MacIntyre nods when it comes to dealing with Mink's point. In the course of his argument against Mink he says:

Consider the question as to what genre the life of Thomas Becket belongs, a question which has to be asked and answered before we can decide how it is to be written. (On Mink's paradoxical view this question could not be asked until *after* the life had been written.)

(ibid: 212)

Surely not. On Mink's view the writing of the life would in itself constitute the question and an answer. And the merit of this activity would lie largely in its making available for objective scrutiny the manner in which such questions had been asked and answered. That is the sense, a quite unparadoxical one, in which the question could only be asked after the life had been written. MacIntyre's attempted elision of the distinction between narrative and life obscures the crucial point at which meaning is being either discovered or created.

In sum, Mink shows Hardy to be insufficiently tough-minded in her speculative hardihood while MacIntyre in turn will not wear Mink. It seems to me that in terms of analytic lucidity Mink has the better of the argument. But I am reminded of the way in which Coleridge's clear-headed critique of Wordsworth's arguments in the Preface to the *Lyrical Ballads* leaves us still with the feeling that Wordsworth nonetheless has the root of the matter in him. And so here Mink states a traditional truth with a clear and sensible pertinence whereas MacIntyre is possessed of a powerful and suggestive theme. In fact, it is MacIntyre's theme which is truly paradoxical and its importance lies precisely in its being so. He is addressing, from his own point of view, the paradoxical nature of literary meaning which is produced by an act of separation, or bracketing, from life; a separation that is necessary yet which can never be absolute. This dependence on an umbilical continuity still underlying the act of separation largely resists analytic treatment; and realistic narrative, of course, sets out to be peculiarly compelling in this respect. But that does not excuse a literalistic elision of the difference between literature and life. It seems that the terms of the discussion need to be reconsidered if we are to avoid the twin errors of elision and dualism with respect to the meaning of narrative.

In this regard it is worth noting that Mink's essay is principally a contribution to a then current debate on the nature, and possible identity, of fiction and history. What this debate largely missed was that the difference between these two kinds of narrative was not necessarily to be found in the formal qualities of the texts so much as in their recognized intentions, their implied contract with

177

the reader. Problem cases don't confound this distinction. They only become problem cases in the light of the distinction. It matters to us, for example, whether Alex Haley's *Roots* is a history or a fiction even if many of us would not be able to determine on purely internal evidence which it was. But the preoccupation with the fiction versus history issue partly explains why the discussion of narrative has often been conducted on a rather two-dimensional, analytically generalized plane.

Such discussion naturally centres on the areas of theoretical overlap in historical and fictive narratives. Hence, for example, a realist novelist and a historian would both reflect contemporary assumptions about human psychology, cause and effect, etc. But whereas a historian would be expected generally to respect these premises, it is often part of the purpose, even of comparatively realist fiction, to challenge or modify them. While some realist writers undoubtedly use the realist mode in a positivist spirit, there are others whose purpose is rather to see how much non-positivistic significance this mode can be made to bear. Great novelists have often been concerned not so much with the depiction of a 'reality' as with producing what we might rather call a reality quotient. They have been concerned with the relative weight and significance of the experiences concerned. But the 'experiences' do not exist in some isolable, or natural, state. They are constituted within the specific understandings of the narrative in question as well as within the general assumptions of the culture. Much of the significance of a novel can indeed lie in the deliberate tension between these two planes. This points to a fundamental problem in using the generalized idea of narrative as the model for lived temporality. There are many gradations of kind, and therefore of meaning, just in the domain of fictional narrative, let alone the historical. Of course, that does not rule out using narrative as a model of the moral life, but it significantly complicates, and relativizes, the value that can be accorded to it.

To summarize the case so far, then, we may say that there are many different kinds of narrative each with its own understanding of its relation to experience. And this understanding will usually be elusive of analytic definition since it is characteristically manifest only as part of the larger significance which it has made possible. The constitutive terms of the narrative experience are only active as part of a complexity that transcends them. Significance, that is to say, is not simply a property of the text but of its impinging on the world of the reader. The narrative seeks to convince; and in doing so it seeks the reader's commitment to its fundamental terms. A complex, implicit negotiation has to be made by each reader between his or her 'real' world and the 'world' of the book. For literary meaning is not strictly contained in either of these, nor is it merely their sum. It lies in their interaction.

To put the point in this abstract way makes it appear perhaps a mystification or merely an empty truism. But, as it happens, an awareness of the relativity and elusiveness of the narrative contract has been a significant sub-theme of the novel in Europe since its inception. Its readers have always had to be persuaded or seduced as part of the very art, and meaning, of the fiction. Hence an understanding of the interrelations of narrative and life is to be found in this self-questioning aspect of the novel form: an aspect which dissolves any generalized principle into a constantly shifting, newly negotiated, practice. But at this juncture I am aware of procedural difficulties. Since the point to be made here only exists significantly within its minute particulars it would properly require a summarized history of the novel as seen from this angle. Yet that history has already been traced in various ways if not in relation to this immediate debate. I have, therefore, compressed into the next two sections of this chapter a synoptic history which bears on two distinct aspects of the present argument.

The first section is on Cervantes. If we had to choose a single founding text for the European novel, *Don Quixote* would probably be the most popular choice and it is no accident that Cervantes is centrally concerned with the elusive relations of narrative to life. *Don Quixote* is a founding text not by resolving, so much as by thematizing, this area. Cervantes therefore provides an exemplary arena for MacIntyre's general concern with narrative. And since the reading that follows here is, so far as I know, original in its particular emphases, I give a proportionate space to developing it.

However, as the argument moves more squarely into the history of realist fiction a different emphasis becomes necessary. All the works to be discussed here fall within the broadly modern period and are therefore contemporary with those developments in moral philosophy which MacIntyre criticizes. In particular, these works are centrally concerned with the issue of ethical feeling which he has identified as a crucial, but problematic, aspect of modern ethical thought. Hence the question of narrative now takes on a more specific relation to the question of moral feeling. As it happens, I have myself written at some length on the interrelations of narrative and feeling from a different point of view.[3] My argument was that, where matters of feeling and responsiveness are concerned, narrative is not just the necessary vehicle, it is itself an intrinsic aspect of our understanding. For there is an important equation, which is not to say an identity, between the feeling dramatized *in* the book and the feeling with which we *read* it. My primary interest at that point was in the issue of feeling rather than of narrative but the equation is of course reversible. Hence in the second of the two following sections I reconsider several instances of this equation as it bears on the nature of narrative. What emerges from this is the impossibility of using narrative as some kind of privileged purchase on the ethical domain in which it is itself constitutively embedded.

On the Pertinence of Curiosity

Cervantes' importance to European fiction arises from his having inherited two powerful, internally coherent, and yet incommensurable traditions: the exemplary idealism of chivalric romance and the incipient realism of the picaresque. The subsequent dominance of realism has helped to create the popular impression that Cervantes was using realism to satirize the romance. This is partly true, of course, but his attitude was more even-handed and the two modes are subjected to a mutual examination. Moreover, his interest in the variety and quirkiness of human psychology, an interest that could be reflected in either of these traditions, provided him with a potential mediating space in which to bring them together. But to say this is to suggest the seriousness of the creative problem that lay before Cervantes and which is now obscured from us by the profound simplicity of his solution. For although a hero like Amadis or Tirant, on the one hand, may be the occasion of realistic episodes while the picaresque, on the other hand, may accommodate romantic behaviour in a sympathetic spirit, this mixture of elements does not necessarily disturb, or even bring to special consciousness, the fundamental premises of the narratives in which it occurs. It is not enough to bring different kinds of character or experience together; it is the different kinds of narrative premises that must be juxtaposed.

The strategic solution to this was to have a character, Alonso Quijano, from the world of the realist novel imagine himself to be Don Quixote, a character from the world of romance. This enabled Cervantes to superimpose within the one narrative frame two incommensurate, but by no means unrelated, sets of premises. One reason why they are not unrelated is that both were read seriously by inhabitants of the contemporary world such as Cervantes and his readers. Each kind of fiction required the reader's adjustment to its terms; a process so familiar as to be subliminal until highlighted by Cervantes' comic unsettling of it. But at this point a further difficulty arises. Given the relationship between the Don Quixote romance and the realistic narrative in which it is contained, there will be a strong tendency simply to identify the containing narrative with an unproblematically 'real' world as in the popular conception. But once the epistemological theme has been focused as such through the figure of Don Quixote, it knows no exemptions. Indeed, much of the life and complexity of the book lies in the way this theme is extended back into the surrounding narrative.

A crucial device here, of course, is the fictitious historian, Cide Hamete, through whom the work's own realistic 'historical' account is thrown into question. But such a device would have no real effect if the narrative texture did not already create an unsettling relativism. One of the ways in which Cervantes achieves this, and disturbs the simple hegemony of the containing narrative as the counter-term to Don Quixote's romance, is to interpose between these two polar narratives a whole series of sub-narratives which are themselves affected by the field of force within which they exist. And they in turn of course modify the dominant narratives of which they are often simultaneously a part. Cervantes uses this multiplicity to create unsettling conflicts not just of narrative action but of narrative premises.

The crucial point here may be seen by comparison with *The Decameron* or *The Canterbury Tales*. In both these works there is a containing narrative for a series of separate tales; tales which in Chaucer's case cover a range of literary kinds. Yet although Chaucer's tales become important elements in the containing story of the pilgrimage, they remain as separately framed fictions. But

Cervantes, having established his strategic use of Don Quixote as a figure inhabiting simultaneously two incommensurable frames, reinforces the effect of this by creating a multitude of similarly elided dualities throughout the text. The book is full of tales, both 'true' and fictional, as well as charades and performances all done with a variety of motives and reactions. That in itself is not significant; the significance lies in the way Cervantes constantly allows a narrative frame to be created and then leaves one side open for characters to step out of it. A digressive episode does not constitute a sub-narrative in this sense unless it is actually given this value, as for example by its being narrated by one or more of its own protagonists. In this book the characters themselves are constantly telling, or listening to, stories, and in assessing the import of such episodes we should attend not just to thematic resonances at the level of action but to the very fact of a narrative mediation. In particular, the effect of such devices should not be confused with Borgesian or postmodernist whimsy by which character and event are thrown into a metaphysical limbo. Cervantes' world maintains an existential solidity and clarity within which he studies the varied impact of narrative in real human lives.

As a case in point I will look more closely at the *Novela del Curioso Impertinente* from Part One. This is a particularly interesting instance in view of the 'authorial' comments in Part Two on the awkward and unassimilated insertion of this story into the main narrative. To what extent, if any, the story is indeed assimilated has therefore been a matter of debate initiated by the text itself with what looks like Cervantes' own authority for a negative judgement. Yet even there Cervantes may have been less concerned to criticize his earlier achievement in Part One than to advertise the different kind of procedure he is adopting in Part Two. At any rate, I wish to argue that the story is highly relevant thematically to the containing narrative not just for its psychological action but for the very way in which it is set off at a formal remove from the larger narrative context. Its being a separately narrated story is part of its significance. But before embarking on such a reading of its impact specifically as a narrative, it is necessary to sketch something of the substantive thematic significance on which this impact in turn depends.

It should be noted first that the *Impertinent Curiosity* is not inserted directly into the main Don Quixote narrative but into the already interwoven story of the four young lovers, Cardenio, Luscinda, Fernando, and Dorotea. Indeed, when the interpolated tale is understood within its relevant context this combined episode extends over a considerable part of Part One from Chapter Twenty-three to Chapter Thirty-seven. Likewise, the story of the *Impertinent Curiosity* is itself interrupted by this doubled main narrative. And these mutual interruptions are not just a way of maintaining the three narrative actions simultaneously; they are precisely placed so as to highlight their parallels. As in a musical composition, Cervantes develops an independent melodic momentum in each narrative while periodically revealing the chordal relationship between them. The *Impertinent Curiosity* in fact relates primarily to the Cardenio narrative and only secondarily to Don Quixote. Hence, to feel the full working of all the interrelations here involves a complex act of separation and comparison but the main shape of it is as follows.

Don Quixote and Sancho first encounter Cardenio as the mad Knight of the Wood. Intrigued by various hints which suggest to Don Quixote a situation of unhappy love, they persuade him to tell his personal history. With some reluctance he begins to do so and brings the narrative nearly to the point of Fernando's perfidy in seeking to have Cardenio's beloved, Luscinda, for his own wife. But Quixote's interruption on a point of chivalry causes Cardenio to relapse into madness and run off into the hills. Quixote, perhaps influenced by what he had inferred about Cardenio's situation, now sets about performing, as a conscious act of madness, his imitation of Beltenebros' penance. This means that when Cardenio later resumes his narrative to the Priest and the Barber instead of to Don Quixote, his reaction to Fernando's real, and Luscinda's apparent, betrayal at the betrothal ceremony strikes a precise chord with what Don Quixote is doing at that very moment. Cardenio rushes from the scene determined to perform some mad act (*desatino*) to demonstrate his feelings. The note of conscious intention here strikes the chordal parallel with the knight while the clinical state of Don Quixote and the emotional immaturity of Cardenio retain their quite different meanings within their separate narratives.

As the action unfolds to bring together all of the characters at an inn, it is Cardenio who first gets engrossed in the manuscript of the *Impertinent Curiosity* which is then read by the Priest to the assembled company. This story concerns a young husband, Anselmo, who is neither clinically mad nor merely immature. In seeking to persuade his best friend, Lotario, to test his wife Camila's virtue, Anselmo reveals a pathological curiosity. Despite his conscious horror at such an outcome, he seems to envisage fully possessing his wife only by a voyeuristic identification with his best friend. The action then proceeds with a closely reasoned logic to its disastrous conclusion.

Now, Anselmo is in many respects the opposite to Cardenio. Where Cardenio partly provokes his own misfortunes by not acting decisively to secure his love, Anselmo wishes to attain security by imposing an absurdly inappropriate and self-defeating test upon his wife. One young man fears reality while the other rushes at it. But both evince a misplaced emotional idealism which provokes their respective friends and forms the point of parallel with Don Quixote. The initial climax of the action is the point at which Anselmo is completely and happily deceived by his wife and his friend, who have been almost driven to stage-manage the charade that he desiderates. By this time, it should also be noted, Don Quixote is himself the victim of a charade involving Dorotea's impersonation of the Princess Micomicon. And indeed this is the moment at which the reading of the novella is interrupted by Don Quixote's attack on the inn's wine-skins in the belief that they are the giant he has undertaken to kill for her. Hence Don Quixote's moment of illusory triumph coincides with the reading of Anselmo's answering moment; and in each case the young woman has taken a leading part in the charade within which this 'triumph' occurs.

Once again, the differences between these narratives are as much part of the overall effect as are the structural similarities suddenly revealed by these moments of chordal recognition. The central theme is qualified as well as amplified. If Quixote, for example, is lacking in an empirical sense of things, we see the opposite danger of a misplaced empiricism in Anselmo. But as we trace the thematic patterns created by this multiple narrative, it becomes necessary to consider not only such personal similarities and differences but also the ways in which the characters' experiences are being placed within specifically narrative perspectives.

When Cardenio, in his persona as the mad Knight of the Wood, starts to tell his story to Don Quixote and Sancho, Cervantes has gone out of his way to enforce the parallel with the Don although this mirror-image aspect of Cardenio is quite quickly shed in the ensuing narrative. This persona may have been used in a purely casual way by Cervantes in order to signal the more substantive, but less obvious, parallel that then emerges. But in fact the shedding of Cardenio's mad persona seems to occur by a more specific process. When explaining his reluctance to tell his story, Cardenio says that he must not be interrupted because the painful events will be lived once again in the narrating and he therefore wants it all over as soon as possible. This amounts to an emotional conflation of the narrative with the events; and indeed the madness caused by the original events is triggered once again in the course of the narration. But when Cardenio continues his story to the Priest and the Barber he conducts the narrative in a very different spirit. He now interrupts himself to express concern that he is wearying his listeners and to affirm the necessity for a circumstantial account. We might say that he sheds his madness in narrating and the change is from a literalistic emotional identification with the events to a more detached concern for their meaning. The act of narration seems partly therapeutic.

If the very recounting of his own history is beneficial, and indeed this is a significant aspect of modern therapeutic practice, it is fitting that it should be Cardenio who first gets engrossed in the tale of the *Impertinent Curiosity*. His own story has been a matter of intense curiosity to all his auditors so far and now the Priest undertakes to read the new story aloud to satisfy the general curiosity. The *Impertinent Curiosity* is being read, that is to say, out of curiosity and this is the moment to remark that the Spanish title *del Curioso Impertinente* does not readily translate into English. The Spanish implies both a high degree of curiosity and a misapplication of it. The Penguin version, *Foolish Curiosity*, catches the general sense by conflating the two aspects but it thereby obscures the aspect of misplacement. For it is not really the degree of curiosity that is in question, so much as the application of it. As it happens, the lively curiosity of the present auditors appears not to be misplaced. The Priest is a little critical of the story as a literary artifact just as the comments in Part Two suggest its lack of assimilation, but the company listen to a story replete with subliminal suggestiveness for their own lives. And in so far as a disinterested remove is in itself part of the transformative quality of a narrative, then the complete formal separation of this tale as a found manuscript is a further positive dimension of its significance for them. Cardenio regained his sanity as he shifted from actor to narrator of his own story. He came to see the shape of the whole rather than relive the emotions of the moment. All of the characters are outsiders to this narrated tale and it may be that the real point of the Priest's comments *for us* is to point up the tale as being *for them* a piece of literature rather than life. Cervantes creates the charged gaps across which the sparks of significance are ignited. Cardenio and Fernando go on to resolve their emotional obsessions after their encounter with Don Quixote and with this story.

All this is not to say that the story has any such exemplary or conscious meaning for the characters who listen to it. Indeed, one should not fall into the trap of expecting Cervantes' thematic elaborations to depend upon later novelistic assumptions of a consistent internal psychology of the individual. Rather, the effect is spread out across the multiple narrative as a significance for us. And so when Fernando undergoes the final change of heart that allows the whole Cardenio narrative to come to a proper conclusion we just have his words without any internal analysis of his thoughts. Hence, although an internal process is implied, we feel that he is to some extent arriving at this decision by accepting his proper role in the action seen as a kind of narrative expectation even if that expectation is perceived more directly by the reader than by him. For this narrative in which Cardenio and Fernando undergo their respective changes for the good is flanked for us by the stories of Don Quixote and the *Impertinent Curiosity*. Each of these has a different kind of narrative fixture to it. Quixote is fixed in his fiction of the chivalric hero and Anselmo is fixed in the completed manuscript of his tale. Cardenio and Fernando, inhabiting the space between these two fixtures, show by contrast a potentiality for change yet our understanding of that change is inseparable from our perception of those fictional *alter egos* whose significance is focused by a separate narrative framing.

The moment in which the company listen out of curiosity to the story of the *Impertinent Curiosity* is typically Cervantean. We may see the inserted fiction as a mirror image of its audience only if we include in that formula a recognition of the inversion, the virtuality, and the dependency of this image. The curiosity inside and the curiosity outside the fictional frame can be neither equated nor separated. This effect, of course, echoes through the whole narrative of *Don Quixote*. In the opening paragraphs we are told that Alonso Quijano first fell victim of his illusions through reading so many books of chivalry when he had nothing better to do which in his case was most of the time. At that juncture we may recollect that the author's opening address was not to the 'gentle', 'learned', or 'noble' but to the 'idle' (*desocupado*) reader. The whole book poses a question about the state of mind in which we are able to read it. In the light of this there is a further point to Cervantes' vindication of a literature of entertainment on the grounds that 'the bow cannot be always bent'. A bow which is always bent will lose its tension and its usefulness. It may be part of the effect of narrative to transpose the inescapable tensions of life into a disinterested, recuperative *use* of the very 'same' energies. It is by apparent similarity that the distinction is most crucially, and significantly, achieved.

It is part of the peculiar genius of Cervantes to produce impressions of psychological depth by superimposing within the same fictive space a variety of the two-dimensional modes of characterization he had inherited. The pre-novelistic nature of his method makes it hard to translate such effects into a readily definable psychological or moral value. But the advantage is in keeping attention on a general speculative theme. Indeed, the theme very largely is the method: the elements of life and narrative are inextricable yet not identical; and their interactions are both dangerous and constructive. It would, I think, be against the spirit of Cervantes to reduce his multi-layered suggestiveness to any single formulation, but one plane of recognition is that, however difficult it may be to define the boundaries of narrative in human life, the drawing of those boundaries is meaningful. The curiosity that listens to the tale is different from the curiosity depicted within it. Curiously enough, even professionally bookish readers such as might nowadays be reading Cervantes find it hard to accept that the company listening to the tale may be having just as significant an experience as if they were fighting, seducing, talking, or engaging in any other activity not regarded as an interruption of the main narrative. Life itself may require occasional interruption for reflective juxtaposition with narrative.

Fiction and Feeling

If we compare the example of Cervantes with the recent discussion of narrative which I have sketched in my opening remarks, he may be seen as addressing similar issues in different terms. He sets out an area of problem rather than argue a particular view of it and by his non-analytic method he suggests the dialectical mutuality of narrative and life. He presents in dramatic terms that abstractly elusive understanding which would arise from seeing the Hardy and the Mink emphases as a complementarity rather than a choice. As a novelist he dissolves any two-dimensional, abstract categorization of experience such as the word 'narrative' may itself come to impose and is concerned to weigh the relative significance and authenticity of particular experiences. Narrative is constitutively involved in this but only as a relational factor within the experience and not as an isolable element or containing frame.

Cervantes was the archetypal and fecund exemplar for subsequent European fiction because, rather than represent a particular viewpoint, he thematized the medium itself as an arena of possibilities. Hence the dialectical relations of narrative and life are for him a central preoccupation. Later novelists who had particular world-views to embody in their fiction were generally less concerned to highlight the problematic nature of the narrative contract and in many cases wished to 'naturalize' it entirely into the text. These instances throw a further revealing light upon our theme because they indicate the stubborn essentiality of the problem. I propose therefore to consider briefly one or two quite different examples from the eighteenth, nineteenth, and twentieth centuries. All of these later instances, however, have a point of commonality which relates to another aspect of Alisdair MacIntyre's argument. For there is now a shift in emphasis from epistemological issues to qualities of feeling: a shift from curiosity to sympathy.

In the interweaving of his multiple narratives, Cervantes notes the sympathetic, and often tearful, response of the listeners but the accent falls rather on issues of belief. By contrast, the major works of later European fiction were produced within or after the eighteenth-century cult of sentiment and tend to be concerned less with the truth-status of the event and more with the ethical meaning of the emotional response. One of MacIntyre's themes is the inadequacy of 'emotivism' when adduced in the philosophical tradition as a basis for virtue. The interest of these later novelistic examples in relation to MacIntyre's argument lies in the way the overt issues of moral responsiveness are themselves constitutively bound up with a more implicit scrutiny of the narrative premises. Since I have discussed that general question at length elsewhere[4] I will give it a more summary treatment here to indicate simply how it bears on the present debate about narrative.

Richardson's *Clarissa* is one of the founding texts for the novel of sentiment. After the rape, Clarissa is kept for some time in the garret of Rowland the bailiff where she refuses to see any man at all. Hence, when she finally agrees to receive Lovelace's now reformed friend Belford, Richardson has engineered, in a completely natural way, the necessity for conveying the situation of Clarissa to the still unrepentant Lovelace by means of a sub-narrative: Belford's letter to Lovelace. This means that Richardson's own narrative, which is really being served by this device, is subjected to an implicit self-scrutiny as Belford struggles to convey not just the facts but the significance of the scene. As it happens, this is not one of Richardson's greatest moments. There is a sense of straining for effect so that the moral climax becomes a kind of set-piece tableau. Yet precisely this quality in the scene exemplifies the peculiar way in which this novel manages to be greater than its author. It is partly that the possible inadequacies are seen as the narrating character's rather than the author's. But, more importantly, any such inadequacies are themselves at the heart of the book's theme.

The struggle between Clarissa and Lovelace is a struggle of rival, incommensurate world-views which are defined in the book through their corresponding literary embodiments. Clarissa is living a religious pilgrimage akin to Bunyan's, while Lovelace is enacting the Restoration rake. One says 'enacting' here because these models are actively used by the characters to dominate the events of Richardson's narrative. The resulting charged atmosphere of the epistolary medium itself enables moments such as the garret scene to maintain a dramatic power not readily demonstrable in isolation. As it happens, Belford's letter does not elicit from Lovelace the kind of response it commands from the implied reader of Richardson's novel. And in this respect its failure enacts the tragic recognition of the book that neither events nor narratives can compel a response unless there is a shared world-view within which to receive them. Part of the power of *Clarissa* lies in the way Richardson has in effect capitalized on both his moral and his narrative problems so that the whole issue of narrative persuasion gives a philosophical cutting edge to his tragic analysis.

Before leaving Richardson's dramatic demonstration of the tragic inadequacy of narrative it is worth pausing on the effect of the tableau already mentioned. For the literature of sentiment frequently privileges tableaux over narrative not just in practice but in principle. While I would not wish to make too much of what are often rather naïve moments in that literature, they have a symptomatic suggestiveness in relation to our larger concern. For they amount to an intuitive recognition that narrative is often underwritten by a prior evaluative commitment for which an immediate, spatialized perception is a truer image. It may be part of the superior cunning of later realist fiction to disguise this fact.

The narrative inadequacy highlighted by Richardson may be countered by an episode from Sterne, writing as the cult of feeling had become fashionable. By the 1760s one might more readily assume the willingness of readers or characters to make the correct sentimental response that Lovelace refuses. But this in turn gives a new urgency to questions that may be raised about the moral significance of such a response. If benevolence, as Shaftesbury claimed, was a natural and pleasurable impulse, then where in fact was its ethical value? Indeed, it might be possible to indulge the sentiment of benevolence without any ethical behaviour at all. Such a question undoubtedly mattered to Sterne but his ambivalence towards sentiment is most typically manifested not by a direct critique so much as by a jokey unsettling of it in action. Like Cervantes, he can make complex discriminations without the possible reductiveness of analytical procedures. This is the light in which to look at the 'Story of Le Fever' from *Tristram Shandy*.

In this instance Sterne has given Uncle Toby an illness especially to ensure that the circumstances of 'Le Fever' are narrated as a story by Trim. At one level, of course, this is a device of contrast whereby the comic setting highlights, and even legitimizes for us, the pathos of the subject. But it also has consequences for the way in which the implied sentimental response is placed. In effect, we listen to the story over Uncle Toby's shoulder so that we both partake of his response and assimilate it in turn to a larger response of our own. Our response is pleasurable. We respond, of course, to the pathos of 'Le Fever' but only as an element in our enjoyment of Trim and Toby. Furthermore, no demand is being made upon our purse. The object of benevolence stays safely within the fictional frame; a frame that Toby and Trim make particularly vivid for us. But Toby is not enjoying the story. As he remarks at one point, he wishes he were asleep, and his pained concern is expressed as a directly practical and sustained benevolence. His benevolence is a crucial part of what we are enjoying.

What happens in this admixture of pathos and humour is that various kinds of responsiveness are being discriminated by the superimposition of the narrative frames. To the extent that Sterne provides us with a different subject from Toby's he legitimizes our pleasurable response. We are not in the dubious position of enjoying a naïvely vicarious benevolence; a dishonesty of feeling which can, after all, arise in relation to both fiction and life. Our pleasure is legitimate here because of its clearly fictional object. It is implicitly discriminated as an exercise in feeling not to be confused with the emotions of a real occasion. And the delicacy of the effect is that this intuitive discrimination is not felt as a separation from Toby or from 'Le Fever'. The ultimate moral root of the experience remains firmly in place and dramatically the reader is more aware of being drawn into solidarity with Toby than the converse. It is only on reflection that we might recognize the narrative means by which that emotional solidarity is being constituted. The intuitive holism of the experience is an important aspect of its significance, for with historical retrospect we can see in this double narrative structure the potential divergence of an ethical and an aesthetic response; a divergence with enormous consequences for nineteenth-century fiction.

In this latter connection Sterne's capacity to indulge sentiment even while subjecting it to critical scrutiny suggests a fruitful example for Dickens. Yet moving our attention into the nineteenth century also focuses what these two opposed examples from the eighteenth century have in common. In effecting their respective narrative/moral discriminations they both assume a rather direct and literalistic relation between the emotions within the fiction and the emotions of the reader. Sterne shows this by the narrative manoeuvres that are required to counteract such an assumed continuity and Richardson shows it by the tragic consequences of its absence. I have discussed elsewhere how nineteenth-century novelists within the tradition of ethical sentiment came to transform the meaning of sentimental rhetoric by transposing it into fictional tropes for the examination of the feeling itself.[5] Feeling is recognized to include a constitutive element of imagination. Hence authenticity of feeling is presented as increasingly noumenal while fiction becomes the appropriate medium for learning to read, or interpret, it. In their very different ways the novels of Tolstoy and Dickens propose a deep affinity between responsive reading and responsive living. But that is not an identity, and without difference there would be no significant affinity.

It is generally agreed that the relation between narrative and life in Tolstoy or George Eliot stands at an extreme contrast from the self-conscious discriminations in Cervantes and Sterne. The nineteenth-century organicist conception allows for a profound homology between fiction and life. Yet these authors do not lose sight of the essential tension between the two orders; a tension upon which the meaningfulness of their art depends. The intrusive narrators of Victorian fiction are perhaps the most striking manifestation of this. These narrators affirm the continuity between their narrative and the world of the reader and yet at the same time they represent a constant subliminal assertion of the narrative frame. This mode of fiction is far from the naïve literalism which a generation of eager deconstructionists would have us believe. The book is a model of life, not a simulacrum. Such fiction is not literalist in spirit and that is actually why it can approximate most significantly to that degree zero in narrative consciousness, in other words the maximum degree of assimilation of life to narrative, which MacIntyre seems to desiderate. It could only do this if narrative meaning were there as a powerful function in the first place. The literalist conception underlying much eighteenth-century fiction, and which gave rise to the counter-emphasis on artificiality in Fielding, Sterne, and Diderot, has been transcended.

Yet the progressive rejection of nineteenth-century realism which occurred from the 1880s onward is comprehensible and manifestly justified. The implied cultural consensus upon which that fiction rested could no longer be assumed. And this consciously formal rejection is the important issue. For it amounts to the refusal of an implied contract rather than the simple absence of a contract.

Gissing's ambivalence towards Dickens, for example, arises from an admiration for Dickens' achievement coupled with a rejection of the Dickensian narrative assumptions.

Now, I have referred to the stance of the Victorian narrator as a mediating one. Of course, in its own context it was not a studied posture but intuitive and natural. Clearly, Dickens, Eliot, and Tolstoy believed in the social consensus embodied in their narrative stances. That is why they are the trickiest cases for our present theme. Their moral and formal confidence gives them a 'naturalness' such that critics can still be found pushing at the open door of their assumed naïve realism. But if they are the trickiest cases they are also the most telling and testing ones. For what all this suggests is that wherever the narrative form gives us the closest apparent approximation to a dissolving of the metaphorical distance from life, precisely there we find the most urgent and understandable resistance of readers to such an assimilation. For present purposes, it hardly matters whether such fiction is seen as controlled artistry or as naïve mimesis, for in either case its subsequent history indicates the danger of merely assimilating the terms of narrative to the terms of life. The Victorian novelists come nearest to MacIntyre's model but if they actually embodied it without any relativizing narrative frame they would indeed deserve much of the criticism that has recently come their way.

In so far as the Victorian novel provides the most testing cases in regard to our theme, it will be helpful to close this selection of instances with a modern novelist who did not adopt the post-aestheticist solution of other modernists and whose attempt to keep faith with the tradition of Tolstoy and Eliot provides an instructive further contrast with all the cases considered so far.

D.H. Lawrence is a peculiarly striking instance of a modern writer who had difficulty in creating a readership. Roughly speaking, we had only learned by the 'fifties how to read his major works written in the teens of the century. The consequences of this were compounded by the nature of Lawrence's demands upon the reader. He could not, like Stendhal, write a book consciously ahead of its time and leave it like a time capsule for the world to discover. The dialogic dimension of Lawrence encompasses the reader as well as competing aspects of Lawrence himself. His well-known injunction to 'trust the tale, not the teller' is a critical principle addressed to readers but its logic, for an author creating within such a conception of literature as a mode of discovery, entails that the author in turn must trust the reader. Lawrence's deliberately vulnerable self-exploration and his attempts to extend the articulation of psychic states make his relation to the reader peculiarly crucial. By the 'twenties he had some reputation and sales but the nature of his reception, particularly after his wartime experiences, is the point at issue here. His major fictions of the 'twenties can only hesitantly be described as novels although they all include moments of novelistic power. One reason for their peculiar generic mode, apart from Lawrence's own unresolved self-exploration, seems to be his difficulty in finding adequate common ground with a reader.

The opening chapters of *The Plumed Serpent* are instructive in this regard. Lawrence raises the central themes of the book, violence, cruelty, and the perversion of sexuality and community, by the description of a bullfight in a manner at once sickening and verisimilar. The Lawrentian protagonist, Kate Leslie, responds to the events in the spirit of this narration but her American companions respond with varying degrees of acceptance. Owen, the elder of the two, feels something of Kate's spontaneous disgust but forces himself to suppress this for the sake of assimilating a new 'experience'. Villiers meanwhile simply enjoys it sensationally. Now the latter half of the book, concerned with the revival of the ancient gods of Mexico, is generally, and I think rightly, regarded as unsuccessful. Yet in many ways the premises of Lawrence's novel are recognized as problematic from the opening episode in that they encompass not merely an external action but the reader's capacity for an appropriately critical and participatory response.

Lawrence is using his observer characters here to define a mode of responsiveness to experience without which nothing in relation to his large theme can meaningfully be said, and this is true whether the object be a real or a fictive one. Hence, in approaching the events as 'experience', Owen and Villiers suggest a mode of response to fiction as well as to life. They embody within the book itself the non-committal manner of reading, or responding, which in Lawrence's case would leave them below the threshold of serious readership. And there is nothing to be done from Lawrence's point of view when faced with such a response. When Kate later attacks Villiers at this personal existential level he merely enjoys her moral indignation as a further sensation to add to his stock. It is possible to read Lawrence's fiction in precisely this spirit as a separable, framed experience in which the existential urgency of Lawrence's responsiveness is itself assimilated as part of the fictional experience as thus delimited. None of these remarks, of course, entails that Lawrence should be read uncritically. They point rather to the peculiarly involved responsiveness that a critical reading of Lawrence requires.

Indeed, the Lawrentian relation to the reader is a complex and shifting matter upon which it is not appropriate to embark more fully here. But enough has been said to indicate once again that, although the emotional and moral substance is being crucially mediated by a narrative model of responsiveness, this is precisely to show that the narrative itself is powerless to impose its terms. The powerlessness is quite conscious and is inseparable from the positive meaning of the narrative. In one sense, Owen and Villiers represent degrees of the problem seen already in Richardson's Lovelace. Faced with events which should compel a given response, none of these men responds in the appropriate fashion. And the way in which both authors have built the issue of response into the tissue of the actual narrative situation enables them to highlight the existential issue without it falling into the limbo of non-meaning represented by the literal, historical reactions of readers.

But to invoke the infinity of possible real readers, as opposed to the implied readers, of these texts is to point up the difference between Lawrence and Richardson. In Richardson's case, although neither the events nor the narration can compel Lovelace's response, there is a clear recognition that the authorial judgement is normative and is accepted as such. Lovelace is the exception. But in Lawrence's case the way in which he introduces the issue of responsiveness into the narrative reflects his recognition that, however normative his response may be, it is not the normal one. I suggested earlier that the kind of formal consciousness I have attributed to Richardson may be seen as a fortunate by-product of his narrative. In Lawrence, by contrast, it points to a genuine predicament consciously underlying, and not ultimately assimilable to, the narrative project. All he can do is forcefully to dramatize his premises; to throw them down as a challenge. My earlier remarks on the sentimental tableau may also be recalled here. The tableau effect in Richardson was rather extraneous to his real dramatic strength. But in Lawrence's novel the strong moments are Lawrence's equivalent of the tableau: those moments that we lamely describe as his 'sheer responsiveness to life' but for which on this occasion Lawrence could find no adequate narrative vehicle. He had no shared world from which to construct it.

Conclusion

The variety of examples sketched here suggests that a problematic consciousness of the narrative contract is not merely an optional extra for philosophically-minded novelists but arises from the intrinsic requirements of the form in use. That in turn suggests some conclusions with respect to the generalized invoking of narrative as a model for the nature of virtue.

MacIntyre uses the amplitude and complexity of the narrative as a telling standard by which to see the inadequacy of 'emotion' when adduced as a basis for virtue. For emotion is itself a relational element taking its meaning from its place in a whole life experience for which narrative provides a model. As a tactical and illustrative device, his appeal to narrative seems to me to work well enough. Yet it is an interesting lacuna in his wide range of enquiry that he does not make much of the novel. This is, after all, the form in which Western culture since the Enlightenment has most notably conducted the education and examination of feeling so as to transcend the reductiveness of any generalized appeal to emotion in the understanding of moral life. Clearly, MacIntyre can read novels cogently, as is shown in his pages on Jane Austen. Yet she is the single novelist discussed in some detail because she is the one who embodies an Aristotelian conception of virtue and lends herself to the same kind of demonstrative use as the Homeric narratives. It would be interesting to have seen his case advanced in the larger context of the novel because, as is evident from the examples discussed above, the novel would provide the most substantial vindication of his argument yet would also highlight limitations and difficulties.

There might be a tactical difficulty for him in that a complex and ambitious argument would then perhaps seem to be leading to a truistic and merely literary conclusion. But behind that stands a more essential issue. I have tried to bring out how, in a wide variety of instances, the narrative authority has had to be negotiated as a constitutive element of the moral or emotional 'content'. This recurrent feature of the novel points us inescapably to its relativity and, therefore, to its consciously limited authority.

It would seem that narrative may indeed provide an objectification for a given form of life, whether individual or communal. Its value in this respect can lie in the compelling power and comprehensiveness of the embodied world view. Or conversely it may lie primarily in the diagnostic possibilities such an objectification provides. But either way a consciously relativistic sense of projecting a specific world-view seems to be characteristic of the novel as opposed to the primary epic. Strictly speaking, of course, it is just as true of the epic, but the novel represents a kind of fall into relativistic consciousness. Hence the exemplary status of Cervantes in the history of the novel. But this overall relativism is merely the collective aspect of what I have been noting about specific texts taken in isolation. Narrative can embody, and thus objectify or vindicate, a form of life but it cannot of itself either create, or compel acceptance of, that form of life. In its fundamental terms it has to appeal to the reader's consent as an existential given.

In sum, then, narrative meaning exists dialectically in the tension between its world and the world of the reader. We must not be mesmerized by the fact that only the former of these appears to be there on the page. The narrative is itself inscribed in a language already inhabited by the reader. That is why the imaginative process of reading may often obscure the constitutive and dialectical nature of narrative meaning, but we need to recognize both planes. To dissolve narrative into life is to dissolve the terms of its proper and important meaning for the sake of a speculative chimera. Given the inescapable relativity of narrative, collapsing the moral life into it can add no significant insight into the meaning or practice of virtue. The problems still reside in the world from which we look into the narrative. And even if a narrative totally embodied a given reader's values, the meaning of that narrative would still only be visible from the outside.

Notes

1 Rev. edn., London: Duckworth, 1985.
2 *Die Philosophie des Als-Obs* (Leipzig: Meiner, 1911) trans. C.K. Ogden (New York: Harcourt Brace, 1924).
3 *The Sentiment of Reality: Truth of Feeling in the European Novel* (London: Allen and Unwin, 1983). The remarks on Lawrence are based on a talk to a symposium on 'Sentimentalism and modern literature' at the Inter-University Centre, Dubrovnik, March/April 1987.
4 *The Sentiment of Reality*, passim.
5 *The Sentiment of Reality*, 111–60.

· 9 ·

Slaughtering the Subject: Literature's Assault on Narrative

CRISTOPHER NASH

Let me set the scene. Here are two brief passages: the first is from a recent review by John Peter, from *The Sunday Times*, of a novel by the Czechoslovak writer Milan Kundera:

The place was Prague and the time the mid-fifties . . . . Now one reason why experimental fiction was a late developer behind the Iron Curtain, and indeed had a lot of trouble being born at all, is not only that it was frowned upon, but also that there was a parched thirst for a specific type of old-fashioned narrative. The land was in the grip of monstrous events. A new order came to power through fraud and intimidation: people were murdered or framed, others simply disappeared; poverty grew, fear reigned. But none of this appeared in newspapers or books: these were stories that were not being told. People wondered if anyone would ever write these stories; if anyone would bear witness . . . . *Life is Elsewhere* is by a rebellious citizen who wanted to tell.[1]

The second passage is the opening of a short prose narrative by Jean-François Bory, published in the early 'seventies:

And after the subject, the verb, followed by an adjective agreeing in gender and number with the subject. The same subject, an adverbial pronoun, an auxiliary verb, an article, a noun, an object of the predicate, an indefinite pronoun and an infinitive verb.

The 'narrative' continues in this way for nearly four hundred words, and ends:

The same subject, an adverbial pronoun, an auxiliary verb, an article, a noun, an object of the predicate, an indefinite pronoun and an infinitive verb.[2]

In Peter's view, Kundera's kind of writing is an enactment of the fact that certain human historical conditions cry out for what he calls 'old-fashioned narrative'; and by that he means, I think, a kind of narrative that has a subject. 'Subject' in two important senses of the word: a 'subject-matter' that demands to be 'told', to be 'borne witness to'; the narrative is about something – something stable, clear, and readily identifiable. And the narrative has in it or behind it a 'subjectivity' – a person, a 'subject' who experiences this truth to which he or she must bear witness; a being, a mind that is in some vital respect stable, clear, and readily identifiable. 'Old-fashioned narrative' wants to be information-full and meaning-full, coming from a solid someone whose intention simply awaits discovery.

The second piece, on the other hand, by Bory, refers repeatedly to a 'subject', literally – the 'subject' of each sentence; but we seem to have no way of knowing not only what kind of 'person' it is, but whether it's a person at all – or a dog, or a lightbulb, an idea, or an absence of an idea. The subject is only the subject of a sentence, one we haven't yet seen and never will see. And what the 'subject-matter' might be, if anything, we can never know, we can only guess. This narrative is a mere syntactical, grammatical shell, designed to be empty of information, meaning-less, referring to further verbal antecedents, to other words that are no longer – if they ever were – there.

What's going on?

Probably no century has ever been so good as ours at producing reasons for being in doubt about what we can know and how we can ever know anything. In the physical sciences, at least since the publication of Heisenberg's paper on the uncertainty principle (1927), and in mathematics, since Gödel's paper three years later on formally undecidable propositions, it has long been thought probable that both our powers of empirical perception and our powers of pure logical conception are inherently incapable by any rational means at any one time of ever 'totalizing', making total sense of – or even of observing – all the facts that make up 'the truth'. Now: the physicist and the mathematician quite regularly keep before them the problem of the uncertainty of what is – or can be – observed. Further still, they remain sophisticatedly alert to the fact that it's difficult to distinguish the object of the experiment from the apparatus with which it is observed. But one thing that is rarely if ever concertedly put into question by them is: who observes what is observed? In fact, one of the things we count on the scientist to do is to declare – 'up front' – who it is, exactly, that saw what it is that's being reported. The scientist – call him or her Professor X – makes it a practice never to say 'A is true', but says instead: 'Experimenters X, Y, and Z observed such-and-such a set of events to take place, and the conclusion (the opinion) of persons X, Y, and Z is that A is true or probable.'

This is of course traditional science's way of establishing its accountability – some person is responsible for everything that's said. Indeed, sociologists of science (such as Rom Harré) have long persisted in saying that, far more than we think, our 'scientific' beliefs are governed not so much by science's narratives of experiments as we commonly think but more by covert narratives bespeaking the relative merits of the scientific persons who conduct and report these experiments. What I'm getting at is that in recent critical literary theory, this very struggle among scientists – or others – to establish their own personal accountability is founded on philosophically naïve premises: that behind the crucial posture of intelligent scepticism (saying that we must know who it is that tells us such-and-such is true) lies the unquestioned assumption that Professors X, Y, and Z, for example, are themselves each accountably clear, readily identifiable and stable subjects. It's the premise that if the experiment is technically repeatable, there is no reason to think that it's not to be – for example – psychologically repeatable. There should be no 'personal' reason, the assumption says, why the person who experienced the event once should not see it the same way again. The notion of personal identity, you see – the identicalness of the observing subject at one moment to what he or she is at every other moment, with his or her unaltered credentials, his or her continuing authority, and so forth – is essential to the credibility, the viability, of the scientific enterprise.

Well – to literary theorists of recent years, there are all kinds of problems here. For one thing, just who is the subject (or the agent) of action, of events, in scientific or any other kinds of narrative – who, even, is the 'true author' – has come to be seen as shot-through with dilemmas and questions.

Let's see what trouble there could ever be with this idea of the subject. For generations, in our schools, in undergraduate seminars, everywhere, it has been the endless custom to speak about, say, *Madame Bovary* as the story of a particular, identifiable woman and her world. We find her complex and we ask questions about her which we may feel we may never live long enough to answer satisfactorily, but – even while we acknowledge the thing's a fiction – nevertheless we speak of 'her' in the very same language, the same terms, that we use in speaking of 'real' people: and we speak of real people as though they were definable centres of experience – in a world solidly existing before we began to speak of it. (Flaubert, in fact, in his correspondence, speaks of Madame Bovary and her world in exactly this manner.) We could, we think, in a complete and unified way, know both the person and her world, if we could only get together all the relevant information and think sensitively and reasonably about it.

But are things that simple? For one thing (quite apart from the problems attaching to our seeking to establish criteria such as 'relevance', 'sensitivity', and 'reasonableness'), if we look at my 'subjectivity', 'objectively' – from the outside, as a biochemist or a neurophysicist might say: the story of my sitting here writing this, my experience of it, is 'really' just the story of a lot of neurons firing in my brain; you are not here in my head, there's no study, no building, no earth, no universe in my brain – just neurons, firing. So which of these stories of mine is more 'truthful', the one about us coming together over this chapter, or that undeniable series of damp discharges in my brain? And where am I, this 'subject', located in all this, exactly? Do I really have an identity, as clear and tidy as my name, neatly contained within the limits of the physical object 'who' (you think) is sitting here writing to you?

Here the literary impact of writers as diverse as psychoanalysts (like Jacques Lacan), cultural historians (like Michel Foucault), critical philosophers or *anti-philosophes* (like Jacques Derrida), and Marxist theorists (like Louis Althusser) come powerfully together for one moment. What we think to be our free-standing identities may be the products, captive agents, of the culture, indeed the language, that has made us think as we do – some 'emperor's new clothes' in which our thinking has been falsely dressed and blandished by a socio-economic-and-sexual hegemony, by a labyrinthine network of forces, sea-changes, of which we may be only anonymously entangled threads, edgeless unbounded currents.

Following from this, some theorists will argue that the only way we can begin to act with freedom is to 'decentre the subject', to shed like the emperor's new clothes that naïve faith in our auto-nomous 'natural' inborn integral individuality. That we must replace that fallacious 'private identity' with the hope of identify-ing ourselves with some collective, and to enter into a permanent struggle with those whom we think to be other than ourselves and inimical to (and hence defining of) our being. Others argue that this too is a mere fable – yet another myth, with its outmoded conservative narrative of heroic struggle, of oppression and its eventual utopian redress; that that notion of being-as-subject, too, is delusory; that, as one literary critic has put it (and you'll recognize the argument, it's a recurrent motif): the 'humanistic concept of the self' has now been eclipsed by theories that shatter many of our most essential traditional 'distinctions, such as rational/irrational, appearance/reality, interior/exterior, fact/fiction'. Mas'ud Zavarzadeh goes on: the function of characteriza-tion, for example – in fiction and in our lives –

has become obsolete today . . . . The individual has lost his centrality in a world where the very survival of the human race is at stake . . . . Character . . . today cannot fulfil its traditional narrative functions, which were to portray a fully individuated person . . . rooted in a 'community of thought and feeling' shared by his fellow human beings . . . . The old organic world of man and the new world of technology . . . 'obey different imperatives, different directives and different laws which have nothing in common' . . . . Such developments create an open-ended and indeter-minable system which defies all historical and totalizing frames of reference.[3]

So, as the novelist Alain Robbe-Grillet had already put it in 1957: where literature is concerned,

all the technical elements of the narrative . . . the unconditional adoption of chronological development, linear plots, a regular graph of the emotions, the way each episode tended towards an end, etc. . . . everything aimed at imposing the image of a stable universe, coherent, continuous, univocal and wholly decipherable

– all this, Robbe-Grillet says, must go. Story as such must be obliterated. And, he says, 'the novel that contains characters belongs well and truly to the past'.[4] Psychology, for example, that very cornerstone of realist narrative, was merely an arbitrary, artificial system of attitudes for the focalization of events through the perspective of a named individualized human consciousness – an outmoded anthropomorphic culture's strategy for the projection of a happily bounded and integrated vision of existence. As Annette Lavers put it, paraphrasing Roland Barthes, 'conceiving a character as the representation of a human person, having a consciousness and an identity manifested in its actions, is an ideological, not a scientific concept'.[5]

For novelists like Nathalie Sarraute, then, like Robbe-Grillet, in the 1950s the contemporary reader 'has watched the watertight partitions that used to separate characters', as she says, 'give way'.[6] There may or may not be such a thing as the human mind, but the old realist concept of person simply doesn't produce a useful model for its representation. A narrative now, then, is bound in no way to laws of identity or continuity outside itself; it is ruled simply by the rules of language. As a 'speaker' phrases it in Christine Brooke-Rose's novel *Thru*,

The notions of subject and object correspond only to a place in the narrative proposition and not to a difference in nature hence . . . the agent is not the one who can accomplish this or that action but the one who can become subject of a predicate.[7]

Narrative is nothing more than a string of linguistic signs.

We've now opened up a whole new can of spaghetti. It's the theme of literary indeterminism as a whole. For if it becomes questionable to 'characterize' a 'character' in a linguistic text, it becomes logically equally questionable to characterize (in language) the author, any author as specific 'origin' or 'originator' of the text; not only his or her intentions, but his or her very being, in any specific relation to the text. Whereas traditionally a narrative was in some sense defined, we thought, by what came before it (a world outside it, an author outside it, an author's ideas of what both meant), contemporary indeterminism begins to say that a narrative is to be described in terms of what comes after it: for example, its reader, and its reader's 'reading' of it.

There are, as we can see if we look closely, two different kinds of arguments here for the indeterminacy of texts. They allude to an undecidability in the relations between texts, between utterances (which we can call 'intertextual' indeterminacy). And to an undecidability lying between a text and the things it appears to refer to as outside it (an 'extratextual' indeterminacy).

In the first of these, the idea is that all utterances are texts whose meanings – produced by the reader – are merely intersections, 'nodes' in the total text, the total 'textile', the whole web of the language of signs inseparably in operation in human experience. Books, traffic signals, advertisements and thence the objects advertised, facial expressions, bottlecaps, thrown stones, all belong to this 'archtext' that is the world of our understandings. And as such they're continually modifying each other. As the novelist Robert Pinget is often quoted as saying, 'what is said is never said since one can always say it differently'. As we write, as we read, what we do is not to find a 'finished' meaning but merely to unfold the seamless fabric of possible utterances which the text draws into the open. Or as novelist Philippe Sollers said in the 'sixties,

every text situates itself at the junction of several texts of which it is at once the rereading, the accentuation, the condensation, the displacement and the inwardness [*profondeur*]. In a certain way, the worth of a text's action amounts to its integration and destruction of other texts.[8]

Intertextual indeterminacy, then, is a function of the multiplicity of possible relations between signs. By its logic, ultimately, the reader too, as Roland Barthes says, 'this "I" which approaches the text is already itself a plurality of other texts, of codes which are infinite or, more precisely, lost'.[9]

Extratextual indeterminists will argue, on the other hand (citing the arbitrary relations between all signs and their referents as well as between every signifier and its signified), that since we discern what words signify only by their 'difference' from other words, and since they always thus bear the latent 'traces' of what they do not signify, words actually call forth not the presence of events (which they never in any case make physically present) but their 'absence'. Texts perpetually 'defer' fixed and final meanings. They generate only 'space' and move ever toward 'silence'. This isn't then a problem of the proliferation of possible 'given things', but rather it's that – in so far as a sign always only signifies something other than itself – signs, texts, always open up chasms between themselves and the things to which they seem to refer. Thus narratives by their very nature as sets of signs create nothing but themselves. And in this sense, ultimately no narrative exists but it destroys itself. (Classic expressions of these kinds of indeterminism can be found in, for example, Derrida, late Barthes and early Kristeva and Sollers, though it's not clear whether they had fixed upon differences between kinds, and for good reason – since here is but another distinction that would be forever deferred.)

So now, in our time, born out of the problem of the indeterminacy of the subject (the uncertainties of the 'who' and the 'what' of narratives) we are confronted with a vast array of fictions whose faith very often is that the most fruitful activity we can engage in, in writing and reading, is the production of utterances that act out this play of contradictions, and of infinite signification. Let's look at some examples.

A narrative may play with our expectations as to what is the proper range of view of a story. Whereas in a traditional realist novel we may be given a description of a stone building on a hill, in a novel by Robbe-Grillet in the 'fifties we might have pages of description of the stonework of a wall, repelling any idea as to the outline or shape or 'meaning of the whole' of which it's a part. Or on the other hand, we may have a narrative like the one quoted earlier by Bory, or like one called 'Genealogy' by Giles Gordon, that begins:

a man a woman a man and a woman lovers a couple a son
a family a man a woman a man and a woman lovers a couple
a son a family a man a woman a man and a woman

and for many lines the 'story' goes on in a similar way, to end:

man a man and a woman lovers a couple a mongol[10]

It's as though the text we're handed were still a 'seeing-apparatus', say a telescope, only one too blindingly powerful for the 'subject' (giving the stone wall but no sense of the 'building'), or – the reverse – a telescope turned round the 'wrong way' (giving the 'building', but reduced to a speck), its power inverted, bringing the subject to nil. We may have the thing, up close, but no sense of its status in the totality of things; or we may have a sense of that totality but it seems now too distant, simple, empty, a void.

Or there may be play with the continuity we've been led to expect. In novels by Pinget, people's and places' names change almost ad lib and, as often as not, anything reported to have occurred in the past is uniformly described as having 'happened ten years ago', putting our normal understandings of chronology and causality into disarray.

Or the text may assert things and revoke them in the same breath: 'The door of the apartment is ajar' (says a typical passage in early Robbe-Grillet), 'the apartment door is wide open, despite the late hour, the apartment door is closed . . .'. Or, in a famous passage in Beckett's *Molloy*: 'Then I went back into the house and wrote, It is midnight. The rain is beating on the windows. It was not midnight. It was not raining.'[11] Or in fiction by Sollers or Brooke-Rose, verbal shifters are made dynamically to dissolve and re-form; pronouns' antecedents oscillate so that we are repeatedly placed in a state of uncertainty (aporia) as to whether, for example, 'I' stands for a character, for the narrator, for the text itself.

Or, in novels by Calvino, Flann O'Brien, Robbe-Grillet, Beckett, the 'story' seems absolutely straightforward – only, finally, some normally crucial event (what was in realist theatre called 'the obligatory scene') is missing: a cipher, a blank is placed where in realism the central, controlling 'truth' would have been. Or, in stories by Borges, Calvino, Pinget, and many others, we may read 'the story', only then to be faced with four or five or a dozen alternative versions (or controversions) of that story within the same text.

Or the narrative may be either recursive or regressive in the way it's built; in novels by Mauriac, Butor, Calvino, Pinget, the protagonist-writer reverts to the times in which he'd written earlier parts of his narrative; there may be an endless series of false starts, or further and further reconstructions of the writer's previous novels, as seen by the writer who is a protagonist in each of those novels. The narrative may refer (regressively) to events from which the current event has sprung or (recursively) to other passages of narration (that is, of discourse) from which the current passage of discourse springs – and these may blur into one another in what is itself an imitation (always an imitation, only an imitation) of infinite regress. Or, in a multitude of novels and stories by, for example, John Barth, Borges, Pinget, O'Brien, Beckett, the narrative may seek to appear circular, as if we'd returned to just where we'd begun, as though progress or change itself were impossible. Or, for example in Nabokov, Simon, Vonnegut, Sukenick, Claude Mauriac, Sollers, Sanguineti, the very linearity which literature can never escape – the 'letters' it is made of and that must be read in series one after another – the sense of eventuation, of things happening – is denied, by a variety of strategies. As in Vonnegut's *Slaughterhouse-5* where characters fantasize novels in which 'there is no beginning, no middle, no end, no suspense, no moral, no causes, no effects'.[12]

Or the 'normal' steady relations between the narrative and the world outside it will be thrown into question: for example in the classic case in a story by Julio Cortázar ('Continuidad de los Parques') where the reader is killed by one of his characters. Or, in another way, in the case of Vonnegut's inventing for his novels a novelist-character (Kilgore Trout) who then 'authors' a novel (e.g. *Venus on the Half-Shell*) which we can buy in a bookshop, published by the writer Philip José Farmer, whose writing Vonnegut endorses.

But the revolution doesn't stop here. The strategies I've mentioned so far would get us to rethink our relation to narrative by provoking us to question our expectations as to what kinds of things ought and ought not to happen in – within – a story. If we speak of 'slaughtering the subject', it's in this sense that we might mean it; quite meticulously, many of *those expectations* have been cut down and carved up. What I'm going to suggest is that in revelling in potent strategies for the dis-integration of some of our illusions, we may have abandoned our larger critical sense in favour of yet more ominous deceptions. But let's not get ahead of the 'game'. The anti-realist revolt goes much further than I have so far declared. Writing can also propose radical alternative ways of thinking about how narratives can come into being, wholly different principles behind the very generation of what happens on the page.

Anti-realism has brought forth an idea about writing so simple that it's very difficult to apprehend at once just how powerful it is and how revolutionary it may turn out to be in the history of literature. And then, it depends on what we mean by revolution.

If narratives are really only made of language, then there's no reason why the events initiating what 'happens' in a narrative may not take place not in '*the world*' but in *the words* of its telling. What we call 'the story', then, may be a narrative not of material or of mental events, but may spring instead from occurrences at the level of the most basic units of language itself. In the idea of writing now at hand – theory purged (by writers like Barthes and Derrida) of conventional notions of some finite 'author behind the work', and buoyed by the confluence of psychological, historical, and political arguments (Lacan, Foucault, Althusser) against traditional realist conceptions of the individual as discrete psychological 'subject' – we can conceive of narrated 'character', too, of anything denoting 'personal being', as instantly constituted by the mere flow of marks on the page, and just as swiftly dissolved by it.

Writers such as Sollers, Federman, Cortázar, Pinget, Rühm, Baudry, Roche, and Brooke-Rose in her iridescently layered parodic mode – following theories from Max Müller to Noam Chomsky on the transformational dynamics of language, braced by the speculative investment in wordplay of, for example, Saussure, and girded with technical strategies engineered by Dada/Futurism/ Surrealism for the disruption and reconstruction of illusion – will build narratives out of bare grammatical and phonetic permutations, lexical variants, orthographic and typographic shifts, and algorithmic manipulations of verbal text according to non-locutionary arithmetical and mechanical procedures such as the arbitrary tabular distribution of text and cut-and-paste collage. The 'motivation' of writing moves from the wearily (and always-at-best hybridly) mimetic to the frankly, wholly, rapturously diegetic. A famous humble quick illustration concocted in English (and highly reminiscent of Müller) is described by Jonathan Culler: the narrative sequence 'the sons raise meat' can by rapid conversion produce an entirely new 'story': 'the sun's rays meet'.[13] Whole novels can be generated by any of a multitude of similar rule-plays (here, one provoked in the ever-present push-pull between spelling and hearing regimes), bespeaking not a 'primary outside world' of events which the words merely 're-present', but out of a 'no man's land' of words – which *may* then evoke, secondarily, such a world beyond, *if* we're disposed to see it (read it) that way. I was going to say 'if we wish', but that's another story and we'll come to it.

The direction is unmistakable. As Stephen Heath put it, writing's project now would be 'not the mirroring of some "Reality" . . . but an attention to the forms of intelligibility in which the real is produced, a dramatization of possibilities of language'.[14] And, we might add, the continual probing of the possibility that (as Vygotsky and Voloshinov/Bakhtin would declare) thought – and indeed that 'reality' of which our thinking tells us – may not exist outside language. So, if our perennial idea that a narrative is about someone, about something, and by a clear someone – if this is deposed, liquidated – Narration itself is made god, reified. 'It is from itself, from its own substance,' says Raymond Federman, 'that the fictitious discourse will proliferate.'[15] Flaubert's dream of writing a book without a subject, about nothing, is finally realized. As Barthes proclaims of a novel by Sollers, 'It is Narration that speaks . . . . The voice is not here the instrument, even depersonalized, of a secret'; the essence attained is not that of a person. The voice is, Barthes says, 'that of literature'.[16] Thus Narration is All. What counts is not what's told, the '*histoire*'s' events, but the eventuation of the '*discours*', the experience of the telling.

It would be perverse to treat casually the enormous attractions of principles like these as background to the act of writing, for writers now. More far-reaching claims will be made for them by their proponents in critical theory than many of the fictionalists themselves raise. There is the obvious mesmeric appeal of the apparently paradoxical: the idea that writing both creates itself out of itself and destroys itself as it goes along; that naming people/places/things lays their absence before us and opens the way toward everything that the text doesn't say; that uttering makes silence. And there's the unparalleled fluidity and freedom promised the writer by the conception that no rules whatsoever need logically govern a narrative – such as those affecting time, place, action, causality, identity – beyond the apparent rules of language itself (and these themselves are always changing, being changed by the activity of our uttering). With a single blow, writing is liberated, in theory, from all the strictures that have bound literature on the one hand to cultural, ideological conventions, and on the other hand to so-called 'natural' material reality. Like a computer virus, by writerly fiat the variation of a single letter (displacing an induced expectation, infecting it with alternatives) may spread its effects throughout a text, playing creative havoc with stories, meanings, breeding new ones as it goes. And writing, now – sheer surface, without 'depth' or 'immanent meaning' – can hope to be pure. Or, seen another way, the text is so seamlessly interwoven with all utterances – from which what we call reality itself is inseparable – that questions not merely of 'fictionality' versus 'truth' but of referentiality versus non-referentiality dissolve altogether. In the absence of a rule by which to discern 'inside' from 'outside' (*hors-texte, hors-la-loi*) all writing becomes innocent.

Can there be such a thing as a pure, innocent text?

It used to be customary – in academe and on the street – to remind one another that it was intelligent 'not to confuse X with Y'. Now it's the convention that it's intelligent to say that we 'can't separate X from Y'. In those days one 'differentiated', now we 'defer'. We have a new meaning for the word 'coherence'. Everything's 'stuck' to everything else – but now, the more 'coherence' the less 'meaning'. Strikingly, out of this proud, seemingly fierce sceptical heroism – in the stoic relinquishment of easy categories, of boundaries – there emerges an often unconfessed metaphysic, an occultist vision, that a Coleridge might have called 'esemplastic': the dream (of which there is unexpected evidence in the work of writers as diverse as Sollers, Borges, Pynchon, Calvino, Fuentes) that everything, that All, is One. Whether we feel it's the sceptic or the mystic that's on top, we can't help but notice that there is here an impulse, often formalist (in search of the formly) if not explicitly aestheticist, that must in theory disavow, disallow – that is, infinitely 'defer' – commitment to earthly, material action beyond the cult of the play of infinite signification. But in practice, does it work that way?

However 'pure' it may seem, however it appears not to tell us 'about' anything (renounces 'subject', in the sense both of the *what* and the *who* 'behind' utterances), every narration visibly represses another narration, the narration it leaves out, an alternative construction of signs. One of the by-products of theory's exhortation that we stop settling easily on what books seem to 'say' (constatively) is the acute realization that we must start looking more closely at what books (performatively) 'do'. This has as much bearing on 'subject-free, story-less narrations' as on any other. Every so-called 'pure linguistic transformation' is the expression of some rule; and every text that seeks to bury its rules expresses commitment to the rule of burial – the ritual of burial, of concealment, as recommended activity. If, as indeterminists, we say these rules are determined by the reader, each reader differently, we're relying, of course, on the rule that readings are bound to their contexts. Troublesome as it seems, we can't show that a text is indeterminate, in general, without committing ourselves to proving that in any actual reading it is bound to its context, that it is determinate. And we can't apply this rule asymmetrically, to readers, without applying it to writers – first (but far from only) because every writer is first and foremost his or her own reader. No writing, then – and no writer – is innocent. Every narration is someone's model of how to behave: of the kinds of things to say to ourselves and to each other, of what comes first, what comes last, what doesn't matter, and what shouldn't be said or thought at all, at least not in public.

An endlessly awkward phenomenon for theorists of art and literature has been the world's abiding lack of interest – in spite of all our vast and costly efforts to educate it – in that evergreen issue: whether works of art are to be held as mimetic or not. As though it were 'purely academic'. This indifference is not a reflection, but it's a matching counterpart, of the fact that in such speculations we have probably always been looking in the wrong direction, have continually misconceived, asked the wrong questions, about referentiality. There is an important sense in which writing never informs us of any fixed (about some past, prior-to-the-text) truth; that it only in-forms our way of thinking about things, that it shapes, *re-models*, our sense of truth – *in the present, as we read it, and for the future* – as we go along. In this respect, there is very little difference indeed between anything we may call 'referential' writing and anything we may call 'pure' writing. Virtually, their effects are identical. They – both, and always – reform the terms of our thinking.

The outcome could have been predicted. One of the great disappointments in late twentieth-century sceptical literary theory and the fiction it has produced, for those of us who were so excited about it, has occurred not in writing's failure to represent 'the outside world', but in its failure, no matter how hard it has tried, not to represent it. Writing's utter inability to stay out of the world, out of readers' thoughts about the world; writing's inability to avoid implicating itself, its reader, and its writer, by its every utterance, in the world – to avoid getting its hands dirty. (We should never have any trouble in perceiving that every 'metafictional' exercise – any semantic-ambiguative strategy, self-reflexive, circular, regressive or recursive discourse, assertion/negation patterning, parataxis, nesting/*mise-en-abîme*, metalepsis, each 'non-semantic regulatory mechanism', et cetera, of which I've spoken in detail elsewhere – can only ever be a metaphor for and never an achievement of the escape from this dilemma, never the Pontian handwashing of which the text dreams. While we're free to treat them as troubling the stability of reference, the more we distinguish texts as purely (internally, linguistically) transformational or as metafictional, the more we are also making them into writings specifically and consistently *about* – fantasies of – power and escape.) And we are afflicted by such otherwise challenging writing's incapacity to lay responsibility at society's door without finding a rationale for denying its own responsibility. Radical thinking may for instance say to its conservative opponents, 'You're a historical phenomenon; look to your history, and see if you haven't died'. Yet, what about those of us who cut our teeth on radical indeterminism in literature – where do we stand? Are postmodernist, poststructuralist forms of indeterminism, for example, so fresh and final as to stand outside history?

What we call 'poststructuralism' was well on its way by 1967, with the publication of Derrida's *De la Grammatologie* and *L'Ecriture et la Différence*. That's 20 years ago, before people going up to university now were born. What we call 'postmodernism' – inasmuch as the word makes sense – was solidly set out with the publication of Sarraute's *L'Ere du Soupçon* (1956) and the first essays (1953) Robbe-Grillet was later to include in *Pour un Nouveau Roman*. Indeed, the seminal lectures and essays dismembering the unified subject by Lacan had already been in circulation a dozen years by 1949 – some four decades ago now, at the same moment that Samuel Beckett was doing his major work in the dissolution of the narrative 'I' in fiction (in *Molloy*, *Malone Dies*, *The Unnamable*). In Russia Mikhail Bakhtin had already invoked the possibilities in the 1920s, and fictionalists as far-flung as Nabokov, O'Brien, and Borges were making ample and explicit *tentatives* in these directions in the 1930s. The *parents* of students going to university hadn't been born then.

The movement for the dismantling of the subject (in both its senses) and all that we come to associate with it that it is customary to call 'radical' in narrative writing is now, by all standards, middle-aged. Far from promoting the permanent revolution it had proclaimed in the 1960s, it's an established tradition. Like many things middle-aged, it's not quite so nimble as it once appeared, it's developing the suggestion of a metaphysical paunch, and it shows signs of a mid-life crisis; it does break out in unexpected hot flushes, hoarse hysteria, myopia, and the general display of nervous defence mechanisms and tics of an idea no longer quite sure of its own sex-appeal. It has done more to provoke the speculative imagination than any other movement in literature since romanticism, perhaps since the cluster of traditions that produced Dante. We have yet to learn all that we've learned and have still to learn from it; and there's definitely no turning back the clock, as colleagues and friends in British universities seem to hope to do. But there may be a thing or two that need saying about its place in our world.

As against traditional realist approaches, radical writing about narrative as well as within narrative today devotes vital attention, yes, not to the 'truth or falsity' of specific works of fiction but to the uncovering of the fictionality in all that used to be called 'non-fiction'. One thing we largely fail to consider is the particular *utility* this line of attack may have for those of us employed to talk about literature, in a world of pragmata in which our talk is increasingly accused of being of no practical use. Just hazarding a guess: could we imagine a better way to shore up the status, the credentials of our salaried dabbling with fictions – against the claims of, say, science and technology – than by neutralizing or purging the truth-test from the realm of worthwhile intellectual endeavour? Is it possible that, beyond its ostensibly 'neutral truths', indeterminism may have its instrumental uses, for the literary community that makes a show of it, just as scientific communities – that uncovered it first – find it useful to ignore it in their everyday practice?

We can imagine a story on this subject, a history. Judging by the names of the writers I've mentioned, one might wager that sceptical indeterminism may initially have been largely the post-war Continental European cry of intellectual sub-cultures sensing themselves washing adrift from an 'operable' universe where civilized decisions had material effect. And that where in America kindred indeterminist thinking took root, it did so in exactly those straitened circles suffering the same malaise, the speculative humanist departments of literature, language, and philosophy – while their flourishing and well-endowed counterparts in the very same universities, those 'hard-science' cadres, sat giggling in the back-waft of all that cobweb-soft fuss about poetry sussuring up from across the quad. A new generation of professionals in letters – finding it tactically unpromising to respond by threatening to withdraw their labour from the world (an offer some institutions might find it hard to refuse) – would by a series of instinctive speculative and discursive manoeuvres withdraw the world from the realm of effective substantive action, professing it wasn't there at all except as a shadowplay of undecidable signs, the proper grist of their very own mill.

The theme is tempting. The literature department – the shelter and principal living of the vast majority of writers-in-revolt in the Western world – under fire for endlessly dragging down from its attics those captured and mounted fictions of yesteryear (its *Paradise Lost*, its *Rape of the Lock*, its *Faerie Queene*), now rushes to appear first to say 'Let us move from the product to the process'. We can only be glad: at long last we're free of the phoney commodification of Literature as a product, that sacred merchandise, the Literary Canon – and with it the confraternity of priests, its custodians and sole authorized dealers who (for the price of a university degree) taught us how to consume it. The Canon, let's say, is gone and good riddance. But what of the marketplace? Is all that swept away too? Is it really true, the rumour we hear, that all 'creative writers' and all literature PhDs are now driving taxis in Milwaukee?

Not quite. The champions of subject-free, storyless narrations, both fictionalists and critics – whose vital function is to problematize meanings, to profilerate more multiplex readings – we're alive and well and delivering lavishly imbursed lectures, doing just these things before packed houses of university students in New York, Rome, Berkeley, Paris, Oxford – and Milwaukee. Our shops overflow with our work: books whose role it is to process books. Not the Word but the word-processor is made flesh – the commodity in demand.

The scenario I've just offered is of course aimed to provoke. At a recent conference a leading British proponent of Derridean deconstructionism, in a spirit of fraternity, took me to task for trying it on, charging me – this will strike as surprising some readers only superficially familiar with deconstructionist thinking – with cynicism. It is incidental that he himself, with Derrida, had already energetically documented an array of uses to which corporate business, government, and the military have in recent years sought to put deconstructionist-orientated academics, for potent wages. What I was getting at then (and now), rather, was not that here was some venal self-interest on the part of writers posing as radical outsiders beyond the mêlée, but – quite differently – that such writers have long now been regarded as those 'on the inside', as the upwardly mobile among 'cultural operators'. And that, in a new academe accorded so headily responsible a place, our *auto*critique – the unwrapping and grappling with the full motives and implications of our 'revolutionary' practices – is long overdue. Not only from within 'the system' but undisguisedly from within the very language we use. Let it begin, we could say, by telling tales on ourselves, and testing the strength of reality's (or 'other' discourses') resistance to them.

The sense of what I'm saying thus requires that I speak 'personally'. My discourse is of an interpretive kind, attributing determinable decisions to what the texts I've referred to say, rather than simply 'letting them be' as instances of the infinite play of signification. It's an irrationally rationalistic (and, it should be noticed, anthropocentric) social and political gesture. And in the long run it is so because I prefer it to be so, because it fits best my definition of myself as subject and the narrative – the life-narrative – that I like for myself. Some of the reasons for my appropriating this narrative are still unknown to me; many are at cross-purposes; none can be defined without reference to society and language and the myths of free self which they induce; all are unquestionably trivial against the background of the ultimate inanity of human normative thinking. But within the frame of reference drawn when indeterminism is claimed to provide a tool of critique, it's literally legitimate for me to say that with any forthright and consistent obliteration of the idea of the experiencing, acting subject – of discrete persons as agents of discrete events and intentions – or with any description of the subject as simply a manifestation of impersonal collective forces, we can't hope either to account intelligibly for change, explain to ourselves how we feel ourselves to be in disagreement with someone else, or hold anyone responsible for his or her acts. Not only do social interaction and political action become incomprehensible; so – if watched closely – does the notion of indeterminacy itself.

We need, then, to notice that the term 'radical writing' can point to at least two quite different kinds of beliefs: one about writing that addresses the roots of writing itself, and another about writing that claims to strike at the root (social, for example) of things 'outside' the text. It has been a commonplace to proclaim that, there being nothing 'outside the text', the first sort has the effect of the second sort; that it generates a critique. All writing when read alters the fabric of the language in which it's inserted, and so plays a transformative role. But nothing is 'criticism' that doesn't nominate some crisis – whether it proposes solutions or not. And this is something that a writing deeply implicated with a notion of All-is-One indeterminism – fictional or theoretical – cannot do. It may be time to ask whether we're not behaving disingenuously when we pretend that such an idea of 'radical writing' supplies the conditions (a 'logic', say) for literary, social, political, or any other kind of criticism we can name. Meanwhile, writers pleased to have their texts regarded as saying anything and everything, or as saying (equally) the inverse of what they 'superficially appear' to desire to say, or who relish being treated as free of responsibility and indeed as gratuitous and fortunately painlessly removable spurious appendages of their texts, can rest content. The restless others will prepare to take corrective action, knowing that 'the Reader' for whom the infinite play of equal significations could be a reality is itself a fiction, the outgrowth of a local historical intellectual delirium from which it is within culture's power to awaken.

Notes

1 John Peter (1986) 'Beastly to be there', *The Sunday Times*, 9 November, review of M. Kundera's *Life is Elsewhere*. © Times Newspapers Ltd.

2 Jean-François Bory (1973) 'Post-scriptum', trans. D. Higgins, in Richard Kostelanetz (ed.) *Breakthrough Fictioneers: An Anthology*, West Glover, Vt.: Something Else Press, 38–41.

3 Mas'ud Zavarzadeh (1976) *The Mythopoeic Reality*, Urbana, Ill.: University of Illinois Press, 17, 30, 19; Zavarzadeh's quotation is from J. Ellul (1964) *The Technological Society*, New York: Knopf, 79.

4 Alain Robbe-Grillet (1957) 'Sur quelques notions périmées', first printed in book form in *Pour un Nouveau Roman* (1963) Paris: Gallimard; trans. B. Wright (1965) as 'On some outdated notions', *Snapshots and Towards a New Novel*, London: Calder and Boyars, 62, 60.

5 Annette Lavers (1982) *Roland Barthes: Structuralism and After*, London: Methuen, 178.

6 Nathalie Sarraute (1956) *L'Ere du Soupçon*, Paris: Gallimard; trans. M. Jolas (1963) in *Tropisms and the Age of Suspicion*, London: John Calder, 88.

7 Christine Brooke-Rose (1975) *Thru*, London: Hamish Hamilton, 69.

8 Philippe Sollers (1968) *Théorie d'Ensemble*, Paris: Editions du Seuil, 75 (translation mine).

9 Roland Barthes (1970) *S/Z*, Paris: Editions du Seuil; trans. R. Howard (1974) London: Jonathan Cape, 10.

10 Giles Gordon (1973) 'Genealogy', in Richard Kostelanetz (ed.) *Breakthrough Fictioneers: An Anthology*, West Glover, Vt.: Something Else Press, 15.

11 Alain Robbe-Grillet (1965) *La Maison de Rendez-vous*, Paris: Gallimard; trans. R. Howard, *The House of Assignation*, New York, 1966, London, 1970, 151. Samuel Beckett (1959) *Molloy, Malone Dies, The Unnamable: A Trilogy*, Paris: Olympia Press, 240.

12 Kurt Vonnegut Jr. (1970) *Slaughterhouse-5*, London: Panther, 62.

13 Jonathan Culler (1975) *Structuralist Poetics: Structuralism, Linguistics and the Study of Literature*, London: Routledge & Kegan Paul, 107.

14 Stephen Heath (1972) *The Nouveau Roman: A Study in the Practice of Writing*, London: Elek, 22.

15 Raymond Federman (1981) *Surfiction: Fiction Now . . . and Tomorrow*, Chicago: Swallow Press, 11.

16 Roland Barthes (1979) *Sollers Ecrivain*, Paris: Editions du Seuil, 21 (translation mine).

Index

Abelson, John 108–9, 114, 120
accountability 201
acquaintance principle 142
'actantial' model 34
actants 34, 36
acteurs 34, 36
actors (discovery narratives) 106–9,
   115–16
'adenovirus story' 108, 113, 117,
   120, 121
aesthetic reading 16
Althusser, Louis 202
American realism 24, 38
analytic dialogue 56, 58
analytic reflection 67–8
analytic theory 56–7
Annual Review of Biochemistry
   108–9
anti-foundationalist theories
   143–4
anti-realism 137, 138, 144, 151,
   206–12
aporia 72, 207
'archtext' 205
artificiality 192
assessment: personal character
   90–4; of probabilitiess 27–8;
   scientific claims 94–9; truth-
   claims 28
audience 12–13, 45, 148; as actors
   107–8, 118–19; addressee 162,
   165

Austen, Jane 19, 196; *Emma* 163,
   166; *Pride and Prejudice* 167
Austin, J.L. 155–8, 168, 170
author 204; dual voice theory 161,
   163–4, 166–8, 170; –reader
   relations 193–5
'authorial audience' 12–13
authorial comment 160, 182
authority 164, 182, 197
autobiography 56, 57, 65–6, 75
autonomy 72, 75
Avers, C.J. 109, 114

'bad guys' 89–94, 96
Bakhtin, Mikhail 213
Banfield, Ann 156, 157, 160,
   161–8
Barthes, Roland 137, 170, 204,
   205, 210
battle theory (of trials) 35–7
Beckett, Samuel 169; *Molloy* 207,
   213
beliefs 52, 59–61, 63–4, 68, 135–6
benevolence 190, 191
Bennett, W.L. 28–31, 37, 43–4
Bentham, Jeremy 140–1, 142–3
Benveniste, Emile 156, 160, 161,
   162
Berget, S.M. 120
Berk, A.J. 120
Berzelius, J.J. 92
'Big Ell' 86–9, 94, 98, 100

biography 56, 57, 150
biological explanations 5–6
Boccaccio, Giovanni, *The Decameron* 181
Bohr, Niels 18
Booth, Wayne C. 164
Bory, Jean-François 199–200, 206
Brannigan, Augustine 102
Broker, T.R. 119
Brooke-Rose, Christine 207; *Thru* 204
Brooks, Peter, *Reading for the Plot* 7
Browning, Robert, *The Ring and the Book* 108
Bruns, Gerald 11
Bullough, Sir George 39
business cycles 7

Camus, Albert, *L'Etranger* 169
case presentation (narrative in) 24–7
causality of fate/tragedy 55, 70–6
Cech, T. 104–5, 115–17, 121
Cell 103, 105, 110, 111, 119
Cervantes, Miguel de 188, 190, 191, 192; *Don Quixote* 179, 180–7
chain novel 44–5
Chambon, Pierre 108, 119
'character', characterization 84, 201–4
characters 160, 168–9, 170
Chaucer, Geoffrey, *The Canterbury Tales* 181
childhood experience 61–2
chivalric romance 180, 181–7
Chomsky, Noam 46–7, 164, 168, 209
Chow, L.T. 119
chronology (of discovery) 110–15, 116
Cold Spring Harbor 104–8, 110–14, 118–19
Collins, H.M. 91, 93
commodification 215
common-sense knowledge 29, 42

common law trials 35–7
communal form of life 174
communication 52, 57, 71, 73, 74
communications model 160, 161, 165, 168
conduct-guiding force 95
'configurational' meaning 175–6
connectedness 149
consciousness 52, 67, 195, 197, 204; reflexive 162, 163; self 72, 74, 75, 76
consensus 52, 192
constructivist theory 143–4, 145
context of culture 84
contracts 39–42; narrative 175–8, 179, 193, 196
conventions (and genres) 16–20
'conversational' constraints 146
correspondence theory 143–6, 151
Cortázar, Julio 208
'counter-evidence' 164–8
'credibility' 93
Crick, Francis 102, 114, 118
critique (self-reflection) 66–70
'cross examination' 36
Culler, Jonathan 155, 209
cultural consensus 192
culture, context of 84
curiosity (pertinence) 179, 180–7

dada 209
Dante Alighieri 214
Darnell 112, 113, 114
de Beaugrande, R. 32–3
decentring (subject) 203–4
decision-making: case presentation 24–7; judicial 38–42; justification (narrative in) 42–5
deconstructionism 192, 215
deep level (text) 33, 34, 36–7, 44
deictics 161, 162, 164, 168, 169
deindexicalization 99
Denning, Lord (Alfred Thompson) 24–6, 41
depth hermeneutics 51–5
Derrida, Jacques 155, 168, 170, 202, 213, 215

Index

Descartes, René 135–6, 146; *Discourse* 132
description, fictionality in 139–40, 142–3
'deviant' judgments 26
Dickens, Charles 191, 192, 193; *David Copperfield* 44–5
Diderot, Denis 192
direct discourse 157
direct speech 157, 158, 164, 166–7; free 169, 170
disagreement (sources) 10–13, 14, 20
discipline (as actor) 108–9
discours 156, 158, 160, 161, 210
discovery narratives: actors 106–9; first reports 105–6; popularizations 115–21; processes 102–5; sequences 110–15
discriminations 190, 191, 192
dispositional state 63–4
'distancing' 148, 158, 159
DNA, *see* discovery narratives
doctrine, legal 38, 41, 43, 45
'documentary comic book' 117–18, 119
dual-voice theory 161, 163–4, 166–8, 170
dualism 177
duties (and rights) 141
Dworkin, Ronald 43–5

economics, storytelling in: advantages 20–1; conventions 16–20; disagreements (sources) 10–13; explanations 5–10; moral order 14–15; reader's role 16; structural approach 13–14
efferent reading 16
egocentricity 85
Eliot, George 192, 193; *Felix Holt* 159
elision 177
emancipation 52, 53, 54–5, 58, 74–5

emotion 191, 196, 197; thought and therapy 58–66, 68–9; *see also* feeling
'emotivism' 189
empirical realism 136, 144
empiricism 141, 184
endophora 84
Enlightenment 75, 174, 196
énoncé–énonciation distinction 162
epistemological: conception 33–5, 65–7, 84, 94; fictions 134, 140, 143–6
epistemology 97, 98, 151
erklären 7
eukaryotic genes 112, 113, 114, 115
events, make-believe 149
existentialism 194–5, 197
exophora 84–5, 89
expectations 30, 186, 206–8
experiences 178, 181, 194, 205
explanations 5–10, 53
explicitness (lack of) 11

fabula/sjuzhet 156
'fact secpticism' 38
'facticity' 81, 99
facts (presentation) 24–7
'facts of narrative consistenct' 44
factual discourse 138
factuality 81
faith 81–4, 91
'fallibilism' 96, 97
false consciousness 67
'false' theories 87
fantasy 17, 136
Farmer, Philip José 208
fate 55, 70–6
Federman, Raymond 210
feeling, fiction and 179–80, 188–96; *see also* emotion; sentiment
Feldman, M.S. 28–31, 37, 43–4
Felman, Shoshana 155
fictionality: limits *see* invention, narrative and; in object and description 139–4
'fictionalizing' narrative 138

fictions: epistemological 134, 140, 143–6; feeling and 179–80, 188–96; logical 134, 140–3; make-believe 134, 143, 147–50; in philosophy 140–6
fictive stance 147–8, 149, 150
fictive utterances 147, 148
Fielding, Henry 192
first reports (discovery narratives) 105–6
Flaubert, Gustave 210; *Madame Bovary* 160, 202
Fleck, L. 99
folk tales 13, 14, 34, 35
fonctions 34
form (narrative) 54–5, 148–9
Forster, E.M., *A Room With a View* 159, 162
Foucault, Michel 202
foundationalist theories 143–4
fraud 39–42
free direct speech 169, 170
free indirect discourse 156, 158
Freud, Sigmund 51, 53–4, 58, 66–7, 70–3
futurism 209

Gadamer, H.G. 52, 58
Genette, Gérard 156, 158, 167
genres (and conventions) 16–20
Gibson, Walker 12
Gilbert, G.N. 93, 94, 114
Gissing, George, R. 193
Gödel, Kurt 200
Goffman, Erving 96
'good guys' 86–9, 96–7
Goodenough, Ursula 114
Goodman, Nelson 134, 144–5, 147
Gordon, Giles 206
Greimas, A.J. 23, 29, 33, 34, 36, 37, 44, 47

Habermas, Jürgen 51–5, 57–61, 64–6, 68, 70–5
Haley, Alex, *Roots* 178
Hamburger, Käte 162
Hanson, N.R. 94

Harberger, A.C. 14
Hardy, Barbara 175–6, 177, 188
Harré, Rom 88–9, 92, 201
Harrison, Ross 141
Harrison, T. 120
Heath, Stephen 209
Hegel, G.W.F. 68, 70, 71, 72–3
Heisenberg, Werner K. 200
hermeneutics (depth) 51–5, 75
Hexter, J.H. 7–8
histoire 156, 160, 161, 210
historical narrative 18
historical reality 73
history 51, 73, 75, 149–50, 177–8, 179, 181
Holton, G. 87
Homer 176
hybridization 110, 111, 117, 118
hypothesis 86, 87, 88, 92

ideal speech situation 51, 74
idealism 136, 145, 180, 184
ignorance 66–7, 68
illocution 157
illocutionary force 82
illocutions *see* narrative techniques
illusions 135, 136, 146, 209
images (popularizations) 117–18, 119
implicit contract (narrative) 175–6
'incomplete symbols' 142
indeterminacy 204–6, 211, 213–14, 216–17
indirect speech 157, 158, 164
inductive indexicality 92, 94
inductive reasoning 144–5
inductive support 85, 88, 92
industrial revolution 7
information processing 32–3
information transfer 119–20
insertion sequences 116
internalization (narrative rules) 42–3
interpretation: discovery and 102–3, 119, 120; hermeneutics 52–5, 57–9, 62, 63
invention, narrative and 131–51

ironic distance 159
irony 161, 167, 170
'irrealism' 144
Iser, Wolfgang 19

Jackson, Bernard S., *Law, Fact and Narrative Coherence* 38
Johnson, N.S. 32–3, 35
jokes (exclusion) 155
Joyce, James, *Ulysses* 159, 160
judicial decision-making 38–45
jury trials 28–31
justification of legal decisions 42–5

Kant, Immanuel 71, 74, 75, 136, 143–4, 151
Keane, Thomas 8
Keegan, John, *The Face of Battle* 18
Kennedy, Edward M. 8–9
Keynes, J.M. 20
Keynesianism 10, 14
Klamer, Arjo 19
Knorr-Cetina, K. 94
knowledge: common-sense 29, 42; constructivist theory 143–4; scientific 95–6, 97, 103; social 29–30, 33, 38
Kucia, Mark 82
Kundera, Milan 199–200
Kuroda, S.-Y. 162

La Fontaine, Jean de 162
Lacan, Jacques 202, 213
language 46–7, 145–6; disagreement and 11–12; *see also* narrative techniques
Latour, B. 90–5 *passim* 99
Lavers, Annette 204
Lavoie, Don 6
law construction 38–42
Lawrence, D.H. 193–6
l'écriture 168
legal decisions 42–5
legal discourse: law construction 38–42; narrative (uses) 23–7; narrative and assessment of

problems 27–8; narrative competence 45–8; narrative as epistemological/semiotic conception 33–5; narrative in justification 42–5; narrative and plausibility 28–31; narrative of psychological processes 31–3; narrativization of pragmatics 35–7
legal doctrine 38, 41, 43, 45
legal reasoning 43
'level of manifestation' 33, 36
Lévi-Strauss, Claude 14
life: communal form 174; moral 68–9, 70–1, 174, 189–90, 196–7; narrative and 176–7, 179, 182, 188, 192, 193, 197; responsiveness to 180, 194–6
literalism 192
literary critics 44, 45
literary example (fictionality) 132–4
literary indeterminism 204
literary realism 137
literary theory 135–8
literature, philosophy and 154–6
literature expectations 206–8; 'pure' writing 210–12; radical writing 212–17; subject in 199–203; 'transformational' writing 208–10; indeterminacy 204–6
lived temporality 174, 175, 178
Llewellyn, Karl 43
Llosa, M.V., *The Real Life of Alejandro Mayta* 132–4, 137, 146, 149–50
Locke, John 141, 143–4
locution 157
logic 86–9, 94, 98, 100
logical atomism 140, 142
logical fictions 134, 140–3
logocentric tradition 155, 168
Lorenzer, Alfred 60
love 71, 72

McCloskey, Donald N. 7, 10
MacCormick, Neil 27–8

MacIntyre, Alisdair, *After Virtue* 174–7, 179, 188–9, 192, 193, 196
make-believe fictions 134, 143, 147–50
Mandler, J. 32–3, 35
Marx, Jean L. 108, 113
Marxism 10, 11, 202
mathematical economics 15, 21
meaning 53, 141, 173; configurational 175–6
meaningfulness 55, 56, 174, 176
Medawar, Peter 17
memory 32–3, 149
Mendel, Gregor 6, 7
'metafictional' texts 212, 213
metaphors 5–6, 7, 9, 15
metaphysics 62, 74, 134–8, 145, 146, 151
metapsychology 51, 53–4, 66, 73
methodological solipsism 136
Miller, G.W. 32–3
Millikan, R.A. 87–8
Mill, J.S. 165
mind-dependence 151
Mink, Louis 175–7, 188
Mises, Ludwig von 6
models and modelling 5–7, 9
modernism 137, 173, 176, 193
modernity 76
monetarism 10, 14
moral: corruption (signs) 89–94, 96–7; life 68–71, 174, 189–90, 196–7; order 14–15, 93, 94–9; philosophy 179–80; reasoning 14–15
motivation 15, 209
Mulkay, Michael 13, 18, 93, 94
Müller, Max 209
multiple narrative 181, 184, 186, 188
myth 15, 173, 176

narrative: assessment of probabilities and 27–8; 'audience' 12–13; authority 164, 182, 197; 'coherence' 27–8, 37;

competence 45–8; contracts 177–8, 179, 193, 196; conventions *see* scientific discourse (narrative conventions); curiosity and 179–87; of discovery *see* discovery narratives; epistemo-logical/semiotic conception 33–5; excess 54; explanation 5, 7–8; feeling and 179–80; form 54–5, 148–9; invention and *see* invention, narrative and; justification of legal decisions 42–5; language *see* language; multiple 181, 184, 186, 188; negotiation 45–8; plausibility and 28–31; praxis 54, 65; 'primordial nature' of 196–7; in psychoanalysis *see* psychoanalysis; of psychological processes 31–3; reason 55–8; role (in judicial decision-making 38–42; rules 42–3; of structure 29–35, 85, 131–4, 149; style 164–8; sub- 181, 182, 189; syntagm 34, 36; term (use) 172–80; theories and legal discourse *see* legal discourse; uses 23–7
narrative techniques: anti-realist 206–10; literature and philosophy 154–6; narrative style 164–8; represented speech and thought 168–70; speech 155–62; thought 162–3
narrativization of pragmatics 35–7, 47–8
narrativized discourse 167
narrator 131, 148, 159, 165, 192 dual-voice theory 161, 163–4, 166–8, 170
naturalism 53, 60–1, 63, 176
Nature 107–8, 112, 119
'neurotic' feelings 59–60
New Criticism 154
New Scientist 108, 113, 119
news articles 108

Nietzsche, Friedrich 76, 170, 174
non-fictional narrative 135, 146,
   214
non-referentiality 210
non-reflective perception,
   consciousness 156, 162, 163
non-semantic regulatory
   mechanism 212
norms 52
nostalgia 149

object 204; fictionality in 139–40,
   145; objectification 197;
   objective world 151; objectivism
   60–1; objects (make-believe)
   148, 149
Ogden, C.K. 141
ontology 139, 140, 144, 151
origin/originator 204
otherness 72

pain and punishment 141
paintings, reality in 46, 47–8
paraphrase 141, 142, 143
parody 161
passé simple 161–2, 169
Pasteur, Louis 88–9
Paterson, Alan 38
Pauling, Linus 12
perlocution 157
person, personal character 90–4,
   201–4
Peter, John 199–200
phatic act 157
philosophy: fictions in 140–6; and
   literature 154–6; of science 95–9
phonetic act 157
phonocentric tradition 168
picaresque 180
'picture picture' of language
   146
Pinget, Robert 205, 206
Plato 154–5, 168
plausibility, narrative and 28–31
pleasurable response 190–1
plot 8, 13–14, 16, 131; structures
   55

Poe, Edgar Allan, 'The purloined
   letter' 120
point of view 131, 167
Polanyi, Michael 82
Popper, Karl 82, 96
popularization (discovery
   narratives) 103, 104, 114,
   115–21
positivism 178
postmodernism 173, 182, 213
poststructuralism 213
pragmatics, narrativization of
   35–7, 47–8
pragmatism 54, 138, 145, 147–8;
   courtroom 30–1
primordial function *see* narrative,
   'primordial nature' of
private identity 203
privatization 59
probabilities, assessment of 27–8
*Proceedings of the National
   Academy of Sciences* 103, 105,
   110
propositional content 149
Propp, Vladimir 13, 14, 33, 34
psychoanalysis: causality of fate
   and tragedy 70–6; critique (self-
   reflection) 66–70; depth
   hermeneutics 51–5; emotion,
   thought and therapy 58–66;
   narrative reason 55–8
psychology and narrative 31–3,
   51–77, 203–4
punishment and pain 141
pure theory 17
'pure' writing 210–12

quasi-causal mechanisms 52
Quine, W.V.O. 142, 144, 157

Rabinowitz, Peter 12
radical writing 212–17
reader: –author relations 193–5;
   role 12, 16, 193–5, 211–12
reading: aesthetic 16; efferent 16;
   theory of 10–12
real, theory of (empiricism) 141–2

realism 146, 178, 180–1, 192;
American 24, 38; anti- 137,
138, 144, 151, 208–10;
empirical 136, 144; naïve 193,
203, 204; psychoanalysis and
62–3, 66–8
realist fiction 17, 18, 178, 179,
199–203
reality 17, 20, 52, 73, 137, 151;
paintings 46, 47–8
realization (logic of) 58
reason (narrative) 55–8
reasoning: inductive 144–5; legal
43; moral 14–15
recognition 71–2
referentiality 210, 212
reflective perception, consciousness
156, 162–4
relativism 193, 197
relevance 202; legal 26–7
reliability 83, 90, 93
representation 62, 65;
hermeneutics 52–5; of reality
151
represented speech 156, 158–70
represented thought 156, 159–65,
168–70
repression 58–9, 66, 67, 70, 71
research community: as actor
107–8; 'bad guys' 89–94, 96;
'good guys' 86–9, 96–7
responsiveness 180, 194–5, 196
results (hypothesis-testing) 85, 88,
90, 93
'retail constraints' 146
review articles 113–14
rhetic act 157
rhetorical presentation (cases) 24–7
Ricardo, David 9, 14
Richardson, Samuel, *Clarissa*
189–90, 195–6
rights and duties 141
Robbe-Grillet, Alain 169, 203–4,
206, 213
Rogers, John 108, 113, 119
romance 180, 181–7
Rorty, Richard 60, 145–6

Rosenblatt, Louise 16
Rosenfield, Israel 117
Ross, John 164
'rule scepticism' 38
rules: narrative (internalization)
42–3; philosophy of science
95–9
Russell, Bertrand 140, 141–3, 144
Ruthven, K.K. 17

Sambrook, J. 108, 112, 119
Samuelson, Paul 12
Sarraute, Nathalie 169, 204, 213
Saussure, Ferdinand de 13
'scenic understanding' 60
scepticism 38, 136, 145, 201, 211
schemata deployment 32–3
schematic arguments (fictionalizing
of narratives) 138
Science 108
Scientific American 104, 115, 121
scientific claims (assessment) 94–9
scientific community 107–8,
118–19
scientific discourse (narrative
conventions): bad guys 89–94;
good guys 86–9; impersonal
techniques 99–100; scientific
writing/speaking 84–6; strict
assessment 94–9; truth, faith
and speech-acts 81–4
scientific knowledge 95–6, 97, 103
scientific writing/speaking as
narrative 84–6
Searle, John 155, 168
selectivity (of stories) 18–19
self 165, 166; -consciousness 72,
74, 75, 76; -deception 97;
-evaluation 55; -formation 53,
54, 56, 58, 61–2, 69, 73, 76;
-identity 64, 75; -interest 10,
215; -knowledge 66–70, 74, 75;
-narration 65; -recognition 72,
76; -reflection 52–3, 55–7,
63–70; -transformation 54, 65,
75; -understanding 56, 61–2,
64–6, 69

'semio-narrative' theory 34, 38
semiotics 32, 35, 43, 45–6;
    Greimasian 23, 29, 33, 34, 36,
    37, 44, 47
sense-data 143
sentences (narrative) 156–65,
    168–9
sentiment 188–92 *passim*, 195–6
separation 71
sequences (discovery narratives)
    108–9, 110–15, 118
Sharp, P.A. 120
signs and signification 204, 205,
    206
Smith, Adam 9, 14
social consensus 193
social evaluation 41, 42
social knowledge 29–30, 33, 38
social reality 52
socio-linguistic levels 33–4
Sollers, Philippe 205, 207, 210
Sontag, Susan 170
'speakable' writing 156–70
speaker 162, 165, 167;
    addressee/hearer 162, 165
speaking, scientific (as narrative)
    84–6
speech: -acts 45–6, 48, 81–4, 148,
    155; direct 157–8, 164, 166–7,
    169; indirect 157, 158, 164;
    represented 156, 158–70; *see
    also* utterances
Spinoza, Baruch, *Ethics* 132
split-off symbols 57, 59
split genes *see* discovery narratives
statement–utterance distinction 162
stereotypes 30
Sterne, Laurence, *Tristram Shandy*
    190–2
stories: economic *see* economics,
    storytelling in; limits of
    fictionality *see* invention,
    narrative and; scientific texts as
    120; selectivity 18–19
story grammar 29, 31, 33, 35
'story of the trial' 37
strict assessment 94–9

structural approach 13–14
structural level (text) 33–4
structure 29–35, 85, 131–4,
    149
sub-groups 42
sub-narratives 181, 182, 189
subject 199–203, 204
subject-free narration 215
subject-matter 200
subjectivity 200, 202;
    transcendental 71, 73, 74, 151
substantive narratives 29, 30,
    47
surface level (text) 33, 44
surrealism 209
Sutton, W.S. 6
symbolic representation 117–18
sympathy 188

tableaux 189, 190, 195–6
tense-system 161–2, 169
textbooks 114
textual indeterminacy 204–6, 211,
    213, 214, 216–17
thematic level (text) 33–4
thematic significance 182, 186
theory 61, 62; narrative reason and
    55–8
therapy 53; emotion, thought and
    58–66; narrative reason 55–8
thought: represented 156, 159–65,
    167–70; therapy and 58–66
time 131, 132–4, 149; chronology
    of discovery 110–15, 116; *see
    also* history
Todorov, Tzvetan 20
Tolstoy, Leo 192, 193
tragedy 55, 70–6
transcendental idealist 136, 145
transcendental subjectivity 71, 73,
    74, 151
transcription 104, 117, 118
transformational texts 213, 217
translation (scientific term) 105
trials: common law 35–7; jury
    28–31
trust 82–6, 91–2, 97–8, 102

truth 18, 27, 53, 58; -claims
28–31; correspondence theory
143, 144–6, 151; narrative and
45–8, 134, 135, 136, 138;
reference and 138; scientific
discourse 81–4; two-truths
theory 154–5; -values 148,
150
Twining, W.L. 24, 26
two-truths theory 154–5

uncertainty, undecidability 200,
204, 207
universal grammar 168
universality 52, 54, 57, 65,
149
'unspeakable' writing 156–70
utterances 205–6, 210–11; fictive
147, 148; *versus* statements
162

Vaihinger, Hans, *The Philosophy of*
'As If' 174
Van Loon, Borin 117
verstehen 7
virtue 174, 196, 197
voice 131, 210; dual-voice theory
161, 163–4, 166–8, 170; *see also*
narrator

Vonnegut, Kurt Jr.,
Slaughterhouse-5 208

Wales, K. 84–5
Watson, J. 105; *The Double Helix*
102–3
Weinberg, Steven 16
Weissman, Sherman 113
Westphal's group 113
Whewell, W. 94
White, Hayden 14, 18
Wisdom, John 141
witness enunciations 31–2
Woolf, Virginia 19; *Mrs Dalloway*
159–60
Woolgar, S. 90–3, 95, 99, 102
Wordsworth, William, *Lyrical*
Ballads 177
'working' notion 87–8
world-versions 144
world-views 188, 189–90, 197
writing: 'pure' 210–12; radical
212–17; scientific 84–6;
'speakable', 'unspeakable'
156–70

Zavarzadeh, Mas'ud 203
Ziff, Edward 117
Zola, Emile, *Germinal* 159